Dear Reader:

The book you are about to read is the latest bestseller from the St. Martin's True Crime Library, the imprint *The New York Times* calls "the leader in true crime!" Each month, we offer you a fascinating account of the latest, most sensational crime that has captured the national attention. St. Martin's is the publisher of Tina Dirmann's VANISHED AT SEA, the story of a former child actor who posed as a yacht buyer in order to lure an older couple out to sea, then robbed them and threw them overboard to their deaths. John Glatt's riveting and horrifying SECRETS IN THE CELLAR shines a light on the man who shocked the world when it was revealed that he had kept his daughter locked in his hidden basement for 24 years. In the Edgar-nominated WRITTEN IN BLOOD, Diane Fanning looks at Michael Petersen, a Marine-turned-novelist found guilty of beating his wife to death and pushing her down the stairs of their home—only to reveal another similar death from his past. In the book you now hold, SEDUCED BY EVIL, Michael Fleeman investigates the unusual case of a normal neighborhood mom with a secret past . . .

St. Martin's True Crime Library gives you the stories behind the headlines. Our authors take you right to the scene of the crime and into the minds of the most notorious murderers to show you what really makes them tick. St. Martin's True Crime Library paperbacks are better than the most terrifying thriller, because it's all true! The next time you want a crackling good read, make sure it's got the St. Martin's True Crime Library logo on the spine—you'll be up all night!

Charles E. Spicer, Jr.
Executive Editor, St. Martin's True Crime Library

SEDUCED BY EVIL

MICHAEL FLEEMAN

St. Martin's Paperbacks

SEDUCED BY EVIL

For information address St. Martin's Press, 175 Fifth Avenue, New York, NY 10010.

EAN: 978-0-312-38176-9

Printed in the United States of America

St. Martin's Paperbacks edition / August 2011

St. Martin's Paperbacks are published by St. Martin's Press, 175 Fifth Avenue, New York, NY 10010.

10 9 8 7 6 5 4 3 2 1

A NOTE TO READERS

This is an account of the investigation and prosecution of a 1996 murder that was still making headlines 14 years later. The narrative is based upon police reports, court records, trial testimony, interviews, and media accounts. As often happens, some early suspects were ultimately deemed to have committed no crimes, and an appeals court would find that seemingly important evidence was not proper for a trial. Most importantly, the guilt or innocence of a central figure remains undecided as of this writing.

CHAPTER ONE

The body lay undisturbed, the ground only now starting to thaw in the morning sunshine. Temperatures had dipped below freezing overnight and there were still patches of dirty snow in the shaded spots beneath the spruce and birch. The grizzlies and wolves had somehow not sniffed out the body, the bugs had not gotten to it yet. It was a perfectly preserved corpse, left literally on ice.

A winding road brought Michael Gephardt to the death scene. A foreman for the Chugach Electric Association, Gephardt and his partner Morris Morgan began their day forty miles away, at the substation in Cooper Landing, a small town at the confluence of the Russian and Kenai rivers. In the summer, the annual runs of sockeye and coho salmon bring hordes of weekend anglers, backing up traffic for miles; but on this Thursday morning in early May, Gephardt had the highway to himself, mindful only of the black ice that could send his truck skidding.

Gephardt and Morgan drove northeast along the Sterling Highway, stopping periodically to read electric meters. They turned left at a spur road, crossed a bridge and headed down a winding road that dead-ended at the settlement of Hope, Alaska. A former mining town that lays claim to two gold rushes, one before and another after the Klondike strike of the late 1890s, Hope spent the better part of the last century fading away into a dim memory, the only remnants of its boom years a few weathered buildings, a collection of rusted mining equipment and about two hundred hearty souls, most of them retirees, some of them still prospecting. Although a place of history and wild beauty, located only ninety miles from Anchorage on the sportsman's paradise that is the Kenai Peninsula, Hope gets little love from the guidebooks. "It's at the end of a 16-mile spur road," observes *Fodor's*, "so it's not on the way to anywhere—you really have to go there on purpose."

It was routine electrical service work that took Gephardt and Morgan to the Hope Spur Road, known to some as "The Road to Nowhere." At least one other crew from the Chugach Electric Association had been here earlier to repair the lines damaged in the winter storms. With each turn, the road descended, the men's truck passing the mile markers on the shoulder and the occasional cabin.

By mile marker 10, the trees cleared and a turnout emerged, offering a spectacular view of the Turnagain Arm, the shallow expanse of water that churns and roars from some of the world's biggest tidal surges, or bores. At low tide the Turnagain Arm is a plain of muddy silt, acres of deadly quicksand, before the tide rolls in with a vengeance, a two- to six-foot wall of water funneled between the high, rocky walls on either side. During new or full moons, when the bore tides are at their most powerful, the waves roar like locomotives. It was about this same time of year, in May of 1778, that British explorer Captain James Cook pushed his leaky vessels the *Resolution* and *Discovery* toward where Hope now is located in his quest for the elusive Northwest Passage, only to hit the channel's fierce winds and tides. Two shore boats journeyed farther, but rather than finding a waterway to the Old World, the explorers encountered only the mouth of a river. They called the river Turnagain and went back again.

From Hope, the city of Anchorage sits just fifteen miles across the Turnagain Arm, but no ferry service exists, so Alaska's largest city is accessible only by a ninety-minute drive all the way around the arm. Isolated and part of a history marked by disappointment, the old mining town has a name that suggests irony but is really a quirk. Founders called it Hope, not for joy and inspiration, but after the name of one of the early gold miners.

Just past mile marker 13, about three miles before the end of the road, Gephardt veered left onto a gravel and dirt access road that dipped then rose steeply into a hillside of Sitka spruce. After pulling the truck to a stop, Gephardt got out, his rubber boots crunching into the half-frozen dirt. His partner stayed behind. One hundred yards up the access road, behind a chain-link fence, stood an old microwave tower built by the RCA Corporation when it controlled Alaska's telecommunications in the 1970s but now the property of AT&T Alascom. The Chugach Electric Association services the two meters on a building next to the tower. Gephardt's job was to read the meter.

By now it was about 10:15 a.m. and sunny on May 2, 1996, the temperature having risen to about forty degrees, about two degrees warmer than the setting on refrigerators, thawing the ground and turning it to mud. Gephardt trudged up the hill toward the tower and its meter, walking to the side of the road in the grass so he wouldn't track mud back to his truck. The road had deep ruts left by the heavy equipment from the crew recently repairing the wooden poles and crossbars of the overhead high-voltage lines damaged by the winter storms.

About two hundred yards up the road Gephardt saw something red and bulky on the ground. He thought at first it could have been equipment that had fallen off one of the repair trucks. He took several steps closer and saw that it was a person dressed in a red jacket lying on the ground.

"Hey, is something wrong?" Gephardt yelled.

The person didn't move. Gephardt walked closer, still staying to the side of the trail. Now Gephardt saw that it was a bearded man dressed in a red jacket, blue jeans, and white tennis shoes. The man lay on his back, his head turned to the left, his arms outstretched and his right ankle positioned over his left awkwardly.

In his years driving the treacherous Sterling and Seward highways of the Kenai Peninsula, Gephardt had frequently come upon traffic accidents. He would report them over his cell phone or truck radio, then direct traffic until Alaska state troopers arrived. He had seen people killed in bad ways, and he knew by this man's gray pallor and gaping mouth that he was dead.

"Don't come up!" he yelled to his partner. "We have a body."

Gephardt walked back to his truck, careful to retrace his steps so that he didn't interfere with the scene.

In the warmth of his cab, he called 911 on his cell phone.

In May of 1996, state trooper investigator Ron Belden was two years away from retirement. His twenty-one-year law enforcement career had all been in Alaska: patrol in the Anchorage suburb of Palmer, then various jobs in the remote hamlets of St. Mary's and Aniak and the commercial fishing village of Dillingham near Bristol Bay before transferring to his current job doing investigations out of the station in the Kenai Peninsula town of Soldotna, known for its salmon fishing and clam digging. It was a typical career for a veteran Alaska state trooper, known as the toughest of the tough. Their agency employs just three hundred officers to enforce laws and investigate crimes in a land mass twice the size of Texas.

Ron Belden had just arrived at work around eleven a.m. when a sergeant informed him that two troopers had responded to a 911 call about a body being discovered in Hope, some ninety miles away and still part of the Soldotna station's turf. Belden's orders were to drive to the scene and determine the cause of death.

When he arrived in Hope at 12:46 p.m., two troopers met him at the base of the side road. One of the troopers had gotten close enough to see that the dead man had not been there long, the clothing was untainted by the elements, and the flesh was untouched by insects, wolves, or bears. The trooper had spotted what appeared to be a wound on the side of the face and, nearby, brass shell casings, shiny, as if recently ejected.

Walking up the hill, Belden could see that the man was bearded and bald and appeared to be in his mid-thirties. He had a long, lanky frame and lay on his back in the red coat and blue jeans. His fingers had formed fists, which meant that rigor mortis had just begun, another sign he had not been here long. Belden noted that the man wore a gold necklace and wristwatch, maybe valuable, maybe not, but certainly not taken. On the right side of the man's whiskered jaw was an apparent bullet wound. Looking over the rest of the body, Belden also noticed what appeared to be a second bullet hole through the man's shirt near the second button up from the belt. Two shots, to the face and belly: an obvious homicide.

A supervisor was en route. Soon a coroner's van would arrive. The afternoon sun had brought temperatures close to 50 degrees Fahrenheit and the ground was mush.

Sergeant Steven C. DeHart had been with the Division of Alaska State Troopers nearly as long as Ron Belden had, his nineteen years on the force putting him three years shy of retirement. His career sent him all over Alaska: academy training in Sitka, two and a half years in the inland city of Fairbanks, and eight years in tiny Talkeetna, before being transferred to the major crimes unit of the troopers' criminal investigative bureau in Anchorage. A promotion four years later made him a supervising sergeant running investigations out of the Soldotna station, working with Ron Belden as one of his investigators.

When DeHart arrived at the station at about noon, the dispatcher told him about the body in Hope and that investigator Belden was on his way. By now one of the troopers there had noticed the gunshot wound to the victim's face and the shell casings, and DeHart didn't wait for Belden's homicide conclusion. DeHart got in the station's crime scene van and set out for Hope.

He arrived at two p.m. Belden had been at work for more than an hour, assisted by troopers arriving from stations all over the region, searching the area for evidence, photographing the scene. The investigators huddled, then went up to the body. By now troopers had found one more brass shell casing—a total of three—all located a few feet from the body. They marked their placement first with yellow proof-of-auto-insurance forms from their patrol cars, later replaced with official crime scene flags from the investigation van. Shell casings meant a semiautomatic pistol instead of a revolver. That they were left at the scene meant the killer was careless—or confident.

The only other physical evidence that troopers immediately found were impressions in the mud near the body. Some of the impressions seemed to match the victim's muddy tennis shoes; the rest were indistinct indentations in the sludge—impossible, DeHart felt, to trace to any particular footwear or tire treads. The impressions were not measured, nor were casts made of them; their only evidentiary relevance was to indicate that the killing must have taken place when the ground was at least partially thawed, in the morning, day, or evening. Overnight, the freezing temperatures would turn the ground to rock. That meant the murder could have taken place at least the evening or afternoon before the body was found, which was consistent with the slow onset of rigor mortis and the fact that scavengers had not yet ravaged the corpse.

Steven DeHart took control of the murder investigation, assisted by Ron Belden.

Over the next five hours, as the mild Alaskan spring day turned back to a frigid night, troopers scoured the crime scene. Near the communications tower, they found bottles, empty bullet boxes, and other debris, but it all appeared to have been old and left there by somebody else and unrelated to the killing. Belden handled the photography, shooting 121 frames, then logging each picture.

It was one of the troopers processing the crime scene who made the first important observation. The brass shell casings were large, apparently coming from a .44—a powerful weapon. The trooper happened to be an instructor on the firing range and noted that it was highly unusual to find ejected .44 shell casings. Forty-fours were the ammo of revolvers, heavy-duty Dirty Harry–style guns that don't spit out the shells after firing. This meant the killer used a pistol armed with .44 bullets. The trooper who was a firing-range instructor knew of only one firearm in the entire world that fit that description: the Desert Eagle.

Manufactured in Israel and marketed and sold stateside by an American company, the Desert Eagle was as rare as it was deadly. A hefty four pounds when fully loaded, it could bring down a charging bear with one shot. Relatively few were sold in Alaska, and none of the troopers on the scene had ever handled a case involving a Desert Eagle .44.

The second noteworthy discovery came from a search of the body. The pockets of the victim's blue jeans were stuffed with papers. In this wad was a checkbook from the National Bank of Alaska, Eagle River branch. The checks were imprinted with cartoon characters, the account in the names of Mechele Hughes and Kent Leppink, with an address in Wasilla, an Anchorage suburb near Palmer.

Also in the front jeans pocket was a New York Life Insurance Company change-of-beneficiary form. It read that Kent John Leppink had amended his life insurance policy to now name his father, Kenneth James Leppink, as first beneficiary for 100 percent of the payout, followed by his mother, Betsy Lou Leppink, as second beneficiary and brother Ransom Gordon Leppink as third. The form bore the date April 26, 1996—one week earlier. With it was a business card for a New York Life Insurance company agent named Steven Leirer in Anchorage.

Another set of papers related to somebody named Scott Hilke. There were two business cards bearing his name with different addresses in California; a luggage tag with his name; a slip of paper with an address for a Scott Hilke in Paradise, California; a Social Security number that apparently belonged to him; and a reservation form in Hilke's name and dated almost a year earlier, August 15, 1995, for a place called Plantation House in Natchez, Mississippi. An accompanying brochure showed it to be a stately two-story home with white pillars converted to a hotel and restaurant in a resort town on the Mississippi River north of Baton Rouge, Louisiana.

Also in the pocket were a set of keys with a Dodge insignia on the key chain, a piece of paper with the name Pat Giganti, and a United States Postal Service receipt for something sent at 2:29 p.m. on April 30, 1996—two days before the body was found.

Finally, there was a folded-up letter, an apparent email from an AOL account that had been printed out that spoke of a computer. The email was signed "Mechele," the same name on the checkbook.

"I think it is finally working, but I am not sure so let me know if you get this, OK?" Mechele wrote. "I've got the rug so don't worry. I was going to have them cleaned, but something came up. It was going to be a surprise."

Mechele went on to request that $3,200 be put into a banking account with an explanation to follow when she got back that night or in the morning. The email ended on a sour note, with Mechele apologizing for "just leaving like that," but saying she "couldn't find you anywhere" since the person had left no messages.

"I drove out to the valley and you were not there. I was a little pissed off," she wrote. "Well, still don't know where you are and I think it's rather immature when you pull these stunts."

There was a postscript with an even angrier tone, with Mechele saying she "did not mess up" the computer she borrowed. "I knew you were smoking pot, taking those pills and drinking," Mechele wrote. "If you were trying to piss me off it worked. But you hurt me more because you damaged the agreement we had about drugs and hurt our trust. I do not want to talk about it again."

After the items were bagged and logged into evidence, the body was ready to be taken away. Now in full rigor mortis, the body was zipped into a coroner's bag and loaded into a coroner's van at four p.m., then driven off to Anchorage for autopsy. A pool of cooled blood was all that remained.

DeHart ordered a canvass of the few buildings that made up Hope, Alaska. They included some cabins and a diner called the Discovery Café, named after Captain Cook's boat, but nobody had seen or heard anything about a murder committed on the side road. They had never heard of Kent Leppink, Mechele Hughes or Scott Hilke.

DeHart worked the radio and cell phone. He wanted to get an investigator to that address in Wasilla printed on the victim's checkbook.

CHAPTER TWO

Today, of course, Wasilla is best and probably only known to people outside of Alaska as hometown of Sarah Palin, the GOP vice-presidential candidate turned conservative activist and best-selling author. In the heat of the 2008 political season, the media would descend on this town of ten thousand in the search for insights into the previously little-known governor of Alaska, and most would come away unimpressed. The Palins—Sarah and her oil-worker, snow-machine-racing husband Todd—lived in a house on picturesque Lake Lucille down the street from a Best Western, not far from the train tracks and main highway. In the distance towered the snowy peaks of the Chugiak, Talkeetna, and Alaska mountain ranges. Outsiders saw the strip malls and taxidermist businesses and declared Wasilla a hick town with great scenery.

But in May of 1996, Wasilla was known best as a bedroom community for commuters to the state's most populous city. Built where the Alaska Railroad met an old wagon trail, Wasilla sits near the northern point of the Cook Inlet, a forty-four-mile drive from Anchorage. Wasilla had five thousand residents, but was growing, and Sarah Palin was a councilwoman gearing up for the mayoral election in the fall.

On Friday, May 3, the morning after the body was found in Hope, investigator DeHart called the Alaska state trooper station in Palmer, whose territory included Wasilla. Located eleven miles to the east, Palmer was another old railroad town about the same size, with a population of five thousand. DeHart reached investigator Dallas Massie and asked him to go to an address on Portage Drive in Wasilla, make contact with a Mechele Hughes, and find out her relationship to a murder victim named Kent Leppink. Leppink, DeHart explained to Massie, had been murdered on a side road in Hope, most likely with a .44 caliber Desert Eagle pistol, and documents found on his body linked him to Mechele.

DeHart would have gone to her house himself—Mechele Hughes was the best lead of the investigation—except that Wasilla was 190 miles away, a three-and-a-half-hour drive. There was no guarantee that Mechele Hughes would be there or, if she was, that she would know anything about the murder of the man whose name she shared on a checkbook. Investigating crimes in sprawling Alaska necessitated this kind of coordination between trooper stations. DeHart also could have called Mechele. But as a key person of interest in the case, Mechele needed to be interviewed face-to-face by a trained investigator (Massie also had two decades of experience with the troopers). Plus, a death notification might be required. That would be Massie's call on-site.

Massie and his partner, investigator Michael Brandenburger, drove west on the Glenn Highway to the eastern edge of Wasilla, where they exited at Hyer Road and drove onto Grantham Road into the spruce- and birch-covered hills with houses on large wooded lots. The road twisted and narrowed until they got to Portage Drive and turned left, coming upon on a long driveway that led to the address on the checkbook found in the dead man's pocket.

The house was one-story with a composition roof and wood siding and a one-car garage. A thick grove of spruce was behind the house. As they drove down the driveway through tall wild grass, they saw three people—a burly bald man with a beard, a teenage boy with a crew cut, and a petite blond woman—looking through a storage shed next to

the main house. The investigators got out of the car, introduced themselves, and learned the trio were John Carlin III,
his son John Carlin IV, and Mechele Hughes.

Up close, Mechele was very attractive. Her hair, blond
with dark roots, tumbled over her shoulders. She had wide-
set blue eyes, thin eyebrows, a well-defined jawline, and a
small, pert mouth with lips that photos would show she
painted bright red. The effect was doll-like. Her driver's license showed that she was twenty-three years old, though
her voice sounded younger, high-pitched, like a child's, with
a trace of a southern accent.

Taking Mechele away from the two men so they could
speak privately, Massie listened as Mechele explained that
John Carlin III and his son were her friends who lived in
Anchorage. She said that she owned the house behind them
but that she and Kent had been temporarily living with the
Carlins while her home was undergoing an extensive remodeling.

"What can you tell me about Kent?" Massie asked her.
"That's what we're here to talk about."

The investigator played it close to the vest. He didn't tell
her why he wanted to talk to her except to get information
about a Kent Leppink. He didn't tell her that Kent was dead.

From the beginning of the interview, which he tape-
recorded, Mechele clearly was suspicious of why the police
were interested in Kent. She had as many questions for
Massie as he did of her. When Massie asked about the nature of her relationship with Kent, she countered by wanting
to know if Kent was in trouble, if he had done something
wrong. Massie didn't answer. When he asked Mechele if
Kent had any enemies, she pressed him on why he wanted to
know. Again he wouldn't tell her. They parried like this for
a while before Massie made it clear that he would be the one
asking the questions. What, he asked her again, was her relationship with Kent Leppink?

"Um, we're engaged," she said tentatively. "We haven't
been getting along so great . . ."

"OK, you said you were engaged?" asked Massie.

"Mmm-hmm," she said.

"You said you've been having some troubles?" Massie asked.

"Well, not troubles—um, we have a very unique relationship," she said. "It's a, um, how do you say, you know."

"Open relationship?" he offered.

"No," Mechele said, "like a conventional, not conventional, it's um, oh, it's a—"

"Well, explain it to me a little bit if you can."

"I have a boyfriend."

His name, she said, was Scott Hilke—the same name on the business cards and reservation form stuffed in Kent's pocket. Kent, she said, was her business partner. Their M&K Enterprises operated a fishing tender, a boat that picks up the haul from fishing boats in open seas and delivers it to port. During fishing season, which was about to begin, Kent captained the tender named *Togiak*—after Togiak Bay, nearly four hundred miles northwest of Anchorage. Mechele said they had no romantic relationship, had never had sex.

"OK, so your relationship with Kent is not as a fiancée?" asked Massie's partner, Brandenburger. "Or is it?"

"It's a fiancée, yes," she said, abruptly contradicting herself. "We don't have any dates set, um, he's in and out with his family, he's not in good relations with his family, so basically I let him tell his family I was his fiancée, only met them once."

"OK," said Massie.

"So, technically," Mechele rambled, "because I said I was his fiancée to his family, I am, but no, we don't plan on getting married."

Mechele was still wary of why she was being questioned.

"Where is he?" she asked.

"Well, we're not gonna mess around with it anymore," Massie said. "It's—he's dead. Ah, his body was found. And that's why we're here and that's why it's real serious."

"How?" Mechele asked, shock in her voice.

"I can't tell you that," said Massie. "We can't, we can't give a—a lot of information out here, OK?"

There was a howl, and then Mechele cried. Her sobs continued as Massie rolled his microcassette—and watched her carefully.

In twenty years in law enforcement, much of that spent investigating homicides, Massie had informed many people about the deaths of a loved one. He couldn't help but think something was off in Mechele's reaction. Later he said that while she "appeared" upset, her reaction to him was "not as genuine" as how other people had responded to death notifications. "It just seemed that it lacked a bit of sincerity," he said.

Mechele composed herself and answered more questions.

Her engagement to Kent, she said, was a front. She said she only allowed him to tell people they were engaged for the sake of his parents.

"Mechele, is he homosexual?" asked Massie.

"I don't know," she said, her voice still choked. "I guess he's bisexual. I don't know."

"Oh, he's never shared that with you?"

"He likes guys," she said.

"He likes guys, OK."

"But his family doesn't know that."

"I see."

"I don't want them to know that."

She said that Kent had lived with her in the Wasilla house, until repairs on the home forced them to move into the Anchorage home of John Carlin III, the man who had been with her earlier, going through the shed where Kent kept some of his belongings. She explained that John was a mutual friend of theirs.

Massie didn't tell her about the documents in Kent's pocket, including the change-of-beneficiary form and her email telling him she was "a little pissed off" about his disappearing act and for "smoking pot, taking those pills and drinking." Nor did he tell her about the Scott Hilke–related papers.

But he did get from her where she said she had been in recent days. She said that she had returned early the day before—the same day the body was found—after spending several days in a condominium in Incline Village, a town on the shores of Lake Tahoe, with her boyfriend, Scott.

CHAPTER THREE

The body of Kent Leppink awaited Dr. Norman Thompson when he arrived at his lab in Anchorage the morning of May 3. After removing the body from the coroner's bag, the fully clothed remains of Kent Leppink were placed on a stainless steel table. The autopsy would begin at about the same time that investigators Dallas Massie and Michael Brandenburger were interviewing Mechele.

Thompson began the autopsy as he always did: by talking to the investigators. Thompson found out the victim's name was Kent Leppink, age thirty-six. The deceased had been discovered at about 10:30 a.m. the previous morning lying faceup in the half-frozen mud. The body remained there for about seven hours while investigators processed the crime scene before it was transported to the Thompson's lab.

The victim appeared to have been shot at least twice, in the face and the stomach, with little blood near the wounds but substantial blood beneath the body when it was moved. Three .44 shells from a pistol were found nearby. The shooting took place in a remote area: There were no witnesses.

Thompson took stock of the exterior of the body. Kent was tall and slender, stretching six feet five inches and weighing 195 pounds. His blue jeans had a mud stain over the left knee, and his shirt had been pierced, apparently by a bullet. A second likely bullet wound was on his right cheek. When

Thompson turned the body over, he found Kent's clothes soaked with blood, a sign of another wound to the back.

Thompson flipped the body back over and undressed the corpse, using scissors to cut away the jeans, white T-shirt, red outer shirt, and red-colored jacket. He worked carefully, watching for a bullet that might shake loose from a shirt fold or drugs stashed in a pocket. He found neither. When the body was nude, Thompson washed it down. Even now, blood continued to flow out of the victim's back and onto the autopsy table. The source: two bullet holes.

Thompson now examined the wounds to determine a cause of death. On the victim's stomach was a "fairly large hole," consistent with a .44 caliber bullet, matching the holes on his shirt and undershirt. Higher up, on Kent's chest, Thompson found a "little bit of a nipple-like elevation" on the skin that had been faintly bruised. When the coroner touched it, he could feel something hard just beneath the skin, most likely a bullet that had entered from behind Kent and lodged beneath his chest. The necklace also left abrasions. On Kent's right cheek, the wound measured more than a centimeter wide, again indicative of a large-caliber bullet.

After recording the two wounds to the front of the body, the pathologist examined the two wounds to his back: one big and jagged, one small and round.

From these four wounds—two on the front, two on the back—Thompson tried to reconstruct the order in which they were inflicted. From the external and a later internal examination, it appeared that Kent had been shot first in the back. This was the smaller wound in his lower back, seemingly smooth and round to the naked eye, but upon microscopic inspection actually ragged and embedded with fibers from Kent's T-shirt: telltale signs of a point-blank shot. The killer likely pushed the muzzle against Kent's back and fired, the clothing fibers lodging in the skin and muscle tissue, the gunpowder granules traveling with the bullet, tearing the edges of the entry wound. The gun was fired so close to the body that expelled carbon monoxide penetrated the tissues and poisoned the muscles, turning the area around the entry wound from a normal maroon to a bright cherry red.

When Thompson inspected the inside of the body, he could follow the path of that bullet. It had traveled up, piercing Kent's aorta, the huge vessel that takes oxygenated blood from the heart to the rest of the body, before lodging itself in the chest cavity just under the skin, creating the nipple-like bump that Thompson had seen near the necklace. The skin popped up so fast from the bullet that the necklace left scratches. With his surgical tools, Thompson extracted the large lead projectile.

Thompson opined that when Kent was shot in the back, he spun around and landed, awkwardly, on his back, bleeding heavily from the ruptured aorta. In no time he'd be dead. But the killer wasn't finished. As Kent's heart continued to beat, even as his blood pressure plummeted, he was shot again in the stomach, this time from farther away, Thompson believed. The shooter probably stood not far from Kent's feet and fired up into the body, Kent now lying on a steep incline, his feet downhill from his head.

Under a microscope, Thompson saw that the stomach wound was clean and round, free of the ragged edges, poisoned tissues, or embedded shirt fibers from an up-close shot. An internal examination found that the bullet traveled upward inside the body, striking the liver, the spleen, and one lung before exiting a foot higher than the entry through that second, bigger wound to the back. In contrast to the neat, clean entry wound to the stomach, which barely stained Kent's clothing, this back wound was large and nasty, with a red-rimmed "shoring abrasion." Blood gushed out, proof he was still alive, if barely, from that first shot.

The mangled nature of the wound suggested that the bullet collided with something hard, like the ground, at the same time it left the body, fragmenting upon impact. "It exited violently and pushed the skin outward," the coroner later said. "The skin pushed against a surface like the ground and created an abrasion." There was nothing left of the bullet, just metal shards. For this reason, Thompson theorized Kent was shot while lying on his back.

From these two shots, Kent Leppink was seconds away from death. Then the killer fired the final, cruelest shot.

To get a better look at the wound to the face, Thompson shaved Kent's beard, revealing a bullet hole surrounded by tiny spots, like a rash, the effect of strippling, which results when gunpowder grains "tattoo" the skin, another sign of a close-up shot. An entire science has been built around the interpretation of strippling patterns: their size and shape can tell how far away a gun was and its angle when discharged (the tighter the strippling pattern, the closer the shot). From the gunpowder tattooing to Kent Leppink's face, Thompson estimated the gun was only nine inches away.

Point-blank to the face.

The bullet traveled up into the skull, rattled around in the brain cavity, and stayed there. Thompson removed the slug.

The tiny amount of blood around the facial wound showed this was the last shot; at that point Kent's blood pressure was almost nonexistent from the shots to the back and stomach. He was alive, but only barely, when the killer delivered the coup de grâce.

From later toxicology tests, Thompson determined that Kent Leppink's system was clean of drugs or alcohol, despite the claims from Mechele in the email in Kent's pocket. His body also showed no defensive wounds, no abrasions from a struggle, no broken fingernails with blood or tissue underneath. He hadn't even put up his hands in a final futile effort to stop a bullet: there was no bullet hole through either hand, often found with gunshot victims. Nor were there rope burns or vestiges of duct tape to suggest he had been restrained. Stone cold sober at the time of his death, with no signs of a struggle or restraint, Kent's killer may have gotten close enough to shoot him in back for the simple reason that Kent knew him—or her.

The last and most difficult part of the autopsy was estimating a time of death. Forensic scientists rely on what they call the "Rule of 12," so called because it takes twelve hours for rigor mortis to set in, starting with the small muscles of the extremities and jaw; twelve hours during which the entire body remains stiff; then another twelve hours for the body to go slack again.

When the first state troopers arrived at the murder scene, Kent's body was still in the initial stage of the Rule of 12. The clutched hand showed that the chemical process of rigor mortis had taken hold in the small muscles. About five hours later, when the body was hauled away at four p.m., the whole body was stiff and in the second stage of full rigor.

Taken together, that would suggest a time frame of around four to five p.m. on Wednesday, May 1, twenty-four hours before the onset of full rigor mortis. But the Rule of 12 is notoriously imprecise and based on the assumption the body is at room temperature, about 68 degrees. The colder it is, the longer it takes for rigor mortis to set in. In this case, the body was subjected to overnight temperatures at or below freezing, and it never got much above 50 during the next day.

Thompson could offer only a big window for time of death, from the night of Wednesday, May 1, and working back to the previous day, Tuesday, April 30—a period during which, Mechele Hughes said, she had an alibi.

CHAPTER FOUR

By the time investigators Dallas Massie and Michael Brandenburger finished their interview with Mechele Hughes, her friend John Carlin III and his son, John IV, had taken off. They headed for their house in Anchorage, and the elder Carlin said police could come by any time they wanted. According to Mechele, she and Kent had lived with Carlin since the previous November. Whatever belongings Kent had not kept in the storage shed at Mechele's house were stored at John's house, as was Kent's car, a Dodge Omni, the same make as the insignia found on the key chain in his pocket.

After the interview with Mechele, Massie relayed this information to Sergeant Steven DeHart, who arranged for another pair of troopers to go to Carlin's house: Michael Sears and Curt Harris, both based in the criminal investigation bureau in Anchorage. DeHart asked them to impound Kent's car for a future search and, if possible, poke around John Carlin III's house to look for Kent's personal effects. They didn't need a warrant for the car, but they needed one to get inside John's home, and DeHart didn't feel he had anything close to probable cause for that. He barely knew anything about Carlin, except that he was a friend of the victim and of Mechele's—and was seen going through Kent's belongings in a storage shed the day after his death. Sears and Harris would have to play it by ear and hope Carlin was agreeable.

Carlin's home was located on Brook Hill Court amid new

housing developments in South Anchorage. The investigators made the short drive down New Seward Highway from the criminal investigation bureau, exiting at O'Malley Road and going past the Alaska Zoo before turning right onto Lake Otis Parkway, then right again into a new subdivision carved out of a birch grove. The three dozen homes had almost identical architecture, each painted in muted yellows, greens and blues as well as tans and grays. John Carlin's house sat at the end of a cul-de-sac, the backyard abutting the parkway.

As the troopers arrived, they noted that parked in the driveway was a gray Dodge Omni. The yellow Alaska license plate number showed it was a 1988 model registered to Kent Leppink.

John Carlin was there as promised, and he welcomed the troopers into the house. The issue of a warrant never came up. John was a heavyset man approaching middle age, with a bald head, a fringe of red hair, a red beard, and sad blue eyes. He led them into the living room, which was furnished with a sofa, and there was an entertainment center in a built-in wall unit. Sears later remembered feeling impressed by the system.

He also remembered seeing a young woman there: Mechele Hughes. She had come down from Wasilla after talking to Massie and Brandenburger.

The troopers made small talk with both of them, not wanting it to feel like an interrogation. As Mechele had done earlier, she and John Carlin III explained the living arrangements: Carlin was a widower with a teenage son, John IV, and owned the home, but had allowed his friends Mechele and Kent to stay there for the last six months, during construction on her home in Wasilla.

The troopers asked if Kent had any other friends or family, and Mechele gave Sears the phone numbers of Kent's relatives, saying his parents and at least some brothers lived in Michigan, where Kent had grown up. When Sears asked if he could see Kent's bedroom, John said that the fisherman had had a room upstairs down the hall from Mechele's room but normally crashed on the sofa in the downstairs living room. Before moving here, Kent had slept either on his fishing boat or at Mechele's house. Kent had had no place of his own and recently hit hard times financially. John said he'd recently loaned Kent $4,000.

Led upstairs by John, Sears looked in the room assigned to Kent. It was sparsely furnished—a bed and little else—so what Sears saw stood out. It was a hard black plastic case. Sears recognized it immediately. In the 1970s, before joining the troopers, he had worked in an Anchorage gun shop and sold many of these hard black gun cases. Getting permission from Carlin to open the case, Sears found a pouch that held an ammunition magazine and a black nylon web belt that served as a holster. The belt was easily big enough to hold a .44 pistol.

John explained that the gun items belonged to him, not Kent. John had brought them to Alaska about eighteen months earlier when he moved from New Jersey. The gun that had gone with the accessories had been stolen back in New Jersey.

Sears and partner Harris next went outside and peered inside the windows of the Omni, conducting what they called an impound search, a cursory look for any electronics or valuables in open view that would be logged at the scene so somebody couldn't accuse police of stealing them. There was nothing of that sort in the car. Nor did they see any obvious clues of murder—no blood or murder weapon. The troopers arranged for a tow truck to take the car to an impound lot in Anchorage. They said good-bye to John Carlin III and called DeHart with their report.

The next afternoon, Saturday, Kent Leppink's Dodge Omni was searched. The trunk yielded nothing of value; the console between the front two seats held an ammunition box, half full of .22 cartridges, and the glove compartment, like Kent's pockets, was stuffed with papers. One stood out. It was a single sheet with two notes, the first written on a word processor, addressed to "Dear Mechele" from somebody named "John."

"The roof on your cabin in Hope is finished," it begins. "It will not leak anymore. The fireplace has been cleaned but as he said, it will have to be redone within the next year or two. It is safe for you to use now." The note goes on to say that the cabin's locks have been changed, with the new key stashed under a stone by a tree, and that the screens are fixed to keep out the mosquitoes that "are very hungry for fair skin [sic] people such as us.

"I am glad that I bought it for you now. It does make a fine getaway," the note says before the writer then muses on where his own future will take him: Australia, maybe, if "the Costa Rica deal doesn't look inviting."

"I do hate going and losing you in my life though," the writer says. "Please be well, safe and Happy. You guys enjoy your stay in the cabin this weekend."

Beneath it was another note in a woman's handwriting, saying, "Please don't let anyone know where we are but you already know that." She added a smiley face, and it was signed, "Mechele."

DeHart got a full report, generating a host of possibilities—and questions. It was a note in all likelihood from John Carlin III to Mechele Hughes, clandestinely arranging for her apparent tryst with somebody—but who?

Clearly not John Carlin. His note affected a tone of both longing and resignation, filled with unrequited love as he played platonic friend helping the object of his affection sneak away with another while John planned to flee to Costa Rica or Australia. And clearly not Kent Leppink, if Mechele was to be believed, since she said he was gay. Was it Scott Hilke, the supposed boyfriend, who was supposedly in California?

Kent clearly knew about it, the note having been found in his car. And he ended up in Hope, dead from three gunshots. What if Kent hadn't really been Mechele's gay business partner but—like John—in love with her? Had he stumbled onto this note and gone to Hope seeking a confrontation?

Or had he been lured there?

The following Monday, May 6, DeHart had Trooper

Michael Sears drive to Hope for a second canvass for witnesses and to show photos of Kent, Mechele, and John. Maria Motoyama, a Hope resident for twenty years and a cook at the Discovery Café, recalled that a tall bearded man who looked like Kent had come into the restaurant the week before—probably Saturday, April 27, since the Discovery Café was open only on weekends that time of year. The man showed Maria a snapshot of a blond woman whom he said was his fiancée and asked if anyone had seen her in Hope recently. Maria told the man she had not. The man then asked if anybody knew of a cabin that was undergoing roof repairs. Nobody did.

A tangled story of love and murder was emerging. At the center of it was Mechele Hughes.

CHAPTER FIVE

Ransom Leppink was asleep in his Michigan home when he heard a rapping on his front door. The clock said it was three a.m. Ransom jumped out of bed and rushed to the door. There stood a local sheriff's deputy.

"Your brother's been involved in a homicide in Soldotna, Alaska," the deputy said, giving the closest town to Hope.

"My brother is dead?" Ransom asked, stunned.

"Yes," the deputy said.

Ransom collected himself, tried to think what to do next. The deputy had little more information to offer; he said an investigator from Alaska named Steven DeHart would be speaking with the family later in the day.

After the deputy left, Ransom knew he had to tell his parents, and not in a phone call. He drove to their house.

Betsy Leppink remembered that it was about five a.m. when she heard the pounding and her third-oldest son screaming. She opened the door and her life shattered.

In a daze, Betsy then called her eldest son, Craig Leppink. When he answered the phone, he could make out his mother's frantic voice but got the meaning: Kent had been murdered in Alaska.

"Let's not talk anymore," Craig told his mother. "I'll get up there to see you in an hour."

There was a fourth brother in the family, Lane Leppink, who was estranged from the rest and hadn't spoken to his family in years. He was surprised to get a call from Ransom, who then told him Kent had been killed.

It had been Steve DeHart's decision to have local law enforcement notify Ransom Leppink of Kent's death. On Friday, DeHart contacted the police in Michigan and asked them to make the notification in person, giving them the name provided by Mechele: Kent's brother Ransom. For the Leppinks, a prominent and wealthy family that owned the Leppinks Food Centers, a chain of grocery stories in central Michigan near Cedar Rapids, the word of Kent's death struck a hammer blow. For so long they had worried about him. Now their worst fears had come true. That his body was found in a place called Hope, Alaska, only deepened the pain. Just days earlier, Betsy Leppink had begged her son not to go there. By the end of that horrible Saturday in May 1996, Kent's parents and brother Ransom had told DeHart all they knew: why Kent had gone to Alaska, how he felt about Mechele Hughes, and how he had ended up in Hope.

Kent Leppink grew up in Lakeview, Michigan, the second of four brothers. Looking back, it seemed inevitable that life would take him to Alaska. As a boy, Kent enjoyed hiking, canoeing, and water-skiing, and by the age of fifteen he was hunting white-tailed deer. As he matured, it appeared he was on track to follow his older brother Craig and their father in the family business. After attending Michigan State University, Kent transferred to Western Michigan in Kalamazoo, studying retail management. Groomed by his father to take over a large share of the grocery chain's management duties when the elder Leppink retired, Kent got experience on the ground level, working in the bakery and produce sections of Leppinks Food Centers.

Kent's transition into the business world would be bumpy. Although he seemed to do well enough in the beginning, his parents couldn't help but be concerned about him. As long as anybody knew him, Kent was an odd duck. He could be polite and shy one minute, then say something that made people squirm the next. Sometimes his comments, couched as jokes, had a strange sexual quality. He seemed awkward around women and never had a steady relationship. People called him weird; his family, more charitably, called him misunderstood. At work, he appeared aimless, distracted.

In 1990, money went missing from the store in Lakeview, where Kent worked with Craig and youngest brother Lane. "We don't know what the total amount of money was," Ransom, who worked at a different store, in Stanton, Michigan, later said in court. Lane thought it was as much as $200,000. "My brothers and I learned of—caught—my brother stealing from the store," Ransom testified. "At the time my parents were gone. They were on a vacation. They were to be home within the next three or four days. We waited until my parents came home. Because my dad was president of the company at that time, and because he's the dad, [we] shared the information with him and he dealt with it."

Kenneth Leppink investigated, quietly and without the involvement of police. The family patriarch determined that Kent had embezzled money from the store. Kent's faults had been tolerated, but this was beyond the pale. In a deal with his father and the rest of the family, Kent signed an agreement to resign as an employee of Leppinks Food Centers and forfeit his allotment of company shares, worth about $100,000 at the time. No charges would ever be filed for the theft, but Kent was out—out of the business, on the sidelines of the family.

Craig and Ransom agreed with the punishment; Lane did not. "I thought police should have been involved," he said. It was a resentment that would fester for years and contribute to Lane's estrangement from his family.

By 1993, Kent had left Michigan for a new career. He ended up in Tennessee, where he studied taxidermy while working on a game farm near Nashville. Although his father had banished him from the family business, Kent's relationship with his parents began to improve in those three years. And in the winter of 1993 he accompanied them on an RV trip to Nevada. In Reno, Kent donned boots and a cowboy hat and attended a meeting of Safari Club International, a large hunting organization. There he met a man who would change Kent's life: Russ Williams, a commercial fisherman who fished the waters of Prince William Sound in Alaska. They struck up a conversation and hit it off. Needing another hand on his boat, Williams offered Kent a job, which he accepted, and he gave Kent a nickname that he would have for the rest of his life: T.T., for "Tennessee Taxidermist."

Kent arrived by car in Alaska in April 1993 to make his living from the sea. Bank records show that he opened a savings account in June with just $300. With no home of his own, he lived with the Williams family when he wasn't sleeping on the boat.

After Kenneth Leppink's retirement in 1993, he and wife Betsy and two of their grandchildren visited Kent for three weeks. They were struck by how much their son had changed. "He finally found a home when he came to Alaska," one of his nieces, Brooke Burlison, later told the *Anchorage Daily News*. "He belonged up here."

At age thirty-three, Kent Leppink finally knew what he wanted. The early hours, the stink of fish guts, the wind and the rain and the weather—everything about fishing appealed to him. He worked hard and his crewmates enjoyed his company. Before long, Kent began talking to his father about buying his own boat, and the transformation in his personality was so complete that Kenneth Leppink, who only three years earlier had banished Kent from the family business, now entertained helping him financially. Kent's brother Lane, however, remained suspicious. He would later tell police that he suspected Kent was really working another scam in Alaska, that he was "out there screwing somebody over." Lane described his brother as having no conscience "or very little."

It wasn't just Lane. The hard feelings toward Kent still lingered among all of his brothers. "Of course, his brothers were upset with him," Betsy Leppink later said in court. In September 1994, his parents visited Kent again, just as he was getting off the water after the summer fishing season and while he was still living with Russ and Shirley Williams. "My husband decided he wanted to bring each of our other sons here," Kent's mother later said. "There had been dissension in the family, and it broke our hearts. And my husband said: 'I am going to bring each of his brothers here to see what he's doing, how he loves Alaska.' We wanted each of the other boys to have that privilege of seeing their brother doing something he was happy doing and living in a place [where] he was so happy."

For all his contentment with his new career, Kent found that Alaska couldn't meet all of his needs. The long weeks spent on the boat weighed him down with loneliness. At ease with the structured life and camaraderie of a fishing boat, Kent still felt awkward in other situations, particularly around women. "He had girls who were friends," his mother later told NBC's *Dateline*. "But my take is I think he had a complex. I think he felt a little inferior to be a boyfriend." As his brothers married and had children, Kent took the role of doting uncle, buying presents for his nieces and nephews, playing games with them, taking them on outings. But he never had a girlfriend of his own.

And so it was with some surprise—shock, even—when in October of 1994, as Kent's parents were ending their visit with him, that he made an announcement.

"Mom," he said, "I've met a girl, and she's wonderful. And her name is Mechele Hughes."

There was much that Kent didn't tell his parents at the time, and some that he would never tell them. They didn't know, for instance, how he had met Mechele or what she did for a living. All they got were the superlatives. In phone calls home, Kent called Mechele "the most wonderful gal in the world" and described her as his fiancée. His family could only feel happy and, at first, relieved. Kent had finally found a career and now, at long last, love.

It seemed too good to be true.

Nine months later, Kent's family finally met Mechele. In July 1995, Kenneth and Betsy Leppink, along with their son Ransom and his wife, Kelly, traveled to Alaska for a ten-day vacation to "see what Kent was doing, hopefully rebuild their relationship," his Betsy later said. "By this time Kent was very, very excited. . . . He wanted us to meet her in person."

The meeting came over dinner at Elevation 92, a seafood restaurant in downtown Anchorage with views of Cook Inlet. It was an important gathering for Kent, and on the surface all seemed to go well. Mechele was beautiful with her long blond hair and in a skirt, dark blouse, and white sweater. She was soft-spoken and friendly. Kent, dressed casually in a blazer and blue jeans, clung to her every word.

But throughout the night, his parents felt uneasy, those old worries about their son resurfacing. While Kent had gushed about Mechele for months, Mechele seemed more restrained at dinner. Kent's mother felt that Kent's feelings for Mechele ran much more strongly than hers for him. Also, Kent had bought Mechele a diamond pendant to present to her at the dinner, but at the last minute she rejected it. She said she already had one. "He was very disappointed," said his mother. His brother Ransom recalled that Kent had purchased what he called an engagement ring for Mechele. The ring, Kent explained to his brother, would suffice for the time being, but later on he'd be buying a larger ring because Mechele didn't like small rings.

"Immediately a little red light went on," Ransom later told *Dateline*.

Most worrisome, though, was that while Kent had earlier told his family that he and Mechele were engaged, she wasn't wearing the ring that Kent had said he purchased.

Despite her concerns, Betsy Leppink didn't say anything to Kent. She didn't want to intrude. Betsy didn't know it at the time, but this dinner would be the only time she'd see Mechele in person.

After they left Alaska, Kent's parents got encouraging reports from their son. In September 1995, Kent called his father to say that an opportunity had arisen to purchase his own fishing tender. After providing the boat's specifications,

Kent said the boat would cost $135,000. The bank had agreed to loan him $100,000 if he had a cosigner with good credit and could come up with the rest. His father agreed to cosign the papers and loan Kent the additional $35,000. At some point Kenneth Leppink loaned Kent another $15,000. The result was that Kent became the owner of the boat he called the *Togiak*, ready for the 1996 fishing season.

Kent's love life also seemed, at least to him, to be going well. He visited his family for Christmas and still spoke fondly of Mechele, although he was vague as to why she had not accompanied him to Michigan.

In March of 1996, Kent's parents were in Baja, Mexico, on an RV camping caravan. Cell phones were not as widely used then, so his parents kept in touch with their sons through a voice mail box accessible by an 800 number and a PIN code.

One day Betsy called the service from a pay phone in Mexico and heard her son say: "Mom, get in touch with me!"

Fearing something was wrong, Betsy called Kent back immediately. Over the course of a conversation that lasted more than an hour, she found that what she had heard was not panic in Kent's voice but joy.

"Mom, I proposed to Mechele, she has accepted and we're going to be married," he said.

Although happy for her son, Betsy was perplexed. Kent had already introduced Mechele as his fiancée over the summer, even though she had said nothing about it during their dinner together and hadn't been wearing a ring. Now, for whatever reason, it appeared that the engagement was legit: Their wedding plans were on under way, and Kent was eager to set a date.

Around the same time, Kent also called his brother Ransom. Kent was "kind of excited because he was making plans to get married," Ransom recalled. Kent, he said, "told me that he was engaged, asked me if I would be his best man, and was trying to pick out dates for a wedding."

Everything was moving fast. Kent wanted to get married on a weekend in April, the next month. But Ransom had planned a trip to Florida to meet up with their parents in their vacation mobile home. "I said if that was the week he wanted we would definitely change our plans," said Ransom. "He thought that maybe they could talk it over and look at other dates."

Kent's parents continued on their RV road trip, leaving Mexico and heading through the American Southwest and South toward their vacation trailer park in Fort Myers, Florida, on the Gulf of Mexico, where Ransom's family was to meet them. When Betsy and Kenneth Leppink got to Texas, Betsy called Mechele from a pay phone. Betsy hadn't seen or spoken in months to the woman her son was going to marry. She knew almost nothing about Mechele except that she was originally from Louisiana. Mechele answered and the women spoke cordially. Betsy told Mechele that their RV trip would take them across Interstate 10, just past New Orleans.

"If you and Kent are going to be married, maybe it would be nice if Ken and I could stop in New Orleans, maybe meet your mother," Betsy told her. "And at least we could become acquainted."

According to Betsy, Mechele said that sounded like a good idea and that Mechele herself might even be in New Orleans at the same time. Betsy gave Mechele the name and number of the RV park in Texas to call back to firm up the plans.

That call never came. The Leppinks drove on to Florida, arriving the first or second day of April 1996. It irritated Betsy that Mechele had not bothered to call back; she had reached out to her and been ignored. Not only did Betsy want to build some semblance of a relationship with her future daughter-in-law, there were pressing logistical issues to address. The way Kent was talking, the wedding was only weeks if not days away.

Betsy called her son to find out what was going on, only to find to her distress that Kent couldn't reach Mechele, either.

"Mother, I don't know where she is again," Kent said, sounding depressed. He explained that Mechele was not calling him back. She had simply disappeared, and it wasn't the first time. "I don't know where she goes."

Betsy asked if Kent wanted to fly out and join them in Florida.

"I can't afford it," he said.

"We haven't given you a Christmas present, we haven't given you a birthday present," his mother said. "May a ticket to Florida to spend a few days with us be that gift?"

"No," he said glumly. "I can't accept that."

Then, the next day, he called his mother. "Is that gift offer still going?" he asked.

"It sure is," Betsy Leppink said.

Kent flew from Alaska to Florida, joining his parents and his brother Ransom's family, who had by now arrived in a single wide trailer in their mobile home park. It was April 3, one month before Kent's death.

Kent's parents hadn't seen him since the previous summer. Always thin, he now seemed to have lost even more weight. In that week he spent with his family, his mood jumped from anger to frustration to depression. He didn't sleep well and was seen walking the streets of the mobile home park at night. "He was in bad shape," his mother recalled. "I was concerned about him."

As Kent's parents had suspected, his finances also were in shambles. After paying for repairs to Mechele's house in Wasilla to the tune of $50,000—a sum that seemed staggering to his parents—Kent said he had to borrow $6,000 to prepare for the fishing season, which was about to start.

But what most upset him was he couldn't locate his fiancée. In his parent's mobile home, he hooked up a laptop to a phone line and sent email after email to Mechele, hovering near the screen for replies that never came. He tried calling her repeatedly and refused to leave the trailer in case she called back.

Ransom's children, not understanding, kidded him. "Hey, Uncle Kent, let's go outside," they said, but he wouldn't budge from his seat, typing more messages to Mechele.

"Hold on," he'd tell the children, "I think I'm going to get an answer." But he didn't.

Like his parents, Ranson had worried about Kent's relationship with Mechele. Kent seemed "infatuated" with her, but Ransom later echoed his parents concern when he said, "She wasn't as serious about Kent as Kent was about her."

At one point, in desperation, Kent said, "Mom, why don't you type a message to Mechele?"

Betsy Leppink knew little of computers and nothing of email.

"You know how to type," Kent told her.

On April 6, Betsy wrote her first email, telling Mechele that it "feels strange typing on this machine." She said the Leppink family was "in sunny Florida" where they were enjoying a break in the humidity and a "wonderful" visit with Kent, who is "getting brown as a berry."

We are sorry that we missed you in New Orleans and here in Florida. We do hope that you have a safe trip back to Alaska. We leave here in a few days and I do believe our little motorhome will be happy to be back in Michigan.

She signed it with "God bless and take care" and her nickname, "Chets."

Kent pressed send, and to his surprise, Mechele replied.

"I was so happy to get mail from you," wrote Mechele. "I bet the weather is nice. We have had our share of rain. It is a little chilly today. I was so surprised to find out the airlines were so booked up. I wish I could have made it."

Mechele told Kent's mother that the "Yucatan is great" and related a story about a spider monkey she played with when she traveled there with her family.

Then she got down to business.

"Kent and I have had some small discussions about the wedding cost and I am not clear on them," she wrote. "He told me that the two of you wanted to pay for everything. I am sure you know that can be very expensive and I don't want you to feel obligated to do so."

Mechele suggested that the wedding be postponed at least until Kent returned from fishing season in the fall. Mechele said she had surgery scheduled for April 12—it was apparently a tonsillectomy—but would then like to go to Michigan to discuss the wedding further.

Soon after this email came, Kent was typing furiously to Mechele, trying to get her to change her mind. He seemed confused and depressed: it was all too much.

On April 7, the family's fifth day together in Florida, Betsy Leppink had a long conversation with her son. She urged him to delay the wedding at least until the fall, after the fishing season, as Mechele had suggested in her email. Kent was in no financial position to get married right away, and Betsy made it clear that he could expect little help from his parents. They would spend only $2,500 on the wedding.

That night, Kent left Florida for Alaska. He took a late-night flight with a stopover in Seattle, arriving in Anchorage after midnight. His mother would never see him alive again.

Spring vacation now over, Ransom Leppink's family went home to Michigan, as did his parents. At some point Betsy spoke to Mechele on the phone. Betsy is unclear on the timing, only that it was after she got to Michigan, and their conversations could have taken place over more than one call. But the subjects were always the same: marriage and money. The actual wedding date remained fuzzy, but Mechele had begun making arrangements, starting with picking out a dress. She told Betsy that she couldn't find a gown she liked in Alaska and was having one made in New Orleans at a cost of $2,600. Mechele said that Kent had told her that the Leppink family had traditionally paid for the gowns for their future daughters-in-law.

"No," Betsy told her, "that is not so."

Mechele then brought up possible locations for the ceremony, suggesting they could get married in Michigan near the Leppinks' home. She said she was planning a trip there to scout locations for a reception. As a Catholic, she also wanted to visit local churches for the ceremony. Betsy mentioned that Kent's father just so happened to be planning to travel to Alaska in a couple of weeks to be with Kent for a few days.

"Gee, maybe you could fly back with him," said Betsy.

Betsy would later recall that Mechele said that that was a "great idea," then began to waver. In one of their phone calls, she said she might not be able to go to Michigan after all because she had minor surgery planned but thought she would heal in time. Betsy and Mechele talked about who would pay the airfare, and Mechele said she could cover it: she had a lot of frequent-flier miles.

Although in disagreement about the dress, Mechele and Betsy did see eye to eye on one thing: Kent's idea of an immediate wedding was unreasonable. Mechele again suggested they wait until fall, and Betsy told her she felt that was "very wise."

After her discussions with Mechele, Betsy called her oldest son, Craig, to tell him that Kent's fiancée, whom Craig had never met, was probably coming to Michigan in late April or early May.

"I would like you to meet your future sister-in-law," Betsy said.

Meanwhile, Kent's father finalized his arrangements to go to Alaska. Three years into retirement, Kenneth Leppink had pent-up energy and big plans for what he'd do with his son in Anchorage. He floated the idea of helping Kent prepare his boat for fishing season, but Kent tactfully said his elderly father would probably just get in the way. However, Kent did need help with his bookkeeping. A whiz with money and taxes, Kenneth would get his son's accounts in order.

On Friday, April 26, Kenneth flew to Alaska on a Northwest flight for a four-day trip. Kent and his friend John Carlin III met him at the airport in the afternoon, and they all drove to John's house. John asked Kenneth if he wanted to spend the evening there watching a movie on what Kenneth recalled was a "humongous" television set, but the elder

Leppink declined. Kent drove him to a Best Western on New Seward Highway. Once they settled in, Kent handed his father an envelope.

"This is for you," he said. It was a form changing the beneficiary of Kent's life insurance to his father, mother, and Ransom, in that order. Kent explained that Mechele's grandfather had purchased the policy as a wedding gift.

"Kent, I don't like the smell of this," Kenneth said. "This is not right."

"Oh, it's OK, it's all right," said Kent, and they dropped the subject.

The next day, Saturday, while Kenneth toiled over Kent's taxes, Betsy Leppink got a call from Kent. He said he was on the road, in Girdwood, Alaska, headed down the New Seward Highway around the Turnagain Arm toward Hope.

"Kent, what are you going to Hope for?" she asked.

"Mom, often I can't find Mechele," he said. "She's missing again, and I want to find her and need to find her, and I have learned that she is in Hope."

His mother's fear rose. "Kent, have you ever been in Hope?"

He said he had not.

"Well, your dad and I have," she said. "We were there in '93, and it's a little village. There's just nothing there. Where would she be in Hope?"

He said she was in a cabin. What's more, Kent claimed she had stolen his laptop and an expensive bronze statue.

"I don't believe that," Betsy said. She told him there were no cabins in Hope that she had seen, no hotel or lodge that she remembered.

"Well, I have reason to believe that's where she is and that's where I'm going," Kent told his mother. "I'm just calling to tell you I'm going there."

The conversation then went from shocking to bizarre.

"Oh, by the way," Kent said almost casually, "we have a first wedding gift."

Betsy was taken aback. Kent and Mechele hadn't even set a wedding date yet, and from her last conversation with

Mechele, it had sounded like it might be postponed until the fall.

"You do?" Betsy asked.

"Yes." said Kent. "Mechele's grandfather bought a million-dollar life insurance policy on my life."

Betsy Leppink was stunned. Kent was making no sense. "What are you saying?"

He repeated it: Mechele's grandfather had insured Kent's life for $1 million as a wedding gift.

"Kent, that's sick," his mother said. "That's absolutely sick. I've never heard of such a thing in all my life. And now you're going to Hope, where she can't be?"

Yes, he said, that's where she was and he was looking for her.

"Don't go," she said. "Don't go alone. And just get out of there."

He refused.

They ended their call and Kent continued on his way.

That night, to his mother's great relief, Kent returned to the motel where his father was staying. Kent laid it out for him: Mechele was in Hope with a friend. Kent couldn't find her, but he suspected that his friend John Carlin III knew where Mechele was, only he wouldn't say.

In the motel room, Kent told his father about the $1 million insurance policy wedding gift.

"Nobody gives a life insurance policy for a wedding present," his father said, overcome now with a combination of fear and that old feeling that his son had gotten himself into trouble again. "This is dangerous," Kenneth said.

"I'm a big boy," Kent said. "I can handle myself."

The next day Kenneth and Kent went to church together, then returned to the motel to finish the taxes. Kent spent that Sunday night in the motel room, and the next morning they visited an accountant, who had two or three more recommendations that Kenneth felt confident Kent could handle on his own. "We had started with a program of putting accountability for his fishing program for the next year, to make his taxes a little simpler," Kenneth recalled.

On Tuesday, April 30, Kent drove his father to the airport. Mechele had never materialized; any plans that she'd go back with Kenneth were now abandoned. With mixed emotions, Kenneth Leppink boarded a morning flight for Michigan, saying a final good-bye to his son.

A couple of hours later, Kent called his brother Craig. The call was a surprise. They normally exchanged e-mails, since Kent was often out on the fishing boat and Craig was usually traveling for his job as a consultant for international trade with Russia. In the ninety-minute discussion, Kent was in a panic because Mechele had disappeared and he was obsessed with finding her. He said he hadn't seen her in a week and that she had stolen his laptop and a bronze statue.

When Kent then told his brother about the $1 million life insurance policy, Craig could hear no more. Until now, the family had held back on their opinion of Mechele. No more.

"I feel you have a bull's-eye on your back," Craig said.

"No, I've got insurance. It's all handled," Kent said mysteriously.

Craig thought he was talking about the wedding present.

"It's not the life insurance," Kent said. "I've got other insurance and nothing's going to happen."

He didn't explain but did say that he had ripped up his will and gone back to an older version.

"I have other information that nothing's going to happen to me," Kent added. "I know things they don't know. I've been reading emails and they didn't realize I read them."

Kent would say no more.

Craig worried that Kent was involved in something and was in over his head—that embezzlement incident all over again, only this time even worse. Craig tried to get more information. Kent said he'd tell him all about it when the time was right.

"I'm going to take you out and get you your first beer in twenty years and you're not going to believe this mess," Kent said. "You're not going to believe what's going on."

Craig had no idea what his brother was talking about, but

knew it had to be something involving Mechele—something bad. He offered some brotherly advice.

"There's other fish in the ocean," he told Kent. "Kent, if it doesn't work out, it doesn't work out. There's other ladies out there."

"No, I really love her," Kent said. "I really love this lady."

It was the last time Craig would hear his brother's voice.

CHAPTER SIX

The package arrived at Kent's parents' house in Michigan on Friday, May 3. It was a bulky parcel postmarked Chugiak, Alaska, a town halfway between Anchorage and Wasilla.

Kenneth and Betsy Lou Leppink opened the package. Inside was another sealed envelope and a letter. The letter was addressed to "KL"—the initials of Kent's father—and "Chets," his mother's nickname:

> *Thanks for coming up. Sorry Mechele couldn't be here to see you. Please put the enclosed envelope in your safe deposit box. Do not open it. I talked to you about "insurance policies." This is mine. If I didn't think that things could get a little rough up here, I wouldn't have sent you this. It'll be safer there.*
>
> *It's not funny to talk about getting killed, but in today's world you have to expect anything. Don't get all nervous and call me on the phone about this. KL and I talked lightly about this. If you think anything fishy has happened to me, then you can open the other envelope I've sent. It's pretty self-explanatory.*
>
> *You don't have to worry about me. I'll be OK. Just want to make sure all my ducks are in a row. By the time*

you get this, I'll have called you. The phone call will
explain everything.

Love,
Kent.

Kent's family, already worried about him from his trip to
Hope and comments about the life insurance policy, now
"became very anxious, upset," Kent's mother later said.
They waited all day for Kent to call, and when he didn't,
Betsy dialed the family's voicemail service and left a mes-
sage for Kent.

"Call me right away," she said. "This is very important."

He didn't call back. The family decided to wait overnight.

The next morning, Saturday, the local deputy knocked
on Ransom Leppink's door to inform him that Kent had been
murdered. By the time the package arrived, Kent had been
dead for at least a day.

Kent's parents then opened the second envelope. It was
filled with bank documents and other papers, including the
paperwork from the $15,000 loan from his father and a copy
of the form changing the beneficiary of his life insurance
policy to his father, mother, and brother Ransom as primary
through tertiary beneficiaries.

And there was a long handwritten letter from Kent with a
chilling beginning: "Since you're reading this, you assume
that I'm dead. Don't dwell on that. It was my time and there
is nothing that can change that. There are a few things that I
would like you do for me, though. I hate to be vindictive in
my death, but paybacks are hell."

In what Kent intended to be a letter from the grave, he
asked his parents to cover his debts with his life insurance
money, give his boat to his friend Gary Brooks, "then go on
a nice vacation" and "act like I am there with you and do
things I would like to do: Lie on the beach, fish, relax. 2
weeks minimum, but not much longer."

Then, he said, "Use the information enclosed to take Mechele DOWN. Make sure she is prosecuted. Mechele, John, or Scott were the people, or persons that probably killed me. Make sure they get burned."

He apologized for asking this of his parents, and if Mechele had married him, this wouldn't have been necessary. Instead, he asked his parents to ensure that Mechele is jailed "for a long time.

"But," he added, "visit her there. Tell her how much I really did—do—love her. Tell her you love her, and help her. She has a split personality, and the part I fell in love with is very beautiful. I really did want to marry her and make her dreams come true."

He signed it, "Love ya, Kent."

Kent's family faxed it along with copies of the other papers to investigator Steven DeHart, who recalled the crime scene evidence. Kent had been carrying a receipt from the Chugiak post office dated April 30 at 2:29 p.m.

He had mailed the letter just two hours after his brother told him he had a target on his back, just days after his fruitless search for Mechele in Hope, led there by a note she and John Carlin had wrote.

"Take Mechele DOWN," Kent had written.

The investigation was now moving in that direction.

CHAPTER SEVEN

There's a saying in Alaska, one the tourism boards don't advertise, but one many women come to know, living as they do in one of the few places on earth where they are outnumbered by men: The odds are good, but the goods are odd.

Such is the history of Alaska and the northern Canadian territories. First came the dreamers and misfits—the miners and the oilmen and the fishermen—followed by the women, the wives and girlfriends, as well as the dance hall girls and prostitutes. Enjoying a numerical advantage, they had their pick, even if the pickings could be slim. The men could be desperate, aching for companionship. Even the rich ones—and there were many—couldn't escape the darkness, the loneliness.

In 1994, a young woman from the South heard from a friend that a lot of money could be made off the men of Alaska, more even than in New York or Vegas or her hometown of New Orleans. Upon arrival in Anchorage, she began tentatively, working only few days a time, staying in motels, then flying home. But she soon found that her skills translated well in the land of odd goods. She called herself Bobby Jo and she plied her trade on the garishly lit stage of Anchorage's premier strip club, the Great Alaskan Bush Company.

The Bush, as locals call it, is built to resemble an old-fashioned western dance hall, cavernous inside with a towering wood-beamed ceiling from which hang chandeliers made of wagon wheels and hurricane lamps. Dancers descend narrow stairs from a second-floor balcony to a large stage with a state-of-the-art lighting system and speakers booming rock and a smattering of hip-hop and country. Against the opposite wall runs a long bar, and in the middle sit the men—hundreds of them, many just coming off work, still wearing their uniforms or coats and ties, their heavy jackets draped over their chairs.

Mechele Hughes didn't have the stereotypical stripper's body. At least one of her detractors, another dancer in the club, would sniff that she was short, with big hips and a small bust, hardly bodacious stuff. But Mechele, in her Bobby Jo persona, possessed talents many of the other girls lacked. When she finished her stage routine, removing her girlish costumes as she writhed around—Mechele never had much in the way of dance technique—she scooped up her dollar bills, then went after the big bucks on the club floor, where the men sat at round tables. Using her youthful appearance to full advantage, she played the role of innocent young thing, the sweet southern girl with just enough spice to make things interesting. She sidled up to the men and talked in a voice one of them would call "captivating." She also listened.

Putting in long hours, often arriving when the club opened at 3:30 p.m. and staying until closing time at 2:00 a.m., Mechele quickly built up a stable of regulars, men who came several times a week dropping hundreds of dollars a night on her. She made so much money that she stopped commuting and settled into an apartment in Anchorage, although she still kept her old apartment in New Orleans. On a good night in the spring or summer, Mechele could make $3,000, which at the end of her shift she stuffed into a velvet Dewar's whiskey bag. It wasn't just cash. Soon men were buying her jewelry and furs. One man lent her a truck.

Her success spoke to a truism of her profession: the real action never takes place onstage but on the club floor and in the lap-dance booths, where the men shell out twenties for a few minutes of a beautiful woman's attention. Like all the dancers, Mechele had to reveal just enough of herself so the men would shower her with money and valuables, but hold back enough so they would come back for more. She did it well—maybe too well. "She played along with men's feelings to keep the money coming her way," Honi Martin, another dancer and friend of Mechele's, later said. "I just don't think she realized how deep these men's feelings ran for her."

In talking to Kent Leppink's family, Steven DeHart found that they had only recently discovered Mechele's stripper past. Betsy recalled that she was on the phone with Mechele one day in April 1996, discussing wedding plans, when Mechele finally revealed how she had made her money when she first arrived at Alaska. Kent's family didn't like it, but they accepted it as they accepted other troubling aspects of the engagement. Kent was in love with her, and by this time she said she was no longer dancing.

Detectives interviewed other dancers and managers at the Great Alaskan Bush Company, filling in details of Mechele's history and character. From these interviews as well as later statements to the media, by her friends and family, a picture emerged of a woman strong, resourceful, and independent, who worked hard, overcame adversity, had a soft spot for animals, and very early on learned how to get what she wanted from men.

Mechele Hughes was the younger of two daughters in a military family. The Air Force kept her father on the move, and the Hughes family never lived in one place for very long, until they finally settled in New Orleans. "As a child Mechele was often quiet and shy," her mother, Sandy Mc-Williams, later said, though those attributes must not have lasted long, for in another interview her mother described her daughter as "active" and so talkative that she'd get in trouble with her teachers. Mechele's sister Melissa Hughes would recall that Mechele had a temper that matched Melissa's own, and the siblings were known to go at each other.

From an early age, Mechele adored animals, getting "much

more pleasure in watching butterflies rather than television," her mother later said. She was always picking up stray dogs, keeping the house full of animals. "The only two things I absolutely refused to allow her to have was a snake and a monkey," Sandy McWilliams later said.

When Mechele was twelve, her parents separated. Melissa left to live with their father in California—he died shortly thereafter—while Mechele stayed with her mother in New Orleans. At about this same time, a doctor diagnosed Mechele with scoliosis, or curvature of the spine, requiring frequent hospitalizations as a steel pin was implanted, leaving her with a small scar on her lower back and perpetually good posture (and poor dancing skills).

When Mechele hit her mid-teens she left home, for reasons that are unclear. Some media accounts said she ran away at age fourteen using her sister's ID to make her seem four years older. Her mother insisted Mechele left with permission at age sixteen to become a model in New York. By age seventeen she got only as far as the secretarial pool at a New York modeling agency—and got a quick education in big-city life. "She quit her job at the modeling agency because she felt the owners were taking advantage of the dreams of young women to become models," her future husband, Colin Linehan, would later tell a judge, as always portraying Mechele in the most positive of lights, "and she felt that she wanted no part of that." Her boyfriend at the time—a Brick Township, New Jersey, deli owner named Pat Giganti—had another story, saying they lived together after meeting in 1990 at the Iguana Club on Park Avenue in Manhattan when he was at least ten years older than she was. "I'm from New York City. I come from a pretty fast place, and let me tell you, she made me feel like I was standing still," Giganti told the *Anchorage Daily News*.

In about 1993, Mechele left New Jersey—and, according to Giganti, left him with payments on a Volvo she had bought in his name. Three years later the car would be found parked at the home of John Carlin III. Police briefly focused attention on him. It turned out that his name resembled that of a famous Genovese crime family member. But authorities established that Pat Giganti had no relationship to the New York mobster and that he had a solid alibi for the time of Kent Leppink's murder.

When Mechele started stripping isn't known. Some reports said she worked gentlemen's clubs in New York and New Jersey while living with Giganti. But her mother confirmed that after Mechele left the East to return home to New Orleans, Mechele confided to her that she was dancing a couple of nights a week in a local strip club to save money for veterinary school. "I didn't approve, but I couldn't argue with her. It made sense," her mother later told the *Anchorage Daily News*. "She didn't go around telling people about it, and it wasn't something she was proud of."

After earning her high school GED in New Orleans, Mechele heard from a friend about the money to be made stripping in Alaska and set off for Anchorage. One of her new friends there was Honi Martin at the Great Alaskan Bush Company. "We hit it off almost immediately," Martin later said. "I had just broken up with my boyfriend, and told her that I was looking for a place to live. Without hesitation, she said I could live with her and that she had a spare bedroom. She hardly knew me, but opened up her home to me."

Honi admired Mechele's work ethic and clean living. Unlike many other strippers, she didn't do drugs, drink alcohol, or smoke. All the cash went straight to savings. "I would go to work and I kept my goal in mind," Mechele later told CBS's *48 Hours Mystery*. "My goal was to make money and leave." Her drive was legendary at the club, her skills at doing that delicate dance with men's emotions as good any as anybody's, always edging herself perilously close to the edge.

"Men who become a dancer's regular often have already been someone else's regular at one time or another," Martin later said. "They are not clueless men who get taken for their money. They only feel burned after they have bought gifts and spend hundreds if not thousands on a girl, only to realize she is not going to fall in love with him. Mechele did nothing different than any of the other girls did that had regulars. I've even done it."

Then one night she crossed an invisible line. She fell in love with a customer.

Since the mid-1980s, James Scott Hilke had sold valves for steam and other gases used in power and petrochemical plants. Going by his middle name, he traveled the western United States, Hawaii, and Canada, pushing his company's products and providing customer support. His home was technically in Paradise, California, near Sacramento, but he really lived on the road, in the hotels and motels of Denver, Chicago, Los Angeles, Phoenix, and, in August 1994, Anchorage.

A job for the George M. Sullivan power plant run by Anchorage Municipal Light & Power took him to Alaska. His task was to train employees how to repair valves while the plant was down for routine maintenance. It was his first trip to Alaska, and when he arrived he was irritated to find out that he wasn't supposed to be there for another two weeks. "But nobody told me," he later said. With time to kill, he paid a visit to the Great Alaskan Bush Company and struck up a conversation with the pretty young blonde with a southern accent who went by the stage name Bobby Jo.

At first, it was a just another approach for Mechele, her target a confident-looking man with sandy-blond hair, maybe a little better looking than most, but a target all the same. Her goal was to get him to open his wallet by making him fall for her. "You don't discourage him. It's not the dancer's fault," Honi Martin later said. "She is at the club to work and make money, not to discourage people from spending it. These men willingly spend money and bring or offer you gifts. There is something wrong with a man who sits night after night in the clubs, hoping to save some damsel from her job."

Mechele used her usual technique, going into her innocent-girl routine. Only this conversation went further than others had. Bobby Jo melted back into Mechele Hughes, her interest in this customer no act, even as Scott handed over cash. At the end of the night, Scott told her he had to leave Alaska but that he would be back in a week or two. "The first meeting was just an introduction," he later said in court. "She gave me her phone number and I contacted her when I got back."

What Mechele saw in Scott would perplex her friends. It wasn't just that as a rule they frowned upon dating the customers: you can't make money if you "give it away." It was that he seemed an unlikely match. For one thing, he was seventeen years older than Mechele, and while he was handsome and charming in a salesman sort of way, he was no matinee idol. His $50,000-a-year salary in 1995 kept him comfortable, but he was no millionaire. He wasn't even technically single. At the time he was separated from his first wife, and the divorce wouldn't be finalized for nearly another year. The other strippers looked at him as another guy in the club with personal baggage, a wallet and a big mouth.

But all signs pointed to a true and growing love between them. Scott returned often to the Bush Company, showed no signs of jealousy, and gave Mechele more than money. In emails he called her his LOML, for "Love of My Life," and before long he was spending the night at her apartment. "It started out as a friendship and dating, and became a relationship," Hilke later said. While they were together, Mechele continued to dance under the name Bobby Jo, making $1,000 to $3,000 a night. "She went to work and on occasion would dance onstage and on occasion would lap dance, and more often than not mostly just socializing with clients," said Hilke. "Her intent was to make enough money to buy a house in The Valley"—where Wasilla and Palmer were located—"and she did exactly that."

Despite Mechele's goal to strip and split, Alaska turned out to be too good to leave. She finally saved enough money to purchase a $64,000 home on East Portage Drive in the hills of Wasilla, populating it with her growing menagerie: dogs, a cat, a toucan, three cockatoos, and an African gray parrot. Scott stayed there when he was in town on business, meeting her at the club and then spending quiet nights watching movies on the VCR. Mechele got a pink dinosaur tattoo on her ankle to match one Scott had, and even Scott's detractors had to admit that Mechele considered him her real love.

Still, for Mechele, whose aspirations ran much higher than working in an Alaskan strip club, Scott Hilke offered something else important to her. His many business trips to the power plants of the western United States and Canada all got recorded on his Alaska and United Airlines frequent flier accounts. The sums were astronomical. At one point he had more than one million miles on Alaska Airlines. James Scott Hilke may not have been rich, but he could literally take Mechele anywhere in the world.

They lived a jet-set style life, the stripper and the valve salesman. An early trip took them to Natchez, Mississippi, where they spent a romantic weekend in August 1995 in the Plantation House hotel.

On Thanksgiving 1994, at Mechele's house, in front of the birds and the cats, Scott proposed to Mechele with a $3,000 ring he had purchased on his American Express card. She accepted, and they made plans for a Thanksgiving 2005 wedding. They talked to a priest. Mechele and her friend Honi went to Natchez to scout places for the ceremony and reception.

By March 1995, Scott had quit his job with the Conval valve company to live full-time in Alaska with Mechele. He tried to start a sales consulting business, naming Mechele as officer of the enterprise to take advantage of tax breaks for minority- and female-owned companies. "She had no hands-on involvement," he later said. It would not be a success. "Business started out slowly and got worse." From April to October, Scott tapped into his 401(k) plan and meager income to help Mechele pay the electric bill and other small expenses. She paid the rest of the bills out of the thousands she brought home in velvet bags from the Bush Company.

As each month passed, the prospect of marriage grew ever more remote. Scott became increasingly concerned about his beautiful young fiancée—and the attention she attracted from other men.

CHAPTER EIGHT

You date a stripper, you have to accept certain things. She comes home from work in the wee hours of the morning smelling of perfume, sweat, booze, cigarettes, and men. In the beginning, it never seemed to seriously bother Scott Hilke. While first dating Mechele, he'd go to the Bush to see her—and was well aware of the men who were her regulars, the men who would one day help pay for that house in Wasilla and allowed Scott to try to strike out on his own as a consultant.

And when one night in September 1994 Mechele, in her Bobby Jo character, introduced Scott to a tall, bald fisherman named Kent Leppink, the valve salesman hardly thought about it. Mechele fawned on Kent the way she did to all her regulars, but Scott felt "it was a dancer/client relationship. She was grooming [him] for economic purposes." Hilke's salesman radar for reading people zeroed in on Kent's social awkwardness. He was an easy mark for Mechele, a walking ATM.

But before long, Kent would become more than just a club regular. Mechele allowed him to be one of the few men to see her outside the confines of the Great Alaskan Bush Co. During the long fall and winter of 1994–95, the fishing off-season when Kent had nothing to do, the man who went by the nickname T.T. started showing up at Mechele's house, spending the night on the sofa, storing his few belongings in a shed. "T.T. was just a customer who had become a friend—but he was still just a friend," Honi Martin later said. "He was never referred to as a boyfriend or lover. They never kissed or hugged or even held hands." As far as anybody could tell, Kent was something of an errand boy for Mechele, doing everything she asked, never questioning.

When Kent spent the holidays with his family in Michigan, he showed them photos of Mechele and of her house, saying he had moved in with her. "I knew that he had met somebody he really cared for," his brother Lane would later say in court. Kent never mentioned anything about the man who really was living in the house and sharing a bed with Mechele. At the time Scott Hilke had been engaged to Mechele for more than a month and was sleeping with her every time he traveled to Alaska. While Kent was singing Mechele's praises to his family during his Christmas trip home, she and her nephew were actually on vacation with Scott at Disney World in Florida.

Mechele's friends thought Kent was pathetic. Night after night he went to the Bush, giving her hundreds of dollars, then subjecting himself to any indignity Mechele could deliver. He cooked, he cleaned, he gave her money, he followed her like a puppy, obsessed with her.

By the summer of 1995, Kent's visits to Mechele's decreased because he was on the water working his fishing tender. But a replacement waited in the wings. One night at the Bush, Mechele introduced Scott to her new regular, an overweight balding, widower from New Jersey named John Carlin III, who lived with his teenage son in a South Anchorage house not far from the club. A former U.S. Marine and steelworker, John had suffered a bout of lead poisoning. He barely slept and his body would be plagued by pain, but he was financially secure, having just received $800,000 out of a $1.2 million legal settlement. The license plate on the Jeep he parked in the Bush's lot read: SUE EM. He was so flush that he could lavish thousands of dollars on the dancer he knew as Bobby Jo. He was another mark: loaded and lonely.

Soon, to Scott's growing irritation, this new loser started

showing up at Mechele's house. Worse, Mechele abruptly announced that John had offered to take her and one of his friends, a lawyer from New Jersey, on an all-expenses-paid European vacation. "I was not enthused," Scott later said in court. Adding insult to injury, Mechele wanted Scott to take care of her birds and other pets while she spent two weeks with another man in Amsterdam, Paris, and London. "I was telling her I wasn't particularly comfortable with her leaving a lot of responsibility in my hands, whether it was the animals or the house, and I wasn't particularly crazy about her traveling with another man," Scott later said in court. He knew he was wasting his breath. "She was going to do what she wanted to do," he said.

But before she left, Mechele tried to put Scott at ease. "Specifically, [she said] that I shouldn't have to worry, if I was worried about them having a romantic or physical relationship, that he was not capable of doing that," Scott said. For all the thousands he spent on her at the Bush, Mechele said, John Carlin III was impotent. It didn't make him feel any better. "I think that was probably about the time I started drifting away."

By the fall of 1995, Scott had stopped going to the Bush and had given up trying to make it on his own as a consultant. His former boss had gone to another company in the interim and invited Scott to join him there. His territory would comprise everything west of the Mississippi, including Canada, Hawaii, and Alaska. The new job would mean more time on the road and less time to spent with Mechele, which under the circumstances struck Scott as fine. He accepted. He began living out of suitcases again but continued a relationship with Mechele, visiting her every two or three weeks for a weekend.

The new arrangement looked good on paper. Scott didn't have to see the two "morons," as he called them, yet could maintain an exciting relationship with Mechele, two gypsies connecting for brief, intense get-togethers. They resumed their travels, going to the Portage Glacier southeast of Anchorage and on more trips back to Louisiana to see Mechele's family, and keeping in touch via email, with Mechele using the email name AkMeWell and Scott going by SHilke99. But Scott soon tired of Mechele's life in Alaska, particularly her continued friendship—or whatever it was—with Kent Leppink. The fisherman's infatuation with Mechele was cramping Scott's love life. During a weekend stopover in Wasilla, Scott suspected that Kent had been watching him and Mechele having sex.

His patience would finally run out, all because of a home repair project. In October of 1995, Scott was in town helping Mechele remodel—he was installing molding—when he made a discovery. He drove a nail through the wall and it went right through, falling into a crawl space. Beneath the house, he found extensive dry rot: water-damaged wood. "I was surprised the house was still standing," he later said in court. "The studs were like sponge. It was terrible." An inspector deemed the house uninhabitable for the winter. An expensive series of repairs began, and Mechele needed another place to live. She chose John Carlin III's house.

For Scott, this was the last straw. Now on the road almost full-time, he didn't want to have anything to do with John or, for that matter, Kent, who followed Mechele to John's house too. Scott visited her two or three times in the fall and winter of 1995, sleeping with her in an upstairs bedroom before hitting the road again. Mechele was like a queen bee, accepting money, jewelry, and furs from John and Kent, playing stepmother to John's son John IV, while dancing every night at the Bush. The men hovered around Mechele, and Scott couldn't get away from them, even when he was on the road. When Scott and Mechele traveled to Metairie, near New Orleans, to pick up Mechele's furniture and Jeep to bring back to Alaska, they ran into Kent Leppink. He had followed them there, driving Mechele's Volvo. "I don't think his appearance down there was expected," Scott testified.

By late November 1995, Scott lost all interest in marrying Mechele. Their Thanksgiving wedding date "came and went" and their engagement "just ran its course," he later recalled. "[She] convinced me that it was my idea that we shouldn't get married," he later said. "It began dawning on me that it was not the way I wanted to spend the rest of my life."

It didn't stop him from sleeping with her. They spent Christmas 1995 together at the Carlin residence, and continued to hook up for weekends in 1996, including several days in a Lake Tahoe condominium in late April and early May.

CHAPTER NINE

Steven DeHart would later insist that despite all the evidence acquired in the early days of the investigation, from Kent's "Take Mechele DOWN" letter to what would be called the "Go to Hope" note, Mechele Hughes and John Carlin III were still not officially considered suspects. But that didn't stop the detective from taking a more hands-on role in the investigation. No longer would he delegate key interviews to surrogates, no matter the geographical obstacles.

On May 5, DeHart and Ron Belden made the three-hour drive from the Soldotna station to John's home for their first face-to-face interview. When they arrived, John welcomed them into the house as he had welcomed investigators Michael Sears and Curt Harris two days earlier. Through the course of the investigation, John would talk to police at least eleven times, never asking for an attorney.

The investigators also found Mechele at the house. They asked for private time with John, and Mechele left the room, although she didn't go far.

They wanted her away from John so they could ask him about the laptop computer that had seemed so important to Kent, and which kept surfacing at different points in the early part of the investigation. Kent had told his mother, father, and brother that he believed Mechele had stolen the computer. He had also told his brother that he had snuck a look at emails, apparently from the computer, getting information that made up his "insurance" policy against those whom he'd later accuse of murder. And in his pocket, after he was killed, was that email from Mechele apparently referencing the computer.

Why was it so important? The detectives told none of this to Mechele or John. Nor did they tell them that they had found the "Go to Hope" note, or that Kent had mailed his parents a letter fingering them, along with Scott Hilke, in his murder.

All they did tell John was that they were interested in Kent's laptop. Did he know where it was?

"Mechele might," he told them, "but I have not seen it."

Just then, Mechele came into the room.

Belden tried to shoo her away. "We would like to keep these separate if possible," he said.

"OK," said Mechele.

"But you're here," the detective then said. "You heard the conversation about the computer. We're trying to locate this computer. Do you know the whereabouts of the computer?"

"Yeah," she said, "the computer is not here."

"Do you know the whereabouts of the computer?" she was asked again.

"Uh-huh," she said, "it's at my sister's in Utah."

"Utah?"

"Mmm-hmm. It's not just Kent's computer. It's mine as well."

The detectives wanted to pursue this further. They made arrangements to interview her separately at her home in Wasilla. She left John's house, saying she was going shopping, and Belden and DeHart turned their attention back to John.

Repeating what he told Troopers Sears and Harris earlier, John explained that he had opened his home to Mechele and Kent since the previous November, though Mechele was about to move back to her Wasilla house, now that the remodeling was nearly complete, and Kent about to hit the water for the fishing season. Describing Kent as something of an oddball, John said the fisherman had deluded himself into thinking he was a smooth operator—his email handle was TangoPI—and that for some time he had the hots for Mechele, who used to strip at the Bush Company, where all three of them had met. Known to everybody as T.T., Kent kept trying to impress her—doing chores, helping her with the remodel—but Mechele was in love with Scott Hilke. In fact, she had spent the days before the murder with the salesman in a place in Lake Tahoe. When she returned late Wednesday night or early Thursday morning, John picked her up at the airport and brought her back to his house; Kent's body was then found later in the morning. The first John had heard of the murder was when the troopers went to Mechele's house on Friday to inform her of his death.

Recalling what Kent's family had said, DeHart asked John if he knew anything about an insurance policy Kent had taken out.

"He had talked about it," said Kent.

"What did he [say]?" asked DeHart.

"I think it was part of trying to make himself suitable for Mechele, getting insurance on himself, getting insurance on Mechele, trying to take care of stuff at the house."

"Was she supposed to benefit from it?" asked DeHart. "I know you understand."

"Oh, yeah," said John, adding that Kent had also changed his will to include Mechele as beneficiary.

"I was with him when he threw out the will," said John. "He had a will made up, oh, back in December or maybe January."

John said that Kent had a plan for Mechele to find out she'd be getting his inheritance: he'd leave the document where she'd find it.

"T.T. is very—I hate to use the word 'sneaky,' but I mean he tries to be slick," said John. "When we got into the truck, he goes: 'Oh, look, that's my will. Would you like to read it?' And I mean, you could just see that he wanted her to see the will."

Along with Kent's awkward attempts to win Mechele's heart by taking out the insurance policy and naming her in his will, he had strange sexual fixations, said John. From the house, John produced a stack of adult magazines and catalogs that he said belonged to Kent, publications with names like *Lovestuff*, *Voyages*, *Adam and Eve Video*, and *Underground Video*. He also gave them a sheet of yellow paper on which, he said, Kent had written suggestive and sexually explicit phrases: "Old one-eyed to the optometrist," "Take a ride on the wild bologna pony," "Enter the holy of the holies," "Slipping her the old salami," "Put the hotdog in the bun," "Tomcat on a prowl," "Meow," "Taking the log to the beaver."

The detectives asked him more questions, which he answered calmly. He seemed neither nervous nor evasive. There was one thing he wouldn't do: allow his son John Carlin IV to speak with the detectives alone.

DeHart and Belden pressed. John refused.

From John's house, the detectives drove separately to Wasilla for the interview with Mechele, her second. Belden arrived before Mechele, waiting out front until she pulled up just after four p.m. In the car with her were John Carlin III and his son. DeHart was still on the road and would show up later.

Belden sat down with Mechele away from the other two and started his tape recorder. He began by asking about Kent's mind-set in the days before his murder. Again the detective didn't tell her about Kent's complaints to his parents that she had stolen from him and then disappeared, or about her email in his jeans pocket in which she had expressed irritation.

Mechele said she had last spoken to Kent on Tuesday, April 30, in a phone call while she was out of town. She summed up his disposition with one word: "Stupid."

April 30 was an important day in the investigation: Kent had dropped his father off at the airport; talked to his brother, who warned of the target on his back; and then mailed the letters to his parents.

Belden gave Mechele a look.

"I know that sounds so cruel," she said. "He sounded stupid."

"Explain that if you will," the detective asked.

"When I used to ask him a question," she said, beginning a rambling answer, "I would ask him a direct question, and I would get answers like—and we joke about it. We used to joke about it. We don't joke now—but I would get answers like, 'Well, well maybe so.' Like my letters, my boxes of letters. [I'd ask]: 'TT, where's my boxes of letters?' 'Oh, it's around.' 'No it's not. Where is it?' you know.

"I want a direct answer," she continued, "and he wouldn't give them to me. So when I called, that's what he sounded like. And I used to yell at him, because, I said: 'T.T., stop it. Don't be stupid. Give me a direct answer.' And that's the only way I could get him to snap out of it, and say, 'OK, this is where it is' or, you know, 'OK, it's in my storage shed. And so when I called, I was, like, umm, I don't remember exactly what I said to him, but I remember him saying—and I asked him, 'Is your dad in town?' 'Oh, I don't know.' 'Well, either he or his isn't. Did you bring him to the airport or didn't you?' 'Oh, well, we took a trip to the airport,' you know. 'So did he fly out?' you know. And I just got frustrated. I remember getting mad, and . . . and . . . that's what I mean by stupid."

"How long was that conversation with him?" asked Belden.

"Not long at all."

"Did you happen to call collect so that we can check on the dates to make sure?" asked Belden.

"I charged it on my Visa card," she said.

The detective now returned to the issue of the laptop computer, asking again where it was. She again told him that she had sent it to her sister's house in Utah to be fixed.

"I had a password on it and I wanted to take the password off so I took it off and when I did, that locked the Norton anti-virus thing up, when I tried to put the disc in to take it out," she told Belden. "Anyway, I couldn't—she's doing that for me. It was either that or send it back to Gateway and they take like months."

By now DeHart had arrived and joined in the interview.

John Carlin III also had walked in and was listening as Belden asked Mechele if Kent had owned a gun. Mechele said that he had in fact kept a handgun that he lent to her about a year earlier when she and other Bush Company dancers, concerned about their safety when walking in the parking lot at night, took a gun safety class. Belden asked if she knew where the gun was now.

Mechele turned to Carlin. "Have you seen that big black gun that Kent had?"

John reacted first with surprise, then he put his head down and mumbled something about not being sure if ever saw such a gun. Mechele wouldn't let it go. She said she was sure that Kent had a big gun. She picked up the phone and dialed the place where she took the class, the Firing Line range, and asked somebody to check the records for the model gun she used. She thanked them and turned to the detectives.

It was a Desert Eagle .44.

"Do you know," Belden asked Mechele, "if anybody has anything to gain from Kent's death?"

"No," she said, "other than, um, life insurance."

"Life insurance?" the detective asked.

"Me, yeah."

CHAPTER TEN

Kent Leppink's murder made hardly a ripple in the news. The local paper played it on page B5 in the "Police Report" section along items about the arrest of a drunken man found sleeping on a church pew and the death of an intoxicated man who had passed out on a bus bunch. "Troopers ID Dead Man Killed by Gunshot," said the short article in the *Anchorage Daily News* written by "Staff." According to the brief, a "passerby" discovered the body of Kent J. Leppink, thirty-six, of Anchorage at the Hope cutoff, an apparent homicide victim. Troopers declined to reveal any more details, but the newspaper cited state records showing that Leppink had a business license for M&K Enterprises Inc., allowing him to operate a "hunting, fishing and trapping service" in Chugiak since the previous fall. There was no mention of his partner in that business, nothing about John Carlin or Kent's letter to his parents.

As little news as Kent's murder had made, it still managed to reach Brian Brundin, a lawyer and certified public accountant who had practiced for thirty years in Anchorage. On the morning of May 5, the same day that article appeared (and while police were interviewing John Carlin III), Brundin knew there was more to the story than the *Anchorage Daily News* had reported. He went through his files. Then he called police.

When troopers interviewed him the next day, May 6, he

told them that Kent Leppink had been a client, referred to him by associates of Kent's grocery store chain owner father, Kenneth Leppink. In the fall of 1995, the father and son consulted Brundin to incorporate M&K Enterprises, a fishing tender business funded by a $100,000 bank loan guaranteed by the elder Leppink (since Kent had no money or assets) and a second $35,000 personal loan from father to son. The first payment on the bank loan was would be a lump sum of $25,000, due a year later, in October 1996. Over the next year, Kenneth Leppink would loan another $15,000 to Kent. The articles of incorporation listed Kenneth Leppink as first representative on the corporate board. Mechele Hughes was listed as "assistant secretary."

Brundin also helped Kent draft a will, the terms of which dictated leaving everything he had—at this point a pile of debt—to his parents.

About five months later, on April 18, 1996, Kent returned to Brundin's office with Mechele, the first time the lawyer had seen her. Kent announced that he wanted to change his will. The primary beneficiary would now be Mechele, who was introduced as Kent's fiancée.

Brundin handled the paperwork, which Kent signed in front of him.

It would have been a routine matter, except that at one point Kent and Mechele got into an argument. The point of dispute had nothing to do with the will or money but with the question of Kent's sexuality. As Brundin sat there, he listened to Mechele suggest that Kent was having a homosexual affair.

"I can't compete," she snapped. "I can compete if it was a girl."

The pair left the dumbfounded attorney's office with the new will, but that wasn't the end of it. The next morning at 10:45 a.m., Kent arrived, alone, with a lot on his mind.

Clearly upset, Kent told Brundin a complicated story about going to North Star Behavioral Health, a local mental health clinic, demanding to talk to a counselor about a friend's son. Brundin couldn't quite catch the name of the boy—he thought it was Callin—but Kent spoke of him like a stepson. Kent complained that the counselor refused to give any information to Kent, citing confidentiality. Mechele then got wind about Kent's visit and berated him for prying. Kent felt that North Star Behavioral Health had tipped her off, violating *his* confidential communications with the counselor. What's more, he thought that Mechele was having an affair with the boy's father.

He wanted to know if he could sue the clinic.

Brundin took it all in and sighed. This recent melodrama, the back-and-forth accusations of affairs, the spat about Kent's sexuality, and the recent change in his will did not bode well for a long and happy marriage between Kent and Mechele. He offered advice, but it wasn't legal. Instead, he told Kent the parable of the turtle and the scorpion: A turtle was about to swim across a stream when a scorpion asked for a ride. The turtle balked, saying that the scorpion would sting him and they'd both drown. No, the scorpion insisted, that would never happen because it was not in the scorpion's interest. The turtle reluctantly agreed, and as they got halfway across the stream, sure enough, the scorpion stung him. As they both sank to their deaths, the turtle asked why. The scorpion answered: It's my nature.

"The moral of the story," the lawyer told Kent Leppink, "is the scorpion is a scorpion, period. He will bite you even if he says he won't."

Brian Brundin didn't hear from Kent for another week. Kent went to the lawyer's office, again angry, this time over something that had happened the night before. His fiancée, Mechele, had disappeared—and so, Kent said, had his car, his computer, his antique rugs, and a statue worth $4,000 that had been kept in a storage area. He was so upset that he had just changed the beneficiaries on his life insurance and now wanted to change his will to remove Mechele. Brundin obliged, telling Kent that in Alaska, if you canceled a new will, it would revert to the old one. In Kent's case, the old will named his parents as the beneficiaries.

Kent tore up the will and gave the scraps to Brundin to throw away.

This all happened on Friday, April 26, when events picked up pace, headed toward murder. Early that morning, Mechele had sent Kent the snippy email, later found in his pocket, about taking the rugs for cleaning and asserting that she "did not mess up the computer" and had got it "finally working"—the computer that Mechele claimed she had sent to her sister in Utah for repairs.

Friday was also the day that Kent's father had arrived from Michigan to help him with his books. It may also have been the day that Kent had found the note from John and Mechele about her rendezvous in Hope, sending Kent there in search of a cabin that apparently didn't exist.

Friday was also the day that Mechele claimed she had been with Scott Hilke in Lake Tahoe.

Following up on the interview with Bundin, investigators went to the offices of Steven Leirer, a New York Life Insurance Company agent whose business card was also found in Kent's pocket along with the New York Life change-of-beneficiary form and other papers. Speaking both to Leirer and his secretary, Marie Homer, on May 7, investigators found that it was Mechele Hughes who had first contacted them inquiring about life insurance back in February of 1996. Talking by phone with Homer, Mechele asked how much the premiums would cost. Homer said she had to refer Mechele to her boss, Leirer, to talk numbers. An appointment was set up for February 11, but Mechele didn't show.

According to Homer's appointment calendar, the meeting with Mechele was rescheduled for February 14. This time the meeting happened, but neither Homer nor Leirer could remember if it was over the phone or in person, although both Kent and Mechele took part. Mechele had been identified as Kent's "associate." Leirer went over the various policies and costs, and two days later, on February 16, 1996, at eleven a.m., Kent and Mechele were in his office to fill out the forms. They applied for $1 million policies for each of them.

Kent was using the policy for business purposes. On the form, he indicated that his business, M&K Enterprises Inc., was a fish tender working in Prince William Sound and Bristol Bay. According to the paperwork, Kent was 100 percent owner of the business and, as a key person in the business, the policy was intended to cover bank loans on an existing boat and possibly on the purchase of a new boat. A policy of that size required that the policyholder have medical examinations, including blood and urine tests, and appointments for these were made. The paperwork was sent to the home office in New York for underwriting.

Within days, Leirer informed Kent and Mechele that the corporate office had approved Kent's $1 million policy, but Mechele only qualified for $150,000. The pair returned to his office on March 1 to complete the paperwork, which was sent back to New York for processing.

A week later, on March 8, Mechele left a message with Marie Homer. Mechele said that she and Kent would be out of town for three weeks but that they would call the following week for an update on the life insurance policies. Homer told troopers that she recalled Mechele saying they were going to Montana. Homer was sure Mechele used the word "they." It was to be a "honeymoon type of vacation," Homer recalled, and the pair referred to themselves as being engaged. Mechele had seemed eager to get the policies into effect and wanted to pay for them now, even though the policies had not come back from underwriting. Mechele was told not to bother. It was too early for a payment.

By April 1, Mechele's policy had been processed, but Kent's was still outstanding. Mechele didn't want to wait. She came into Leirer's office alone and dropped off a check for $2,606, covering the premiums for both policies: $266 for her policy, the rest for Kent's premium. The check was drawn on Mechele's personal account, not the joint account she held with Kent.

Kent picked up his policy a week later, on April 8, signing the last of the papers. His life was now worth $1 million, with 20 percent going to Kenneth and Betsy Leppink, and the remainder—$800,000—going to Mechele Hughes, identified on the policy as his "intended spouse."

The policy had only been in effect for two weeks when Kent returned solo to Leirer's office. He wanted to make some changes. A form was signed, dated April 22, 1996, and sent to the local processing center in order to make Kent's parents full beneficiaries. Mechele would get nothing.

Then the next day Kent changed his mind again. He called the office and told Homer to stop the processing of the paperwork from the day before. Returning to the office, Kent now removed his parents entirely from the policy and made Mechele the 100 percent beneficiary of the $1 million. Calling Mechele his "fiancée" on the form, Kent was insistent: he didn't want her to know that just the day before he had written her out of his life insurance policy. Kent even asked if he could destroy the now outdated form. Homer said that was unnecessary, that the new paperwork would supersede the old, but to appease him, she put a big X through it.

Three days later, on April 26—a day proving to be pivotal in the investigation—Kent was back in Leirer's office. He once again removed Mechele from his policy and named his father as first beneficiary, his mother as secondary, and his brother Ransom as tertiary.

Kent gave no explanation. He filled out the new paperwork and left, making his way, police now know, to his lawyer's office, where Kent then removed Mechele from his will. In her last police interview, Mechele made reference to the insurance policy and how she would be the one who could benefit from Kent's death. Did she know she'd been written off the policy?

According to Homer and Leirer at New York Life, on Tuesday, April 30, Mechele called Leirer's office at 3:12 p.m. and reached Homer. The secretary took this memo for Leirer, based on the conversation:

Wedding postponed for two months, short of cash, can they get their money back. Call her Friday, she is currently out of town, back late Thursday.

As Leirer later read the memo, it occurred to him that Kent probably hadn't told Mechele she was off his policy. He called her that Friday, May 3, but couldn't reach her. Leirer didn't know it yet, but Kent was already dead.

Tuesday, April 30, was another day of significance in the investigation. That morning Kent had brought his father to the airport for the flight back to Michigan, then talked to his brother Craig about the "target" on his back before sending the package to his parents.

This was also the day, Mechele claimed, that she had spoken with Kent by phone, their last conversation. She had thought he was acting "stupid."

Steven Leirer finally reached Mechele by phone on Monday, May 6. It was morning and she seemed "distraught." She told him that Kent was dead.

As investigators DeHart and Belden continued to reconstruct Kent's final days, more evidence mounted to indicate that the lovesick, deluded fisherman had started to get wise. In addition to removing Mechele from his will and insurance policy, Kent began to have second thoughts about the thousands of dollars he was pouring into an extensive remodeling project on Mechele's house.

And for good reason: Kent was going broke. Investigators subpoenaed bank records and found that by mid-April, Kent's balance had dipped so low that with his father's help he borrowed another $10,000. According to the loan documents, the money was intended to "gear up for fishing season in Prince William Sound." The money actually went to Kenneth Leppink, then was credited to the checking account for Kent's fishing business, M&K Enterprises.

But additional police interviews found that the money wasn't going to the fishing tender. Employees of Eagle Hardware in Anchorage told investigators that just days after the loan money arrived, Kent and Mechele came into the store. They had been there the previous February with another, unidentified woman—probably one of Mechele's stripper friends—to draft plans for a new kitchen with bath and kitchen designer Jerry Leon Faulkner (during one awkward moment, Mechele had accused him of looking down her shirt; he denied it).

Now, on Wednesday, April 24, Mechele and Kent were back in the store, ready to buy a set of kitchen cabinets, only to get into a heated argument over which account the money would come from. Faulkner, who had experience with bickering couples, excused himself to get a drink of water. He told investigators the argument "got fairly vocal" and "there was definitely friction there."

Ultimately, Mechele and Kent came to an agreement and purchased the cabinets for $4,284.90. Kent paid with a check on his joint checking account with Mechele—the bank book that had been found in his pocket at the crime scene. But bank records showed the money really came from elsewhere. The day of the cabinet purchase, $4,284.90 was transferred from the M&K Enterprises account to the joint account. The $10,000 loan intended for fishing was actually funding Mechele's home remodel.

Two days later, Kent returned to Eagle Hardware by himself and told designer Faulkner that Mechele wanted to cancel the purchase because she had found cabinets she liked better elsewhere. Faulkner referred him to another manager in loss prevention. The check was under both names and Faulkner wasn't sure if Kent alone could cancel.

Michael Hull, assistant store manager in charge of kitchen and bath at Eagle Hardware, told investigators that Kent was "adamant" about canceling the sale. Wanting to save the deal, Hull pressed Kent on where these other cabinets were and what they looked like. Kent wouldn't say. "He wanted a refund and that was it," recalled Hull later.

Company policy dictated that a cash refund couldn't be made until the check cleared. But Kent wanted the money immediately. So Hull faxed the corporate office in Seattle with a refund request.

This all happened on Friday, April 26, the same day that Kent had received the email from Mechele later found in his pocket, the same day he had removed her from his will and life insurance policy.

Hull, meanwhile, wasn't yet prepared to lose the big cabinet sale. He repeatedly called the number that Mechele had left on the order form to see if she really did want to buy her cabinets someplace else. He finally reached a man who was clearly John Carlin III—he remembered that his first name was John and last name started with *C*—who said that Mechele was traveling and would be back within a week.

Hull eventually reached Mechele by phone and arranged to meet her on Wednesday, May 1. At some point she called back to reschedule. She explained that she was working on her house and wanted to meet instead on Friday of that same week. She wanted the cabinet order reinstated.

Hull spoke again with Mechele, probably on Thursday, May 2, or Friday, May 3. She mentioned almost in passing that Kent had been killed. "It was pretty much no emotion, no anything, that he was deceased," Hull later said, "and she wanted her cabinets."

Kent's death, it seemed, would not stop her from remodeling. Mechele went back to Eagle Hardware on Sunday, May 5, and spoke with designer Jerry Leon Faulkner. By now, Faulkner knew that Kent had been killed, but told investigators that all Mechele wanted to talk about was her new kitchen. "[She] said the cabinets were not his to cancel and she wanted to put them back on order again," said Faulkner, who referred her again to Hull, who put the order through.

Faulkner told investigators Mechele had come in during the afternoon. That meant she had stopped there the same day that DeHart and Belden had interviewed her. They recalled she had left John Carlin's house to go "shopping," she said, then was interviewed later at her home in Wasilla.

Kitchen cabinets weren't the only things on Mechele's mind that day. Troopers interviewed a jeweler Dana Lumetta Danford from Megagem in Anchorage, who said that she also had spoken with Mechele on May 5. Danford had a long association with Mechele, having sold thousands of dollars in jewelry to Kent Leppink and John Carlin, who in turn gave it to Mechele.

The transactions dated back to about the summer of 1995 when Kent and Mechele came into the store and Kent purchased a diamond pendant and a pair of matching earrings for $500. "They were definitely a couple," the jeweler later recalled. "She would be hugging on him and talking to him." The purchase had occurred around the time that Kent's family met Mechele over the dinner at Elevation 92 in which she rejected his offer of more jewelry.

A couple of months later, in September 1995, Kent looked at a loose diamond worth $11,000. He didn't purchase it, but two days later John Carlin III did. "He came in and asked for a particular stone," Danford recalled. "It was a one-carat round diamond, D color, flawless, the best nature produces. He knew that I had it in stock and he purchased it." He wrote her a $5,000 check and returned in two days with $6,000 in cash. The diamond was set in a solitaire setting. "It would be your typical most common engagement ring that's sold, just a stone and a plain ring by itself," said Danford. Later she saw Mechele wearing the ring in the store when she was with John.

Mechele had said nothing to the troopers about being engaged to John. Was she engaged to him at the same time as Kent?

The last jewelry purchase came just days before Kent's murder. Mechele had ordered a chain and bracelet. Danford called to say it was ready, leaving a message, and Mechele got back to her either by phone or in person—Danford couldn't recall which—on May 5, the same day Mechele had been interviewed by DeHart and Belden. Mechele wanted to pay using credit for a pair of earrings Kent had earlier returned before his murder, which she called a "very creepy thing."

"She went on and told me that they were never going to get married, that she was in Nevada, that she had left town," Danford said later. Danford wouldn't let Mechele use the credit, since it had belonged to Kent, and now might be part of his estate because he was dead.

While troopers conducted interviews with Mechele, John, and the people from the hardware store and jewelry shop, Robert Shem, a forensic firearm and tool mark examiner for the Alaska state crime laboratory, was busy in his lab. He had received a package on May 9, 1996, with a handwritten note: "On 5/2/96, victim located deceased on power line 13.5 Hope Road. Three gunshot wounds. Suspect weapon possibly Desert Eagle." In the envelope were two bullets extracted from the chest and head of a man named Ken Leppink, and random pieces of metal.

Shem had spent twenty-one years peering through microscopes, identifying projectiles and linking them to weapons. Before him on this day were at first glance relatively common bullets, both .44s, both manufactured to weigh 240 grains but now smaller after losing mass from being fired.

The rest of the material was metallic but did not come from a gun. It appeared to be the remnants of tooth fillings.

Inspecting the bullets through the microscope, Shem saw something unusual in the grooves, or rifling, around the edges. As a bullet is blasted down the barrel of a rifle or handgun, it spirals along the tracks of the raised and lowered areas inside of the barrel. This allows the bullet to gain gyroscopic speed, like a top, to keep it steady in flight. Without the spin, the bullet—which is pointy at the top and wider at the base—would turn around and fly backward led by the heavier end. Those raised and lowered surfaces in the barrel are called lands and grooves, and a typical firearm has six of them, spiraling clockwise, or with what examiners call a right-handed hook. As the bullet passes through the barrel, it picks up these six right-handed indentations, which are easily seen under the microscope.

But the first bullet that Shem saw was different. The six lands and grooves were not distinct but faint, the transition from raised and lowered marks subtle. This is the sign of hexagonal right rifling, the bullet coming from a barrel with more gradual changes between the lands and grooves. In his two decades of experience, Shem had never seen that before in a .44 caliber bullet.

He flipped open his 204-page guidebook—the FBI's *General Rifling Characteristics File*—and on page 194 it listed a single weapon that leaves these characteristics: the Desert Eagle .44 handgun. The literature says the Desert Eagle is a heavy gun, about four pounds when fully loaded, and that the slide that opens the main chamber can be hard to pull back. When the trigger is pulled, the weapon has a powerful kick.

The murder weapon's identity was corroborated by Shem's examination of the brass shell casings found near Kent's body. He found tiny indentations from where the gun's mechanism grabbed onto the casings and ejected them during firing. This is the sign of a semiautomatic pistol. In a revolver, the shells must be removed by hand and therefore have no markings.

Shem's ballistics examination confirmed what the troopers at the scene had suspected and matched what Mechele had related about a "big black gun" she had used in her handgun safety course. Lead investigator Steven DeHart assigned a trooper to scour all of Alaska's gun shops, looking for somebody who may have purchased a Desert Eagle .44 in the last year or two. DeHart also wanted to speak again with John Carlin, who had denied owning such a weapon but acted strangely when Mechele said that Kent had owned one.

For the next three weeks DeHart continued to go through Kent's financial records and interview more people with details about the fisherman's life and final days. On May 10 he placed a call to Mechele and asked her again about the laptop that she said she had sent to her sister's for repair.

"Do you know when your sister's going to have the computer back?" he asked.

"Probably within a couple of days, I mean a week or so," she said. "Why do you need the computer? There's nothing on it."

He didn't answer.

While DeHart waited for the laptop to come back, he received reports from the canvass of gun dealers: nothing so far. Alaska has among the nation's most lenient gun control laws, and that gun could have been sold in any number of ways without leaving a paper trail. If it was a private-party transaction at a gun show or a sale between friends, there would be virtually no way to track it down.

By the first week of June 1996, after a month of police work, DeHart had only the outlines of a case. But DeHart had no strong physical evidence. He still had no eyewitnesses, no murder weapon, no confessions—a lot of smoke, but no fire. The longer the investigation dragged on, he knew, the slimmer the chances any more evidence would emerge. Even the laptop was a long shot. Anything incriminating would have been scrubbed from its memory by now. Still, he moved forward. DeHart planned to talk yet again to Mechele and John—neither had refused to speak and neither had hired lawyers—and thought of obtaining search warrants for their homes. As he considered his next steps, word came back to him that John and Mechele had plans of their own. It looked like they were leaving Alaska.

CHAPTER ELEVEN

When Douglas Hendricks, senior RV salesperson with Johnson's RV in Anchorage, spotted John Carlin III coming onto the lot, he went into salesman mode: Establish a rapport, find out what the customer really wants—a pop-up van? a midsized RV? a monster-size class A motor home with all the bells and whistles?—hook them on that product, learn how much money they really have, then close, close, close.

On this particular day Hendricks was fortunate. He recognized John from a previous transaction: the burly man had bought his fancy Jeep there and, just the week before, sold to Johnson's a Chevy Blazer that had been driven by his son. A repeat customer meant an easier path to making rapport, and after the two chatted, Hendricks moved to the next step, trying to find out what John wanted. This would be more difficult, for John said he was making the purchase with a female friend, who wasn't there. Hendricks sighed.

"You're not allowed to go buy paint unless your wife tells you what kind," Hendricks recalled later. "Same with an RV. It's very hard to get specific on an RV when you're talking about a couple without involving the woman's point of view."

John said he'd have to come back later and left the lot.

When police talked to Hendricks, it was nearly a week later. For the interview on Tuesday, June 11, troopers and Hendricks sat down inside one of the lot's RVs. Talkative and friendly, Hendricks expounded on the art of RV sales, telling them that it's considerably more complicated than selling a car—closer to a real estate transaction—and that the process can take several days and require large amounts of paperwork. But the payoff for a salesman can be rich. Along with a hefty commission on what could be a mid- to high-five-figure sale, Hendricks stood to gain another $500 bonus—or spiff, as they call it in the business—if he could close before a weekend.

As promised, John had returned to Johnson's RV the next day, Thursday, with the woman he identified as Mechele Hughes and his son John IV, according to Hendricks. After going into a number of RVs, Mechele honed in on a Thor Industries class A motor home with expandable sides. "When Mechele saw this motor home she truly admired the beauty of it," Hendricks recalled.

The retail price was $86,000—more than what most houses in Alaska cost—but it was what Mechele wanted. The group retreated to Hendricks's office to haggle on price. They settled on $72,000. For Hendricks it was a "skinny deal"—very little profit—but worth doing because it stood a good chance of closing.

They then went about finding out whether they had the cash, assets, and credit rating for what would be a sizable loan. Mechele said she would finance the motor home and John would provide the down payment and secure the loan, putting up his house in south Anchorage as an asset. But because the loan would be in Michele's name, it had to be secured by her assets.

Mechele said her Wasilla home was the biggest asset. At one point she turned to John and said, "What about the jewelry you bought me?" Based on her estimates, the jewelry was worth a whopping $42,000. They also discussed selling John's Jeep back to the dealership, which John estimated was worth about $31,000. The used-car department reps took a look at it and only offered $19,400, which John rejected. "It ended up being an insult to him," Hendricks said.

Hendricks, motivated by his $500 bonus if he closed before the weekend and feeling like he was on the verge of closing, pushed the pair to come up with the down payment that day. Mechele and John conferred and said they probably would buy the RV but needed to go to Mechele's house in Wasilla to review her financial documents. They all made the forty-minute drive, Hendricks driving John IV in one vehicle, John and Mechele driving in John's Jeep, which had a trailer filled with carpeting, part of Mechele's remodeling project.

By the time the last papers were signed, it was after midnight. They talked some more: Mechele told Hendricks she was thinking of selling her house, and Hendricks said he had a brother who might be interested. They eventually said their good-byes, and Hendricks got home at 2:30 a.m.

The next day Mechele drove off the lot in her new $72,000 palace on wheels. She had paid for it with an $18,000 cashier's check that John dropped off and $57,000 in financing. To secure the loan, Mechele listed her assets as a 1989 Volvo worth $19,000, a 1995 Jeep worth $32,000, a home valued at $125,000 with mortgage payments of about $800 or $900 a month, and "other assets" worth $45,000.

For the next few days Mechele stopped returning Sergeant DeHart's phone calls, so the detective sent a trooper to drive by her house to see if her car—or the new RV—was in the driveway. On June 19 the trooper spotted a bearded man who fit John Carlin's description in front of the house, and a Jeep Cherokee with Louisiana plates, DQW793—Mechele's car—but no massive motor home. A check of local auto dealerships found that John had in fact sold his matching Cherokee to another lot on June 7, the same day Mechele picked up the RV.

DeHart continued to try to reach Mechele in the days that followed, but her whereabouts were unknown. She had disappeared, just as Kent used to complain about, only it didn't take long for investigators to find out where she had gone.

On June 26 a woman called the Division of Alaska State Troopers, saying she had information about the murder of Kent Leppink. A trooper named Donald Bowman took the call and wrote down her name—Melissa Hughes—and passed it on to DeHart.

When the lead detective called her back, Melissa explained that she and her husband lived in Moab, Utah, where they managed the Slickrock Campground. She said that in mid-May, a heavy package arrived in the mail: a laptop computer from her sister, Mechele Hughes.

According to Melissa, the laptop wasn't the only thing that arrived in the campground. A week earlier, on June 19, Mechele drove up in a big RV filled with her pets, including a cat and some birds, and a teenager named John Carlin IV whom she identified as a friend's son. A day or two later a blond-haired man arrived in the campground in a rental car he had picked up in Denver, where he was on business. He said his name was Scott Hilke and he also was a friend of Mechele's.

For the next couple of days, according to Melissa, her sister Mechele and Scott enjoyed themselves, renting wave runners and going rock climbing, before Scott had to return to Denver. The visit was going well enough until at some point Mechele and Melissa sat at a picnic table to discuss the laptop. The discussion turned into an argument. Mechele wanted Melissa to reformat the hard drive, saying she had purchased the laptop from Kent Leppink and wanted it to be like new. Sensing that something was off, Melissa angrily refused.

The argument then turned to Kent's murder. "While we were sitting at the table and discussing the laptop," Melissa recalled later, "she told me . . . that people didn't like him, that he hunted and stuffed animals and that she felt that he got exactly what he deserved." Stunned, Melissa listened to her sister rant against the dead man. "She said that it was too bad that someone didn't torture him first," Melissa recalled. "She was sitting at the picnic table and she slammed her hands down on the table. The words were quite strong for me to hear." The teenager with Mechele also shared her low opinion of Kent, expressing no concern over his death. "I remember him saying that no one likes T.T. anyway," recalled Melissa.

Mechele then talked about the investigation into Kent's murder and how she had been questioned by the police. She seemed to have a lot of inside information. "I seem to remember her saying that he had sent a letter to his parents saying that if something happened to him she was responsible," according to Melissa.

DeHart had not released that information to the press and never mentioned it in the interviews with Mechele or John Carlin. How had she found out?

Soon after talking to Melissa Hughes, Steven DeHart was busy obtaining search warrants. The first was served three days later on June 29 at Mechele's house in Wasilla. When the three troopers arrived, Mechele was still out of town, but a man was working on cabinets in the kitchen, continuing the renovation project in her absence. The troopers seized a Packard Bell computer and discs and took feathers from a large birdcage. They also went under the house in the crawl space, where they saw clothing in a box marked *Hilke*.

In one of the bedrooms, the troopers also saw a document called an earnest-money agreement from somebody named Brett Reddell and a mention of a $10,000 cashier's check. They also saw copies of Kent's loan papers for his fishing tender. They made note of the documents but didn't seize them.

While the troopers were in the house, the phone rang. It was a woman identifying herself as Mechele Hughes, saying she was calling from a campground in Louisiana. Somebody—perhaps the workman—had tipped her off that her house was being searched. She told them that if they were looking for Kent's belongings, they were in a shed outside, and that if anybody needed to reach her she'd be at her mother's house in New Orleans.

Next, a pair of troopers searched John's house. Nobody was there, but they saw moving boxes filled with belongings. Upstairs, a trooper found the same gun case and nylon pistol belt that Trooper Sears had seen nearly two months earlier. The items sat in the corner of the upstairs bedroom, under a pile of bedding.

Then a warrant was served on Mechele's green Jeep. Inside, the troopers found a gun holster.

That day the troopers tracked down John in Anchorage and pushed him harder than ever on what he had been doing the night before Kent's body was found—and who might have been driving Mechele's Jeep.

John said he had gone to the airport to pick up Mechele, who was arriving late in the early morning hours of Thursday, May 2, because of a missed connecting flight in Seattle. She had driven there herself, but while she was out of town John had picked up her Jeep from the airport parking lot.

"Do you recall if she called you from outside [the airport] or here in Anchorage when she got in?" a trooper asked. "How is it she made arrangements for you to pick her up?"

"She probably called," John said. "No—she wouldn't have called from Anchorage. She could have called from Seattle. I'm not sure if that was the call where she missed her flight and came an hour later on the next flight or what. I don't know."

"But you had enough advance notice that you were waiting at the airport for her?"

"I knew she was coming in."

"OK, did Little John go with you when you picked her up, do you recall?"

"No, he did not. I do recall. I don't think John's ever—I could be wrong—but I don't think John's ever come to the airport and picked her up or dropped her off."

"She thought Kent was going to pick her up? Do you know at all why Kent did not pick her up?"

"Kent," said John, "wasn't around."

The troopers then pressed him on the murder weapon.

"John, what would you say if I told you that I've been told that you had a .44 gun in your house," said Trooper DeHart.

The question was a ruse. Nobody had said that.

"I would say that's a bunch of crap," John shot back.

"You deny having a .44 caliber handgun in your home?" the trooper asked.

"Absolutely."

"Never owned one there?"

"Nope."

"At any time?"

"Nope."

"Or possessed it for anybody else?"

"No."

"Here in Anchorage?"

"No," he said. "I have in Jersey."

"Why would someone tell me that you had a .44 gun in your house here in Anchorage?"

"I don't have the foggiest idea."

John had not taken the bait. But the investigation seemed to be picking up steam.

Two days later, Louisiana police spotted a motor home in New Orleans with Alaska plates registered to Mechele. Acting on a warrant obtained by Alaska state troopers, the local police searched the RV and found a Gateway laptop computer and a parcel shipping order for $27.50 with an Alaska postmark. When Steven DeHart and Ron Belden had interviewed Mechele on May 5, she told them that she had already sent the laptop to her sister. The postmark showed it was actually sent the next day.

On July 25, DeHart and Belden flew to Louisiana, where they took custody of the laptop from local authorities. While in New Orleans, they also spoke to Mechele's uncle and grandfather, getting no information of value. They decided against speaking to her mother but wanted to do another interview with Mechele. However, she wasn't in town: the day the investigators arrived, she boarded a flight for Anchorage.

DeHart and Belden left New Orleans with the Gateway laptop in their luggage. The return trip included a stop in Sacramento. It was time to talk to Scott Hilke.

CHAPTER TWELVE

Scott Hilke lived by a code: he minded his business and expected others to mind theirs. For nearly three months, he had refused to take phone calls from Steven DeHart and his investigators, calling their attempts to extract information out of him "an infringement on my privacy." So when he finally agreed to appear at the Sacramento Police Department on July 29 for an interview with DeHart and Belden, he made no effort to hide his disgust. Terse and prickly, he answered the questions as directly and briefly as possible. He offered no additional information. "I was," he recalled later, "not pleased."

Under persistent questioning, Scott acknowledged having a relationship with Mechele Hughes, first as a fiancée now as something of a weekend lover. The more the detectives pressed him about his getaways with Mechele over the last two years, the more he took offense. The detectives suggested it was an odd relationship; Hilke thought the detectives were rude.

But he did confirm that he spent the days before Kent's murder with Mechele in a condominium in Incline Village on the shores of Lake Tahoe. Mechele had obtained the condo through a friend whom he didn't know. Scott mostly went golfing. Mechele joined him for one round, making for a spectacle on the links in her short skirt and high heels. It was, he said, just another weekend like many others.

Mechele typed on the laptop and made phone calls, just as she always did. She brought her birds along, her cockatoos Sybil and Sarah, but Hilke explained that Mechele frequently flew with her pets, stashing them in an animal carrier under the seat. He would have to pay the airlines extra for the birds, but Mechele loved her animals. She spoke of one day building a bird sanctuary and had even gone so far as to travel to Costa Rica recently to see if she could make her quixotic dream a reality. Costa Rica brought to mind a fact from the first days of the investigation: the "Go to Hope" note found in Kent's glove compartment had John saying he may go to Costa Rica or Australia. Aside from complaining of being a little tired, Mechele's demeanor was not out of the ordinary. She'd been living with John Carlin for months while her home was being remodeled and was eager to move back in.

The only wrinkle in the trip was that after a day or two, friends of the condo owner unexpectedly showed up. It seemed the owner had also promised the condo to them for the same weekend. But their arrival caused no intrusion, the trip went as planned, and Scott drove Mechele back to Sacramento and put her on a flight back to Alaska. He said she probably returned on that Sunday or Monday, April 28 or 29, but he wasn't sure.

At no time during their stay in Tahoe did Mechele act like somebody involved in a murder plot.

Scott added emphatically that he wasn't part of one, either. He said he had only known Kent slightly. Scott thought he was an idiot—and, in answer to the detectives' pointed questions, had no idea if Kent was gay, only that he was strange. If Kent had been engaged to Mechele, that was news to Scott. But he did know that he hadn't killed Kent and didn't know who had.

As for Scott's whereabouts, the day after taking Mechele to the airport, he went on a business trip to Cleveland.

The detectives asked Scott if he placed any significance on Hope, Alaska, and if he knew anything about a letter making Kent think there might be a cabin there. This was the first he had heard of it. They asked him if he knew anything about a $1 million life insurance policy on Kent. Again Scott claimed to know nothing.

For Scott, the interview was getting to be a bore, the detectives annoying. When they asked him if they could look through his house, he said no. He even refused to tell them where he lived. The more the salesman claimed to know nothing, the more frustrated and nasty DeHart got, Scott later claimed. The interview ended with Scott thinking that both of the Alaska lawmen were fools.

Scott was driving home when he spotted the tail. He stormed back to the station, upset that police were following him. DeHart, who had requested the assistance from the local police, exchanged heated words with Scott, explaining to him in no uncertain terms that this was a homicide investigation and that it was imperative that Scott cooperate. The salesman backed down. He said the investigators could come to his house, but they had to call first.

The next morning DeHart phoned Scott to tell him he was on his way. When DeHart and Belden arrived about a half hour later, Scott allowed them to search. The most provocative finds were a stack of newspaper clippings. Asked about this, Scott claimed he liked to keep up on current events and was something of a crime buff. Scott also acknowledged that he had spoken to Mechele recently but wouldn't say what was discussed. However, to get the Alaska state troopers off his back, he offered to take a polygraph. The detectives said they'd take him up on that.

After two days in Sacramento, the investigators boarded a flight in Sacramento for Anchorage, their luggage containing the Gateway 2000 laptop computer seized from Mechele's motor home in New Orleans. During a layover in Seattle, they received a fax from Alaska Airlines: Mechele's itinerary for the days before the murder. It showed that she had left Anchorage for Sacramento on Thursday, April 25, her ticket charged to a credit card of John Carlin, with an added $50 "kennel fee" for her birds. Her return flight left Sacramento the night of Wednesday, May 1. After a connection in Seattle, she arrived in Anchorage at one a.m. on Thursday, May 2.

Kent's body was found nine hours later in Hope, a ninety-minute drive from the airport.

CHAPTER THIRTEEN

For weeks Mechele had refused to talk again to investigators, demanding that they return the laptop that had been seized from her motor home in Louisiana. In several phone calls with Mechele, Sergeant Steve DeHart told her that the computer was evidence and she couldn't get it back until the investigation was complete. And even then she would need permission from Kent's family, as executors of his estate, which owned the computer.

Reluctantly, Mechele agreed to one more interview.

On July 31, 1996, Mechele sat across from DeHart at the trooper station in Palmer. By now DeHart had talked to Scott Hilke and to Mechele's sister Melissa. It quickly became clear that Mechele had been talking to at least one of them too. When DeHart asked Mechele about her stay with her sister Melissa in the campground and whether they had discussed anything, Mechele knew all about what her sister had told police.

"Oh, that if I would have done it, I would have tortured him? Is that what you're talking about?" Mechele said.

"No," said DeHart, "what she shared with me was that you were glad that he was dead, which seems pretty cold to me."

"Yeah" was all Mechele said.

"That it's unfortunate that he was not tortured, which sounds pretty cold to me."

"That wasn't exactly words like that I said," Mechele said.

"But words to that effect?"

"When I was cleaning up in the shed," she explained, "I found the dead animals that were stuffed. I looked at their eyes, and it was odd that T.T. died in the woods like those animals that he killed. And from the animals' point of view, yeah, he deserved it. And I told her, I wish he were—I would torture him."

DeHart asked her what her real relationship was with John Carlin:

"You have always been just strictly friends?"

"Um, we were strictly friends," she said. "It was strictly a platonic relationship, until I can't tell you exactly when, it was probably—hmmm—I don't know, I don't know. But if you're asking if we've had sex, yes, we have had sex three times. And it was, it was months and months and months ago."

"OK, and did he propose marriage to you?"

"Uh-huh."

"And what was your answer?"

"Which time?" Mechele asked.

"Well, how many times did he propose to you?" asked DeHart.

"It depends on what you consider a proposal," Mechele said. "If somebody hands you a ring and doesn't say anything, is that a proposal? I mean it's obvious. It looks like an engagement ring."

"Depends on what kind of ring it is," offered DeHart.

"It obviously looks like one," she said. "But if somebody gives it to you in a box and says open it later on—"

"Generally speaking, Mechele," said DeHart, losing patience, "people think of a proposal—somebody's asking you to marry him. I mean most people think that's a proposal and that's essentially what we're talking [about]. Did he ask you specifically—or would you marry him—and what was your response to that?"

"Um, we've talked about getting married a couple of times. Um, never really seriously until the last time, right before I left."

"And who proposed at that time?"

"I brought it up."

"You wanted to marry him?"

"Well, I asked him if he wanted to get married before I left, yeah."

Before she left, she said, for Lake Tahoe.

"OK, so you and Scott Hilke are not going to get married?" asked DeHart.

"At this time, I'm not getting married to anybody," Mechele said.

"At the time that you were talking to John, your intentions were not to go back to Scott Hilke at that point?"

"My intentions were not to marry anyone. I asked John if it would make him feel better, OK, if we were to get married before I left," Mechele said. "Did I really intend on getting married? I doubt it. But at that point it was just a conversation and it wasn't—we didn't have a date, a calendar out, you know."

"OK, he gave you a ring?"

"Uh-huh."

"What type of ring was it?"

"You know what type of ring it is," Mechele snapped. "You saw it. It's an engagement ring."

"You know what it costs?"

"Yes."

"How much did it cost?"

"I think it appraised at $14,000, costs about $10,000."

"OK, did he give you any furs?"

"Uh-huh. You know that too," said Mechele. "He gave me a Christmas present. It was a fur."

The detective also asked about Brett Reddell, the man who had loaned her his truck and whose name was on the earnest money agreement spotted in her house.

"Is that another person you had a relationship with?"

"Brett?" she said. "No, no."

"But, Mechele, you're smart—"

"But, I mean, yeah, he sends me money. He comes to the Bush Company every time he comes to town. I've gone to see him."

"You're a smart—"

"He doesn't even know T.T. He's never even seen him."

DeHart then asked her about the weekend before the murder. Mechele corroborated what Scott Hilke had said about the condo. She said it was offered to her by a man named Tony Dawson, an airline pilot who had been referred to Mechele by a mutual friend.

"Did you ever see Tony in person prior to going to the condo?" asked DeHart. "Or did both of you just talk to him on the phone?"

"No, I had dinner with him the night before I left—two nights before I left," said Mechele.

For the Tahoe trip, DeHart wanted to know how she got to the airport.

"Did you take T.T.'s car?" he asked.

"Never, never, never, never," Mechele answered.

"How did you get to the airport?"

"I drove my Jeep," she said.

And it was "Big John" who picked her up.

"He got my Jeep from the airport."

"OK, so he came and got it?"

"Uh-huh, something was wrong with his Jeep," she said. "He went and got my car from the airport so it wasn't there when I got in."

DeHart asked Mechele about the large gun she had used in her concealed-weapons course.

"Was there a holster for the gun?" he asked, knowing that one had been found in her car, "although you didn't have [it]?"

"I don't know," Mechele said. "I never asked."

"Well . . ."

"There was a gun in a case and it had bullets," she said.

"Isn't it in fact true that the gun belongs to John?"

"No, the gun belongs to T.T.," Mechele said, "and I'm sure of that."

CHAPTER FOURTEEN

Mechele Hughes returned to Louisiana, and most hopes of solving Kent's murder seemed to go with her. Over the next few weeks, as the summer of 1996 turned to fall, the investigation sputtered and the list of people to interview dwindled.

Detectives did find Anthony Dawson, the man who owned the condominium in Lake Tahoe. A pilot for UPS, Dawson said he was referred to Mechele by a friend. "He frequently contacted her, communicated with her. He had suggested I contact her," Dawson said later. "He said she's an attractive, nice individual and you should meet her." Dawson called Mechele and they arranged to meet at a Thai restaurant in Anchorage during one of his weekly trips there for UPS, though he said it was lunch, not dinner, as Mechele had said. She arrived for the late April lunch date in a light-colored fur coat—not the first time, investigators noted, that Mechele had worn fur despite the animosity she directed toward Kent for his taxidermy. John Carlin III had also acknowledged buying her a fur coat, perhaps the one she was wearing. Dawson described their meeting as "cordial, very pleasant," and insisted it was lunch only—no sex. As they spoke, he happened to mention that he owned a condominium in Incline Village that he often rented out to friends. He allowed Mechele to have it for the weekend for free.

After Dawson, the next person to interview was Brett

Reddell, an oil worker. When he spoke to an investigator in September 1996, Reddell said he was still in contact with Mechele. More surprising, he said he considered himself Mechele's boyfriend.

Brett explained that he had met Mechele a year earlier, in September 1995. At the time, he was a recent divorcee raising two children in the remote North Slope community of Barrow, the northernmost town in the United States, where the sun doesn't set in the summer and doesn't rise in the winter. During business trips to Anchorage about three times a year, he and local pals and subcontractors would hit the Great Alaskan Bush Company, where he would spend a lot of money—between $1,000 and $3,000—the "biggest part" of it to Mechele. "It was the way she talked," he said later. "She was magnetic."

They became friends outside the club, and she soon asked him for money for house and car payments. "She would call. She would need some money. I would send her money, wire or mail the money orders," he said later. He also let her use his credit card. She needed the money, she told him, to help remodel her house in Wasilla. In all, he estimated he spent $6,000 to $9,000 on her. "She always said she was going to be rich. Her goal was to have lots of money."

In a year, Brett slept with Mechele only once, he said. He never proposed to her, but as far as he knew he was her one and only boyfriend. In that interview the investigator didn't tell Brett about John Carlin or Kent Leppink, and Reddell never said anything about knowing about a murder.

When Brett was asked when the last time was he had seen or spoken to Mechele, he said it had been a few weeks before, in late August 1996. She was planning a long trip to the "lower forty-eight" and wanted to borrow his truck, a 1994 Chevrolet four-wheel-drive pickup he left in Anchorage for transportation when he was there on business trips, but lent it to Mechele. "When she needed to it, she'd borrow it. She'd ask to borrow it," he said later.

This time, Mechele wanted to take the truck to her sister's place in Utah. He agreed, but wanted her to get a trailer in Arizona on the way back and tow it up to Alaska, where Brett was going to place it on his brother's property. Brett even agreed to provide her with spending money, giving her his ATM card and secret code.

Brett thought that when she returned, they would move in together in his house in Barrow. "She mentioned she was going to quit work."

It was now a month later, September 10, and Brett Reddell had not heard from Mechele—or seen his truck. The investigator didn't tell him—and he never mentioned—anything about Mechele buying a motor home for the trip. The whereabouts of Brett's truck were unknown.

And that's how it would remain for another month. In October a detective interviewed Brett Reddell again. Mechele had still not returned with his truck and his brother's trailer, but he held hope that she would. He was, after all, her boyfriend.

Investigators asked him if he knew of a man named John Carlin. Brett said he did and had even met him once. "I thought they were friends," he said later. "They were just good friends, that's it." For a time Brett had considered buying John's house in Anchorage and living there with Mechele. "The company was going to transfer me back to Anchorage within the next year or whatever," he said later. "I didn't know how it was going to work out, if it was going to be me or her buying [it]."

The investigators asked Brett if he knew of a man named Scott Hilke. The name was familiar. He seemed to recall Mechele saying that Scott was dating one of her friends.

Then he was asked about Kent Leppink. Brett claimed to know nothing about the fisherman and had never heard, from Mechele or anybody else, that he'd been murdered.

"I think that either you know or [at least] you know more than you told me," one of the investigators said.

"That's not true," Brett said.

The investigator said that the Leppink family had put out

a $10,000 reward for information leading to the conviction
of Kent's killer. Maybe Brett could call Mechele and pump
her for information about the murder.

Reddell resisted. He didn't want to cooperate.

"Well, what if it happened to you?" the investigator said.
"And you know it could've been you."

"I have two little girls, and them without a father or
mother . . . ," his voice trailed off.

The troopers never got Brett Reddell's help in building a
case against Mechele, and Reddell didn't see his truck for
months. Mechele didn't return and they didn't settle down as
boyfriend and girlfriend in Barrow or Anchorage. Instead,
one day the next year, John Carlin III called Brett from New
Jersey, saying his truck was there. A friend of Brett's who
lived nearby offered to drive it back to Alaska. Brett instead
had the friend sell it for him in New Jersey.

There was one last witness statement to consider. It came
from a woman named Lora Aspiotis, who said she used to
be one of Mechele's closest friends. Lora came to investigators on her own, calling them to say she had information
about Mechele's life on—and off—the Bush Company dance
floor.

For the previous six years, Lora had made her money as a
stripper in Alaska and Las Vegas, using the stage names
Zoey, Allison, and Mystique. She had met Mechele at the
Bush shortly after Mechele arrived from Louisiana, and appraised her as short and flat-chested and not very good at
dancing. Soon, though, Lora marveled at Mechele's ability
to extract money from men, collecting thousands of dollars
a night, mostly by just talking.

The two dancers worked the same shifts, and by the winter of 1995–96 Lora would hang out at Mechele's house,
watching movies on video. The fisherman Kent Leppink,
off the water for the winter, was a constant—and strange—
presence. Mechele used and abused him, took his money
and made him do chores, then ridiculed him behind his back.
She recalled that one night in the winter of 1996, Lora's

husband—who worked at a restaurant—made a big meal for Lora, Mechele, John Carlin, and John's son. With wine and beer, the bill came to "probably a couple of hundred dollars," Lora recalled. After the meal, Kent showed up and Mechele told him to pay the bill. He didn't ask any questions; he just did it, Lora said.

One man did seem to own Mechele's heart: Scott Hilke. Lora said it was clear that Hilke was Mechele's boyfriend. Lora had no use for the big-talking salesman, calling him an "asshole."

By now investigators knew most of this already, with Lora's portrait of Mechele as a manipulator of Kent and John while being in love with Scott coming out in other interviews. But Lora had new information.

The first related to the life insurance policies that Mechele and Kent had taken out. In February 1996, Lora said, Mechele told her that she had no intention of getting a life insurance policy on herself: she only wanted to insure Kent. When Mechele returned from the agent's office, "she was very, very upset," Aspiotis said later. "She told me that they got insurance on T.T. but he wanted to get a policy for her and . . . she wasn't happy with that. . . . Probably the most angered that I had seen her, pretty angry, very much beside herself."

By February of 1996, Lora had grown weary of Mechele's "manipulation and lies" and broke off their friendship. In her diary, Lora wrote, "Called Mechele. Put me off. Finally talked to her, told her deal: conniving, scheming, deceitful, manipulative, living in a fantasy world."

They never spoke again. But when Lora found out about Kent's murder, an episode from her friendship with Mechele—at the time routine and innocuous—now chilled her and prompted her to call police.

In January or February of 1996, during one of the long Alaskan winter nights when Aspiotis and Mechele holed up in her living room, they watched a video of *The Last Seduction*, a 1994 movie starring Linda Fiorentino. In the movie, Fiorentino is a beautiful woman, Bridget Gregory, who manipulates her lover into killing her husband for money—then walks away unscathed with the cash, letting the lover take the fall.

Lora said Mechele "wanted to be like her."

CHAPTER FIFTEEN

The plot: The beautiful and manipulative woman conning an older, insecure man into gunning down her pathetic and annoying fiancé for his $1 million life insurance so Mechele could jet off into the sunset with her real true love. If Mechele had really wanted to use *The Last Seduction* as a road map, she did a good job. Had Detectives Stephen DeHart and Ron Belden come across a real-life femme fatale worthy of Cain or Chandler?

If only real life were as tidy as a Hollywood thriller. Hunches, appearances, and leads can propel an investigation, but they aren't proof. By the fall of 1996, after more than four months of detective work, hundreds of hours of interviews, and several search warrants served, DeHart and Belden didn't feel they had enough cause to arrest anyone.

Not even another break in the case—the results of Scott Hilke's polygraph—convinced them. According to a report from the Sacramento Police Department, the examiner "determined that Hilke's overall rating was 'deceptive' and that Hilke's most deceptive answer was to the question: Did he shoot [Leppink]?"

He had answered no.

Scott, meanwhile, had still not provided flight manifests, receipts, or other documents proving he was on a business trip to Cleveland at the time of Kent's murder.

But like everything else the detectives had uncovered,

from the "Go to Hope" note, to Kent's letter to his parents, to Mechele's apparent lies, the polygraph raised suspicions but couldn't take the place of hard evidence. No judge in Alaska would allow the results of a lie detector test. Without corroborating evidence—or a confession—a polygraph is useless in court.

Not even the seizure of the laptop computer proved helpful. Technicians found that all the emails and Word documents had been erased, and all they could uncover were scrambled words and phrases. For all Mechele's concern about the computer, it proved worthless to the investigation.

By early 1997, Mechele had settled back in Louisiana, enrolled at Loyola University in New Orleans, and begun taking undergraduate classes toward becoming a veterinarian. She talked briefly by phone with DeHart on January 17, then stopped returning his calls. DeHart now focused on other cases, doing only sporadic work on the Leppink investigation. The sheriff in Incline Village found the name of one of the people who showed up at the condo at the same time Mechele and Scott were there, but DeHart didn't pursue it. U.S. Customs officials, who had been asked by DeHart to keep an eye out for Mechele if she left the country, reported that on April 4 she had arrived in New Orleans on an Aeromexico flight; her traveling companion was Scott Hilke. DeHart made a note of it but didn't follow up.

Mechele filled her new home with parrots, dogs, and cats. She kept in shape by jogging with her dogs through Audubon Park, a former plantation across from Tulane and Loyola universities, bordered on one side by the Mississippi River and the other by St. Charles Avenue. In the spring of 1997, a little over a year after Kent Leppink's murder, Mechele and her dogs caught the eye of a young medical student named Colin Linehan, who was jogging with his own dog. They struck up a conversation, and Colin felt an immediate attraction. "She would always be by herself, walking and playing with her three dogs," Colin recalled later. "I was struck by her beauty and joy for life."

They started dating and soon found they had much in

common besides jogging and dogs. Mechele told him she
had recently relocated from Anchorage, and Colin told her
that he had lived there as a doctor's son. When Colin was
eight years old, the family—including his five siblings—
moved along with his father's medical practice to Olympia,
Washington. Following in his father's footsteps, Colin was
now a third-year medical student at Tulane, his education
funded by the U.S. Army. He was nearing graduation and
his residency.

Like Mechele, Colin had also lost his father: he died
when Colin was fifteen. And like Mechele, Colin was close
to his mother. Judy Linehan was a nurse. After Colin's father died, he worked hard to support the family in Olympia.
"Life abruptly changed from upper middle class to the very
bottom," he later said. Colin told Mechele that he had
largely supported himself through his teens, just as Mechele had (although it's not known whether at this early stage
of their relationship she told him she was a stripper). While
an undergraduate, Colin held down forty-hour-a-week jobs
because he couldn't get much financial aid due to what he
later called "arcane rules at the time." "There were sacri-
fices too innumerable to count," he would say, "but I worked
hard towards a nebulous goal, that turned out to be medicine."

These two fatherless, self-sufficient college students who
loved pets and their mothers grew closer. About eight months
after they met, at the end of 1997, Colin brought Mechele to
Olympia to meet his mother and other relatives. "I was drawn
to Mechele and her zest for life from our first meeting," Colin's mother, Judy, later said. The love between her son and
the beautiful young southerner was immediately apparent.
"Both had lost their dads at the same age," Judy later said,
"and this seemed to be an element of their growing bond."

In early 1998, Colin's mother visited her son in New Orleans, seeing Mechele's mother for the first time and getting
a tour of the city from Colin and Mechele. Judy Linehan's
second meeting with her son's girlfriend impressed her even
more. Judy said that one moment during their driving tour of

New Orleans stood out, as it revealed Mechele's character. Colin was pulling from an intersection when Mechele spotted a stray dog approaching her window.

"Colin," she pleaded.

"No, Mechele," he gently chided, "we can't bring home every dog that wants to jump into our car."

As much as Mechele wanted to save the dog, Judy Linehan recalled, "she accepted this realistic pronouncement, but it was obvious she would if she could. And so began my initial glimpse into the magnanimity of this young woman's heart."

Less than a year into their relationship, Colin proposed marriage, and Mechele accepted. On May 31, 1998, just one day after Colin graduated from medical school, they were married in a simple ceremony.

Those close to the couple saw it as perfect match, their love unconditional and true. Colin had no money; Mechele paid for her own engagement ring. "She married a poor medical student," her friend Ann Gassga, who met her at Loyola, later told the *Anchorage Daily News*. "If she was out for the money, he was not a catch."

Colin's family couldn't have been happier for them, seeing in Mechele a warm and giving soul, completely selfless. "During a walking tour of the downtown area," Judy Linehan later recalled, "Mechele greeted a homeless man by name and exchanged brief good wishes. To this day, I'm still incredulous at that moment."

After the wedding, Colin got a civilian deferment from his active duty commitment so he could do his residency at the University of Maryland Department of Family Medicine in Baltimore. "I had a start date for a new residency . . . almost immediately," he later said in court. "Graduation, wedding, a big move to a new house—it was a pretty wacky time." Mechele dropped out of Loyola and put her veterinary plans on hold while Colin embarked on a young doctor's rite of passage: a grueling three-year residency, working one hundred hours a week for the first two years. At home, he had the unwavering support of his selfless wife. "Mechele never ceased to amaze me with her energy and dedication," he later said. To help make ends meet, Mechele worked as a waitress at a chophouse while volunteering at the Red Cross, teaching CPR, and taking classes at Howard Community College in Columbia, southwest of Baltimore.

Two years after they married, Mechele became a mom, welcoming daughter Audrey on June 30, 1999.

A new marriage, a new baby, a new house, a new life. Mechele's life in Alaska—and Kent's murder two years earlier—was now ancient history. The investigation had all but been abandoned, the investigators moving on. Shortly after Mechele arrived in New Orleans, Ron Belden was reassigned from the Soldotna station to an understaffed drug unit. By the time she was married, Belden had retired from the Division of Alaska State Troopers altogether and taken a job with BP, the British-owned oil giant with vast operations, including pipelines, in Alaska. Steven DeHart had also left the Soldotna station, heading courthouse security in Anchorage in the fall of 1997. His caseload went to other detectives.

Mechele kept only superficial ties to those she once knew: she had sent wedding invitations to John Carlin III and his son, but they didn't go, and emailed a birth announcement to Scott Hilke that wasn't acknowledged.

Then one day in late 1999 or early 2000, as Colin was completing his residency and Mechele was at home with the baby, the past crept back. A patient came into Colin's clinic at the Maryland Department of Family Medicine: a heavyset man who complained of back pain. He said he had driven south from his home in New Jersey specifically to see Dr. Linehan.

Years later, Colin said that when he first treated the patient, he had no idea who John Carlin was or how John knew Mechele. It would become one of the unanswered questions of the case: Just how much did Colin know about Mechele's past? He would later insist she told him about what he called "the tragedy that happened in Alaska" early in their relationship. "This came about when our courting conversations

turned to biography, and she told me why she left Alaska
and moved to New Orleans," he said later in court. "Her
story has never changed." Colin added to NBC's *Dateline*
that Mechele spoke of a man who "she's really close to" but
who "ended up getting killed. . . .

"And she was investigated," he told *Dateline*. "She said,
'They thought I had something to do with it.' And she was,
like, 'It really shook me.' "

But in talking to Colin, Mechele apparently left out a key
detail: namely, her relationship with John Carlin III. Colin
later said he didn't know that Mechele had been acquainted
with John in Alaska "until I saw him as a patient," and that
it was from Carlin—not Mechele—that he got this information. "He told me he was a friend of Mechele's," Colin said.

Otherwise, it was a routine examination. When John
arrived at the clinic, he not only related his medical history but gave Colin MRI printouts. "He basically said he
didn't trust any of the doctors up in New Jersey and he
thought that because I was Mechele's husband he could
implicitly trust me," Colin later said. "He had a distrust, he
said, for the medical profession. . . . He trusted that I would
give him sound advice on the MRIs." Diagnosing him as
suffering a bulging disk pushing against a nerve, Colin recommended surgery, which John refused. Colin prescribed
Percocet for the pain and told him to return for follow-up
visits, which he did, two or three times.

When Colin returned home after the first visit, he told
Mechele about treating her old friend. "She didn't like it,"
Colin later said. "She discouraged it."

After three years in Maryland, Colin's residency was up and
it was time to repay his medical school debt by going on active duty for the U.S. Army. The military could have sent
him anywhere, but to his joy he was deployed to Madigan
Army Medical Center, near his old hometown of Olympia,
Washington. In 2001, the Linehans—Colin, Mechele, and
daughter Audrey—moved into a fixer-upper on Bigelow Avenue, eight blocks from Colin's mother's house. Nearby were

his brother, sister, grandmother and aunts and uncles. As Colin later said in court: "I was very, very pleased to be stationed in a place where I had family."

The house, though, needed work. "When I first saw it, I was terrified," Colin's sister-in-law Kerry Mrazek later wrote in a note to a judge. "It was such a sight. But [Mechele] quickly transformed it into a beautiful home. I could not see it, but she did." Mechele, it seemed, had a practiced hand in home renovation.

Placing Audrey in Catholic school, Mechele returned to school, finally finishing her bachelor's degree at Saint Martin's College, studying biology and psychology, before going on to earn a master's in public administration from The Evergreen State College in Olympia. While at college, she worked at a medical spa in Tacoma and interned with the Washington State Executive Ethics Board, telling people it was her passion to help those afflicted by poverty and injustice. She took her daughter to a soup kitchen.

Between her work and studies and raising Audrey, Mechele became the neighborhood Martha Stewart, baking cookies, joining the PTA, throwing backyard barbecues, charming the neighbors.

Neighbor Kristina Hermach met Mechele at a local bakery in 2001 and they quickly became friends, as did their toddler daughters. "Mechele invited my daughter and I to see *The Nutcracker* in Seattle," Hermach later recalled to the court. "My daughter treasures those trips we had. Mechele's parenting wisdom helped me through many frustrating moments—and always with advice that allowed me to be kind and patient with the teachable moment."

Mechele did twelve-hour shifts Friday nights at a crisis center in Olympia, counseling suicide and rape victims. She approached Bob Zeigler, then the coordinator of the social justice committee at St. Michael Parish in Olympia, about getting involved with the church's social justice programs. "She had called me about what she could do to make a better world," Zeigler later told the *Anchorage Daily News*. People marveled at her patience and ability to defuse difficult situations. "She treated the rude with 'southern charm,'" her friend Hermach later said, "continually showing me that grace and humility improve the situation and indulging anger does not."

Neighbor Terri Plewa said their children played together and spent holidays together. "When we moved to the neighborhood, Mechele and her daughter were the first people to welcome us, baked goods in hand, and have been warm and open with us the entire time we've known them," she later told a judge. She picked up dogs on the street, helped the neighbors, babysat. "She is loving, yet has high expectations," Plewa continued. "She is fun, but also tough. She pays attention to the small things with her daughter and is an ever-present shaping force in her life, from making sure she is not hurt by thorns on rose bushes to seeing to it that her daughter wears her bike helmet and writes thank you notes for gifts."

Mechele kept a busy schedule, but always had time for her daughter. When Mechele opened her own business, she had Audrey help her design the office. She went biking with Audrey, gardening, even delivered puppies with her. She put Audrey in ballet and taught her the finer points in doing a Christmas tea party. People who had no place to go for Christmas or Thanksgiving were welcomed into the Linehan home for a holiday meal.

Colin's mother Judy recalled a Christmas in which the family gathered in Olympia from around the country. "Mechele was in the forefront of instigating a trek up Mt. Rainier for sledding," said Judy. "She rounded up snow gear for the kids, food for the journey, mobilized us with her energy and enthusiasm, and up the mountain we went in our caravan. I still see the faces and excitement of the children at the wonder of snow." Colin's sister, Kerry Mrazek, said Mechele's house was a "place of refuge for friends and animals who had no place to stay for a while," with Mechele making time to be gracious despite her busy schedule of work, volunteerism, and parenting. "Mechele seems to have two days to my one," said Kerry. "I could not understand how she could fit it all in. I have known in one day for her to bike ride with her daughter, blueberry pick, knit, volunteer, cook/bake, get a little work in, garden, invite friends to dinner, care for her menagerie of animals, and watch a movie at home with Colin and her daughter, and probably get some reading in. Somewhere in there she probably got a trip in to Goodwill to recycle/salvage some time for one of her multiple ongoing art/craft/home projects."

Even the local authorities admired her. When a home contractor stole from her, the Thurston County, Washington, prosecutor on the case was impressed with Mechele's forgiving attitude. "She was very compassionate, very understanding and very forgiving," deputy prosecuting attorney Mark Thompson told the *Anchorage Daily News*.

If there was anything that put people off, it was Mechele's beauty. Some women felt threatened by her at first: her sexy figure, pretty face, and soft southern accent always caught the attention of men. But once people got to know her, she won them over quickly with her graciousness, kindness, and parenting skills.

And no one adored her more than her husband. "No marriage is perfect, but Mechele and I have a great partnership, and our mutual love and respect has kept growing," Colin later told a judge. "Mechele is a great wife and amazing mother. Our daughter is so full of spirit and so caring to all living things. This is a direct reflection on Mechele as a mother. She has instilled in Audrey her own values that love and kindness apply to everything living."

The couple had big plans. For the day when Colin finished his Army obligations, they considered opening a medical day spa, tapping into Colin's medical experience and Mechele's administration training.

It was a family as perfect as a Christmas card, whose future was bright. Then events halfway around the world intruded, and Mechele and Colin faced the first serious test to their marriage.

* * *

In the end, it was Mechele who broke the news to four-year-old Audrey. "Mechele explained to her that her daddy was serving his country and protecting her as well as everyone's freedom," Mechele's mother later told the court.

Army doctor Colin Linehan was about to be sent to Iraq with the Stryker brigade. His deployment date was September 2003.

"In the months before Colin left for Iraq, I indeed felt the tension in their home," Colin's mother later told a judge in a written statement. "I understood the angst, as I myself was a basket case over my son's imminent departure to a war zone. They allowed me to accompany them to Fort Lewis the night of his unit's deployment. I assure you it was a time of utmost grieving and tenderness as we let him go and the three of us faced into the unknowns of the separation."

Colin spent thirteen months away. Mechele, alone with a daughter in a house that still needed extensive repairs, faced her own rite of passage: that of a military wife. The isolation and uncertainty of a spouse left behind can test the strongest of relationships. The Linehans were no exception.

Colin came home, safe and unharmed, in October 2004. The same couldn't be said for their marriage. "We all shared the indescribable relief at Colin's safe return from Iraq," Colin's mother later told a judge, "and yet tensions between the two of them remained obvious. . . . I don't know how long it was before they told me they were seeing a marriage counselor, but I remember my relief, especially as little by little I observed affection and easygoing playful banter coming back into their interactions."

Mechele attended a military wives' support group, whose numbers dwindled as each one got divorced. "I felt immense gratitude for Mechele, intuitively knowing in my heart of hearts that it was her efforts that assured they got to counseling," Judy Linehan later said. "I knew Mechele as a person who always faced into issues of conflict rather than let them simmer. Indeed, she is hardwired that way." Her son saw it too. "He would have done whatever it took to keep his family together," Judy said, "but he was still reeling from the war, so it was Mechele giving the counseling demand that put them on [the] road to healing in their relationship."

Little by little, they rebuilt their relationship and restarted their plans. At Madigan, Colin was now a military doctor but not with active military commitments. "I didn't have to go to the firing range and shoot guns," he said. They built their savings and pushed forward with starting their own business. Counseling and the passage of time brought them closer than ever, and nothing—not even war—would pull them apart.

But once again events far away from home would intrude, this time in a way even more devastating than Colin's war service.

It seemed that in the state of Alaska, concern in political and law enforcement circles was growing about the large number of old and unsolved murder cases that had begun piling up.

CHAPTER SIXTEEN

In the summer of 2002, Jim Stogsdill lived the outdoorsman's dream. As operator of Fish Happens in Soldotna, he took fishermen out on the Kenai River to snag the king salmon that run from May through July and the salmon and rainbow trout of August through September. "You can rely on our assistance for locating a processor or taxidermist to take care of your trophy catch!" the Fish Happens Web site says. Just bring your king salmon stamp, warm clothing, and a "strong desire to experience Alaska and catch some BIG fish!" A half day on his twenty-foot motorboat costs $225 and includes not only fishing but an up-close view of eagles, caribou, moose, and sometimes bear. Coffee, donuts, soft drinks, bait, and tackle are provided unless a fisherman wants to bring a favorite rod.

It was a good business and made for a fulfilling retirement. Then came September, when the days turned colder and shorter, the salmon finished their annual breeding runs, and another brutal Alaskan winter loomed. When Stogsdill was still a cop, these winters kept him busy. "All the things started happening when people were shut up and it was 40 below," he says—things like drinking and drug abuse, assaults, stabbings, and shootings as nerves frayed and domestic violence raged during those punishing eighteen-hour nights.

Stogsdill had had a long career, starting as a patrol officer in the 1970s in Sitka, Juneau, and Glenallen and moving to the Criminal Investigation Bureau in Anchorage, before transferring to Soldotna as a supervisor in a regional investigative unit. In 1993 he retired and went fishing.

"I always wanted to do that," he said. "I was having a good time with that, some success. But things in the wintertime are a little slow in the fishing area. In the wintertime, you're looking for home projects and things like that, and there's only so much of that indoors. I was bored."

In the decade after his retirement, Alaska underwent change. The population, which first surged with the oil boom of the seventies and eighties, steadily increased through the nineties. So, too, did crime, straining the state's far-flung trooper stations. If a murder case went cold, an overworked investigator often was forced to put it on the shelf and focus time and resources on the next series of cases. Communication between departments was poor, so if there was an unsolved case outside of Anchorage, for instance, that's how it would remain: unsolved.

For years, the head of the Division of Alaskan State Troopers, Colonel Randy Crawford, had wanted to start a special unit dedicated to investigating unsolved homicides. But it wasn't until the early 2000s, with the bodies literally piling up—there were by now some 90 unsolved murders in the state—that the legislature finally approved funding for a statewide cold case unit. It was to be a small operation—just four part-time investigators—but the state wanted to hire the best and most experienced people.

In 2002, Stogsdill got the call from Crawford, who was a longtime friend. Bored and antsy, he jumped at the opportunity—but with conditions. "I did not want to move to Anchorage," he said. He also wanted to keep his summers and early fall free for the fishing guide business. Otherwise, he told Crawford, "I'll do anything you want." The Division of Alaska State Troopers gave Stogsdill the biggest office in the Soldotna station and left him alone.

Success came quickly. Stogsdill first reviewed a case from the 1980s, building a case against a man who had gone on a violent rampage, robbing shooting and severely wounding a shop owner before killing a woman during another robbery, then finding another man to help him assault somebody with a tire iron. In between this, the suspect also allegedly killed somebody in Kansas.

Stogsdill had just returned to Soldotna from Kansas, where he had testified before a grand jury. He was looking for a case close to home when one of the investigators told him about the 1996 murder of a fisherman in Hope. The detective had picked up after Steven DeHart and Ron Belden, both long since gone from the Alaska state troopers, and had gotten as far as reading the case file. "[The detective] was in the same position of a lot of investigators: He never really had any time to do anything about it," recalled Stogsdill. "He brought the whole thing into my office—about 12 volumes—and I sat down and read every page."

Stogsdill was three years into his retirement when Kent Leppink was murdered, and he knew nothing about the case. The old homicide file provided crime scene reports and photos, a detailed autopsy report, ballistics reports, and hundreds of pages and hours of tape recordings of interviews. Stogsdill admired the effort and the organization on the part of Steven DeHart, now retired. Many case files weren't nearly as good. Then he went about seeing how he could succeed where DeHart had failed.

"I needed to read every word basically to see what the investigators were thinking and why they went off in whatever direction they went off," Stogsdill said. "I'm looking to see what was done initially, any gaping holes that you might be able to fill. Looking at evidence, what physical things accumulated over the years, to see if any of those things can be re-examined. That's your initial look; once you've done that, just proceed whatever fashion you think most productive."

The case unfolded in chronological order in the volumes— something that doesn't often happen in old cases—and it was easy for Stogsdill to follow not only the course of the investigation but the thinking process of DeHart. By the end,

DeHart thought that the shooter was John Carlin III but that the mastermind was Mechele Hughes. Although not explicitly stated in the files, Stogsdill could also sense DeHart's mounting frustration at never getting enough evidence for an arrest. The case was never presented to a prosecutor for possible charges.

After reading the case file, Stogsdill went through it a second time in order to to answer questions that came up during the first reading. He made note of what little physical evidence was found: the brass shell casings at the scene, the bullets in Kent's body, the various notes and documents. He read the transcripts of the interviews with Mechele, John Carlin III, Scott Hilke, as well as the other witnesses, from Kent's family to Mechele's stripper friend Lora Aspiotis.

Then Stogsdill built his own case file, creating profiles of the various people involved—a who's who of the Leppink murder investigation—and a detailed timeline. "I wanted to present the case in compact form to the other cold case people and see what their thoughts were," he said.

Key problems jumped out, starting with the murder weapon. "First of all, we didn't have it, and we never could prove that Carlin even owned it," Stogsdill said. "Even though Mechele had it, she claimed it was Kent's." The original detectives found those gun accessories at John's house and the holster in Mechele's car, but could never directly link either one of them to a Desert Eagle in general or the murder weapon in particular. It wasn't for lack of trying. The case file had page after page dedicated to a fruitless search of gun dealers in the Anchorage area. DeHart was so intent on finding the gun that he had considered reading every classified ad in the *Anchorage Daily News* in the years since Carlin had moved to Alaska, but in the end "he just never got around to it," said Stogsdill.

Another big missing piece was Carlin's son, John Carlin IV. Throughout the case file, it was clear that DeHart and Belden felt that the teenager had something to say—and that that was why his father had shielded him from investigators. The boy had appeared troubled but also close to Mechele, whose efforts to get him counseling had so unnerved Kent. Within weeks of the murder, as investigators zeroed in on Mechele and John, Mechele abruptly left Alaska in the motor home, taking John IV with her. According to the file, DeHart had arranged for police in New Jersey to contact John IV when he turned eighteen years old and his father could no longer protect him. The report from the New Jersey locals boiled it down: John IV told the cop to get lost.

Then there was the laptop computer. The case file noted how Kent had complained to several people that Mechele had stolen it and police believed Mechele lied about its whereabouts. When DeHart and Belden finally got their hands on the laptop, the crime lab's 1996 forensic software could retrieve only gibberish.

After Stogsdill brought himself up to speed on the facts, he poked away at the case, working part-time and billing the state hourly for his services. He spent the remainder of 2003 and early 2004 tracking down the major players in the case. Scott Hilke still lived in the Sacramento area but appeared to have remarried. Mechele had a new address in Olympia, Washington, and word came back that she also was married, to an Army doctor said to be on deployment to Iraq. John Carlin III continued to make Elmer, New Jersey, his home, and he, too, had become married again in 2000 to a Russian dentist, Julia Chernikova, whom he met through a matchmaking service: they had had a long-distance marriage for three years until she moved to the United States in October 2003. John IV's whereabouts couldn't be determined, although Stogsdill had a line on the boy's old girlfriend in Alaska.

And sitting in an evidence room, gathering dust, was Kent's Gateway 2000 laptop and a Hewlett-Packard PC taken from John's house.

The technical aspect of the investigation was handled by a second detective. Linda Branchflower was also a retired Alaska state trooper who, like Stogsdill, had vast experience in law enforcement, including patrol and investigating crimes against children, adult sexual assault, homicide, and robbery. She had retired to Anchorage with her husband, longtime prosecutor Stephen Branchflower. (He would make news in 2008 by overseeing what became known as the Branchflower Report, which found that then-governor Sarah Palin had violated ethics laws in a trooper firing scandal.) Linda Branchflower had grown restless in retirement—"pretty bored, actually," she later said—and when she got the call to join the new cold case unit, she signed on. One of her first duties was to draft the search warrant, first for the laptop.

In March 2004, a judge in Alaska approved a search warrant to peer into the laptop and retrieve anything on its memory. Then Christopher Thompson with the computer and financial crimes unit got to work. Thompson primarily investigated white-collar crimes, using the latest forensic software to extract information from hard drives and other storage devices.

He reviewed the search warrant, retrieved the laptop along with zip discs and floppy disks—the precursors to CDs—from storage, and photographed all the items. He then removed the hard drive and connected it to a special forensic computer that powered the drive without risk of copying any new data on it. Using the EnCase Forensic program from Guidance Software of Pasadena, Thompson made an image of the data on the disk drive, including the so-called blank space, copied that image onto a new drive, and disconnected the laptop drive. In this process, the original computer never had to be turned on, which could contaminate the evidence. He repeated this process, making copies of whatever was on the zip disks and the floppy disks.

Thompson now launched his search through the copied image, relying on a list of keywords and short strings of text provided by Detective Branchflower. Advances in forensic software since the late 1990s, when the computer was first examined, allowed Thompson to find not only untouched data that remained on file or in in-boxes but also data that the computer user had deleted. This was the realm of what technicians call unallocated space: those strange and dark places on the hard drive where things are both there and not there. As long as new data had not been written over material on unallocated space—making it allocated space—even deleted data, from emails to Word documents, could be retrieved. It was just a matter of poking in the right corner, using the right keyword as a guide.

As any detective knows, time can be both an enemy and an ally. Conventional wisdom dictates that if a case isn't solved in the first forty-eight hours (from which the CBS program *48 Hours Mystery* gets its name), it may never get solved. If witnesses aren't going to talk in the beginning, they probably won't ever talk. As time passes, memories fade, motivation wanes, lawyers get hired. But cold case detectives know that time also offers advantages. A change in life can mean a change in attitudes and perspective as people mellow, mature, and release—or forget—their anger and fear.

In March 2005, when Jim Stogsdill approached Scott Hilke, the salesman first expressed surprise. A decade had physically changed Scott little. He was still the blond, trim, confident salesman with whom Mechele fell in love at the Great Alaskan Bush Company in 1995. But something inside had changed. Although Scott still held the same low opinion of John Carlin III and Kent Leppink, calling them morons, now he said, "I place myself in that category."

Mechele, he had come to believe, had not only manipulated the weak-willed John and Kent, she had manipulated Scott too.

Hilke continued to maintain he had had nothing to do with Kent's murder, no matter what that polygraph said nearly a decade earlier. He repeated that he was in Lake Tahoe with Mechele in the days before the murder prior to leaving for a business trip. He said again that Mechele's demeanor was the same as it ever was, aside from her seeming a little tired and eager to get back into her own house after the renovation. As always, their relationship was casual, with no long-term plans to be together, although he acknowledged they did see each other after Kent's murder.

In June 1996, after Mechele and John had purchased the

motor home and Mechele left Alaska, her drive did not take her directly to Utah but through Sacramento, where she and John Carlin IV stayed with Scott for a couple of days. While at his house, Mechele picked up a teal leather sofa and love seat combination that Scott had been storing for her, and before she left they had a brief conversation about Kent's murder. "I confronted her and gave her my opinion of what I suspected may have happened," he later said. He wouldn't divulge what his suspicion was, but he implied that he felt that Mechele had information she wasn't sharing with anyone, including him. "I was shut down," he said. "At that point, that was the end of my ever bringing it up."

While she was still there, he left for another business trip, then later hooked up with her at her sister's campground in Utah. Months passed, Mechele set up residence in New Orleans, and Scott remained in Sacramento, but they kept in touch. In the spring of 1997 they hooked up in Cancún. "It was the vacation from hell," Scott later recalled. "We just didn't get along. It was not a pleasant trip."

The pair went snorkeling, and Mechele acted like a pill, treating the other divers rudely and embarrassing Scott. Then, Scott believed, when she had stopped by his house with the RV on the way to Utah, she had stolen a framed print his sister had given him and a candy dish from a female friend.

"As soon as we got back to New Orleans, I was gone," he said later. "I was angry with her. . . . I found a crummy motel outside the airport and flew out the next morning."

This was the trip documented by U.S. Customs officials, and it was just around this time that Mechele met her future husband in Audubon Park.

For the next several years Scott said he only heard directly from Mechele once, when she emailed him a birth announcement in June 1999. He described it as an impersonal form email and he didn't respond. But at around the same time, his parents told him that Mechele had contacted them "to find out where I was, under the [pretense] of getting information about the ring that I had given her," he said later. "Apparently, something happened to that ring and she was

looking for the information about the receipt or appraisal."
Whether the ring was lost or whether Mechele wanted to sell
it (at the time, she and Colin were a struggling young couple
with a new baby) couldn't be determined, but Scott was irritated by the fact that Michele had contacted his parents.

By now Scott didn't want anything to do with Mechele. He
had reconnected with a longtime friend—the same woman
who had given him the candy dish. "She's just always been
the person who's been there for me through two marriages
and numerous relationships," he said later. "I was always in
contact with her. I was in Sacramento. She contacted my
parents and was having a fiftieth birthday party for a friend
of hers. She contacted me and I called her and we started
seeing each other." In April 1999 they were married. Scott
never replied to Mechele about the ring.

Over the next five years, Scott settled into married life in
Northern California and heard nothing from Mechele. Then,
in 2004, he got a message on his 800-number service. It was
Mechele.

Things had changed. Scott was married now and so was
Mechele (though when she contacted Scott her husband was
off at war). Still, the passion was the same. A meeting in a
park near her home in Olympia led to a dinner in Tacoma,
which resulted in a tryst in a hotel room in Seattle and then
another two nights in a hotel in Minneapolis.

After ten years, history had repeated itself, with Scott
and Mechele sleeping together on the road—only when they
got together in Minneapolis, Mechele's daughter was asleep
in the next-door hotel room. They might have continued to
be frequent-flier partners, except that Scott's wife found a
suspicious email and confronted Mechele in an angry telephone call that Mechele took while she was working at the
Washington State Executive Ethics Board offices, and that
was the end of that. Scott patched things up and the marriage continued; it wasn't known whether Colin ever found
out, or how much of his and Mechele's counseling—if
any—dealt with Mechele's infidelity.

If word of Mechele's indiscretion ever got out, the revelation would certainly tarnish Mechele's image among her in-laws and Bigelow Avenue neighbors. But beyond that, it served little value to Stogsdill. Although Mechele had reached out to Scott not long after the cold case investigation had begun, Scott said his dates with Mechele were for dinner and sex, not to compare notes or advance a murder cover-up. It was something of which Scott wasn't proud and reinforced his conviction that Mechele was a master manipulator. He said that as unsavory as it was, he was prepared to testify about it to a grand jury or even in a trial if it came to that.

Given Hilke's willingness to testify, combined with his other statements, Stogsdill was not inclined to believe that Scott had anything do with Kent's murder. However, that didn't mean that he was telling everything he knew. There was also that failed polygraph. Even if Scott hadn't been directly involved in the plot to murder Kent, he could be still holding back information. To the end, Stogsdill was never really sure how he felt about Scott. "Hilke isn't a number one citizen," Stogsdill later said. "In the back of mind, I thought: Hilke is alive and well and Leppink isn't."

CHAPTER SEVENTEEN

From the first time Stogsdill read Sergeant DeHart's case file, a question nagged at him: Where did John Carlin IV fit in?

"You just have a feeling that this seventeen-year-old kid who was around there all the time knew something," said Stogsdill. "That's reinforced by the fact that Carlin III shoves him in a motor home after the murder and sends him away."

But first, detectives had to find him. They started with Adella Perez, who for a few intense months nearly a decade earlier was one of the most important people in John Carlin IV's life.

Stogsdill and Linda Branchflower tracked Perez down in November of 2004 in California from a birth announcement she had posted on a baby Web page. She recounted how she and John Carlin IV began dating in June of 1995, two months after his mother died and around the time that his father first met Mechele Hughes at the Great Alaskan Bush Company. The younger Carlin was "introverted, very intelligent," Adella later said in court. "I had felt that with [*sic*] a situation like that would explain why somebody would be a little quiet and introverted."

The loss of John's mother and the stress from the move to Alaska from New Jersey manifested itself in other ways. "He seemed a little bizarre at times and didn't necessarily want to be up here," Adella said. "He's not from Alaska and he didn't want to be up here."

Adella told the cold case detectives that her relationship with John IV had long since ended, but she still obviously cared about him and didn't want to get him in trouble with the police investigating a murder. In trying to get Adella to talk, Branchflower chose her words carefully. "I told her that he might have some information and that the information would be helpful to the investigation," Branchflower later said in court. "He was not a suspect in the murder, but we were concerned. The information from the 1996 investigation indicated it was possible he might have had something to do with the evidence after the fact."

Adella agreed to tell them everything she remembered. She recalled that not long after she started dating John IV, his behavior went from occasionally odd to worrisome. One incident from 1995 stood out. Adella said that although John IV loved dogs, in a strange fit of frustration and rage he once tossed a Labrador retriever off the second-floor balcony of his house onto a sofa below. "It didn't scare me as though he would do something to me, but it definitely concerned me," she said. "He would have moments where he didn't seem to know what to do with his life and was not happy here at all."

She also remembered the time he punched his fist into a wall of the house. "We were goofing off after school, playing music, and I was kind of dancing around and I did something that made him mad—not exactly sure what it was—and he punched a hole in the wall and got extremely scared about what his father was going to do," she said later. "At that point we tried to patch the hole and make it look as if nothing had happened." They used packaged noodles, of all things, and "it turned out pretty good." But the episode left John IV on edge. "He was so scared that it really surprised me," she said—scared of what his father would do if he ever found out. Luckily, she said, he never did.

John IV's bursts of anger were often accompanied by

periods of depression. More than once, Adella said, he had put a pistol to his head and threatened to kill himself.

Branchflower asked if Adella could remember what the gun looked like—hoping that she'd describe a big black Desert Eagle .44. Adella said she didn't remember.

By October of 1995, John IV was out of control. He started "tweaking, acting irrationally," Adella said, recalling the time period when Mechele and Kent moved in with them. "He had always made so much sense and thought things through before he would say things, and I felt that he simply wasn't doing that at times. He would just be in a really bad mood and act really different than he had been." He developed a jealous streak and constantly wondered whom Adella was with and what she was doing.

At the end of 1995, their six-month relationship ended. It was not a bad split: they kept in touch. In fact, Adella said, she had his cell phone number.

Linda Branchflower wrote it down. Then she obtained a subpoena.

John Carlin IV's cell phone records did not reveal a home address for him, but from the lists of incoming and outgoing calls and texts, Branchflower saw a recent flurry of activity: eighty text messages in one day, all to one person, a student at the University of Washington.

In May of 2005, Branchflower and Stogsdill flew to Seattle to speak with her. A UW campus police officer was sent to the young woman's class, and returned to confirm she was there. At about noon, as she was leaving, Branchflower, Stogsdill, and a female deputy sheriff from King County approached her. They asked if she would come with them to the campus police office. She agreed. There, they sat around a table with a fourth officer, a sergeant from the campus police, and "basically had a discussion," Branchflower later said.

The woman confirmed that she was John Carlin IV's current girlfriend. As the investigators asked her questions, they were vague as to their interest in John. They asked her if he had ever talked about something that had occurred in Alaska in 1996. Like what? she asked. A crime, they said.

"He indicated to her that he didn't believe he was necessarily involved," Branchflower said, "but might have known
about it." John's girlfriend didn't say what he might have
known but suggested that he had told her very little. They
ran names by her, including Scott Hilke's, and she said she
had never heard John mention them.

When they asked the woman if she would tell them where
John was, she said he was probably at work, but she didn't
have the address. She invited them back to her apartment,
where she gave them John's business card. By now she was
worried. She didn't want to talk to the detectives any more
and asked for a ride back to campus so she wouldn't miss
her next class. The detectives obliged, then went looking for
John.

The address on the business card took them to an office
building where, the detectives later learned, John made
three-dimensional composite drawings of pipes. The three
investigators—Stogsdill, Branchflower, and the King County
deputy—went to the reception desk and asked for John Carlin IV.

When John emerged from his office, shock flashed across
his face, followed by anger, then panic. People from other
offices started looking at them through the windows. For
more privacy, Stogsdill suggested they go to the parking lot.

Outside, John lit a cigarette, the first of many. Branchflower remembered him looking "very nervous, very upset."

At this point John wasn't under arrest and therefore
wasn't informed of his constitutional rights to remain silent
or get an attorney. He could have walked away at any time.
The investigators played it as carefully as possible. They
didn't want to push him too hard, but they didn't want him
to feel at ease. They didn't tape-record the interview or
even take notes. They said they just wanted to have a little
talk about some things that had happened when he was a
teenager.

As John chain-smoked, he resisted saying anything, telling them he wasn't happy to see them and was extremely
unhappy that the detectives had spoken to his girlfriend.

The investigators pushed harder. John would later say that they threatened him with charges of obstruction of justice if he didn't cooperate. He was, he was later embarrassed to admit, intimidated.

And so, for the first time, he talked.

CHAPTER EIGHTEEN

John acknowledged that he had reconnected with his old friend from Alaska, Mechele Hughes, now Mechele Linehan. He said that one day in September 2003 he got an email from her "literally out of the blue"—and the timing couldn't have been better. Living in Pennsylvania, John had made plans to move west with his roommate, then the roommate changed his mind and left him hanging. Now here was Mechele, inviting him to live with her, saying that her husband had been sent to Iraq and she had plenty of room at her house in Olympia. John, she had said, could pay her back by doing odd jobs and babysitting her daughter. It was the least she could do. Once John's father had offered Mechele a place to stay; now she could do the same thing for the son.

John arrived in Olympia in early 2004 and stayed with Mechele for eight months. For most of that, they got along well, two old friends with a shared past. John felt that he was earning his keep with odd jobs and babysitting. But by late September or early October 2004, with Mechele's husband's tour of duty nearly done, tensions rose and Mechele's temper grew short. John recounted the incident about the thieving contractor, the incident that had so impressed the local prosecuting attorney, but John had a different version. Mechele believed the workers refinishing the floor had stolen CDs, DVDs and a router, and reported them to police. By the time the case got to the prosecutor, Mechele was described as compassionate, understanding, and forgiving. But when it first happened, John said, "she was pretty agitated by it, and was upset and cursing and hooting and hollering."

That incident, however, paled in comparison to a dispute between John and Mechele. After months of working for her for lodging but no pay, the pair had "a conflict of opinions," John said. Mechele accused John of not upholding his end of the deal, and John complained that she hadn't compensated him enough for all that he had done. Frustrated, John left. Not long after that, Colin returned from Iraq.

The argument stood out in John's mind because he had usually gotten along well with Mechele, even during his toughest times. He recalled that when he first met Mechele— his father introduced her to him—he liked her immediately. That Mechele was a stripper made no difference to the teenager. Mechele made no secret about her job, and to John she seemed like successful businesswoman, coming home from her shift with velvet bags full of cash that she dumped on the table. John would help her count it, and it was not unusual for it to reach $1,000. Young and beautiful, Mechele made John's recently widowed father happy, and for this he was grateful and relieved.

Kent Leppink, however, was another story. John IV told the investigators that the tall, bearded fisherman started living with him and his father at the same time Mechele did, in the fall of 1995. John IV found Kent odd, even a little perverted, a "sexual deviant to a certain degree," as he later said in court, repeating what he had told the investigators. Ken did strange things, like thrust out his pelvis in front of John IV in a sexual manner. Kent didn't so much as scare or threaten John as disturb and confuse him.

The detectives noted that John IV's account of Kent's behavior was reminiscent of what his father had told troopers years earlier when he provided them with what the elder Carlin said were Kent's sex catalogs and the sexually explicit writings on the legal pad. The remarks also coincided with what Kent's family would tell investigators: how his sense of humor could be seen as strange and disturbing by those who didn't know him. Yet, John IV told the detectives that Kent's antics never got out of hand. John IV finally told his father about it. It was not known if John III confronted Kent, but the behavior did stop.

"As far as I know everybody was OK with everybody in the house," he recalled, saying that for the most part he had gotten along with Kent. They watched TV together and played video card games on a laptop computer that he believed Kent and Mechele used for the fishing business.

One thing that was evident in the household, John said, was that Kent "had a crush" on Mechele and followed her around "like a little puppy," doing everything she asked. As a teenager preoccupied with his own problems, John wasn't the most observant eyewitness of other people's behavior, but he could tell that Mechele didn't have the same feelings for Kent that he had for her. Mechele, he said, treated Kent "like a houseboy."

John's father, on the other hand, had a closer relationship with Mechele, a friendship that appeared to become a romance. Around Christmas 1995, about a month after Mechele moved in, John's father called his son into the master bedroom. The elder Carlin was there with Mechele. John IV couldn't remember the exact words or who actually said them, but the gist of the conversation was that his father and Mechele "were engaged to be married."

John IV embraced the news. Mechele did more than ease his father's loneliness. She served as the buffer between him and his father, a role his mother had once had, settling disputes between the two headstrong men. Mechele was one part surrogate mother, one part big sister. This became particularly important as John IV's emotional problems worsened. In early 1996, after he got kicked out of high school for missing too much class, it was Mechele who punished him, forbidding him from driving his Chevrolet Blazer—and removing the distributor cap and spark plug wires to make sure that he didn't. When John IV entered North Star Behavioral Health for counseling, it was Mechele who encouraged and went with him.

After Kent's murder, however, John IV and Mechele's relationship changed. Within weeks, his father announced that John IV was leaving Alaska with Mechele. The news struck him as "fairly sudden" and he remembered that "I didn't have much choice in the matter." For all his problems adjusting to Alaska, he had come to believe that that was where he would live for some time and had begun to make peace with it. When his father told him in June 1996 that he would be leaving, John IV didn't challenge him, even though his father suggested John might be headed to New Orleans to a Catholic school, a horrifying thought. "After growing up with my father I learned not to ask questions," John later said.

They loaded up a motor home with belongings and pets— Mechele brought her cat and at least two birds, and John was allowed to bring his dog, Roscoe. They drove south to Sacramento for a couple of nights at Scott Hilke's house—John had no recollection of Hilke—then headed toward Utah, with a stop in Southern California, where Mechele spoke to a bird expert about breeding one of her toucans. John had hoped to see his old girlfriend Adella Perez, who lived in San Diego at the time, but for one reason or another that didn't happen. Their drive took them through Houston, where Mechele collected a small amount of money one night working in a strip club. They spent a few days at the campground, then drove to New Orleans.

Upon their arrival, their plans changed. Instead of Catholic school, John went back to New Jersey to finish out high school in a public school. He said he had to leave behind his beloved Roscoe, whom he had raised from a pup and who had always slept in John's bed. "I left Louisiana under the impression that [Mechele] was going to ship Roscoe to me in New Jersey," John said later. Instead "she kept Roscoe." John asked her repeatedly to give him back his dog, but he never got Roscoe back.

"She did steal my dog," he said.

John Carlin IV didn't see or speak to Mechele for years, although his father went to Baltimore a couple of times to be treated by Mechele's doctor husband. So it was with some surprise when she sent the email inviting him to live with her in Washington. They were friendly, but John IV was now on his guard with her. As he pointed out later, "She had stolen my dog. I'm not going to trust her completely." Then came that final argument and his move out. He has not seen or spoken to her since.

The detectives then broached the subject of John's father—and the older man's actions around the time of the murder. John had spoken openly of tangling with him and of his frustrations, yet seemed to hold back. "He still felt loyalty toward his father," Branchflower later noted. "He seemed very conflicted in talking to us."

"We picked up little hints along the way that the relationship between him and his father was strained at best," said Stogsdill, "and so I think for a fleeting moment in his life he thought he would do the right thing."

So they spoke some more—a lot more—and when John Carlin IV had extinguished his last cigarette and said his last word, the three investigators rushed back to their car, drove around the corner, parked, and recounted their recollections into a tape recorder while their memories were fresh.

John IV had just blown the case wide open.

CHAPTER NINETEEN

Early in the cold case investigation, when Jim Stogsdill had located Mechele's new address in Olympia, he dispatched local police to drive by her house on Bigelow Avenue and then to follow Colin to work one day at the military base. Investigator Linda Branchflower checked up on Mechele with an employee at the Washington State Executive Ethics Board. Branchflower also spoke with military investigators to confirm that Colin really had been deployed in Iraq, as Scott and John Carlin IV had said. Local deputies set up a loose surveillance on Mechele to get a feel for where she worked, shopped, and brought her daughter, and to establish the best time to pay her a visit.

Stogsdill also wanted to find a place to talk to her where she wouldn't be comfortable, where she would be alone.

"I discovered that she was taking classes at some local college there and they required a parking permit," Stogsdill said. "One of the detectives in Olympia was acquainted with the chief of police of the college. He called that fellow to provide a parking permit number, which told us what lot she would park in. I thought maybe we could catch her in that area. So one day we actually went out there, hung around, and didn't see her."

It was in the second week of May 2005, shortly after they spoke to John Carlin IV—and almost exactly nine years after Kent was murdered—when Branchflower and Stogsdill

Dear Mechele,

The roof on your cabin in Hope is finished. It will not leak anymore. The fireplace has been cleaned but as he said, it will have to be redone within the next year or two. It is safe for you to use now. I also had all the locks changed and the key is under the stone by the tree, where the old key was. It has dead bolts now as well, so you will feel safe when you are there. The one key is universal and will fit all the door locks. I could not find someone willing to go to Hope and clean it though, so it will still be a little dusty. Also, the window screens are all fixed so there will be no mosquitos that will get in. I believe they are coming out now and are very hungry for fair skin people such as us. I am glad that I bought it for you now. It does make a fine getaway. I think when you come back from there this weekend, I would like to spend a couple of days there myself, if that is okay. I need time to figure out where I am going with my life when I sell the house. I have been thinking of Australia, if the Costa Rica deal doesn't look inviting and I don't like it. I sure am going to miss you but I know if something happens or you become unhappy here, you will call me and we can spend time together where ever I am at. You know how much I would like that. I do wish you all the happiness and joy in the world. I am sure you will be happy and raise a fine family. I do hate going and loosing you in my life thought. Please be well, safe and Happy. You guys enjoy your stay in the cabin this weekend.

With all the love I can have for a wonderful woman as you,

John

The "Go to Hope" note found in Kent Leppink's car written by John Carlin III and Mechele Hughes allegedly to lure him to his death.   *State of Alaska*

The Turnagain Arm looking toward Hope, Alaska.
Michael Fleeman

An Alaska Trooper car parked on the turnoff from the Hope Road; Kent Leppink's body was found at the end of the gravel road.
State of Alaska

Kent Leppink's dirty Dodge Omni, where police found the "Go to Hope" note in the glove compartment.

State of Alaska

Kent Leppink and Mechele in 1995.   *State of Alaska*

Mechele Hughes's house outside Wasilla, Alaska, undergoing renovations that Kent Leppink paid for. *State of Alaska*

The Great Alaskan Bush Company, where Mechele worked as a stripper and met Scott Hilke, John Carlin III and Kent Leppink. *Michael Fleeman*

Kent Leppink and Mechele Hughes at dinner in Anchorage with Kent's family in 1995. *State of Alaska*

A gun case found in John Carlin III's house after Kent Leppink's murder; a witness said it was originally purchased to hold a Desert Eagle .44. *State of Alaska*

John Carlin III's mug shot after his arrest on a murder charge in 2006.

State of Alaska

Alaska Trooper cold case detective Jim Stogsdill at the Discovery Café in Hope, Alaska. *Michael Fleeman*

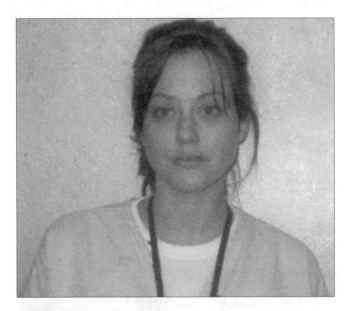

Mechele Hughes's mug shot after her arrest in 2006.
State of Alaska

The courthouse in Anchorage, where both John Carlin III and Mechele Hughes went on trial. The totem poles are of a raven and an eagle.
Michael Fleeman

A brass cross memorial to Kent Leppink near the site of his murder. *Michael Fleeman*

went looking for Mechele. After the community college, they went to the church where Mechele's daughter attended preschool. They observed Mechele in the parking lot, waiting for her daughter. But they didn't want to talk to Mechele with the child there. "We decided: Enough of this," recalled Stogsdill. "Let's just go to her house and see what happens."

After leaving the church, Stogsdill considered making a surprise visit to Mechele's house. To make sure she was there, he arranged for an Olympia detective to knock on her door. When Mechele answered, the detective lied and told her the police were investigating a burglary in the area. After the detective reported to Stogsdill that Mechele did in fact live at that address on Bigelow Avenue, Stogsdill had the detective return and give Mechele one of Stogsdill's business cards with the phone number of the local police station. Mechele called back, incensed at Olympia police for lying to her. Stogsdill asked Mechele to come to the station to talk to him, but she said she wanted to do it at her home. "She made it clear she wanted no Olympia police on the premises," he said. "I did not want to interview her where she was most comfortable, and we ended up doing it in her living room."

The next morning, on May 13, Stogsdill and Branchflower arrived at Mechele's house. Mechele brought them in, then berated them for prying into her personal life. As he spoke to her, Stogsdill was surprised at how much Mechele already knew about the cold case investigation; he later found out that somebody at the college police had tipped her off that authorities were looking into her. Mechele said she considered it harassment.

Stogsdill was blunt.

"These kinds of intrusions often occur when you're a suspect in a murder," he told her. "Get used to it."

He told her the Division of Alaska State Troopers' cold case unit had reopened the investigation into Kent Leppink's murder and that they were talking to everybody again.

"And that," he told her, "means you."

Mechele listened and said little. Stogsdill asked her questions about the case and she offered nothing she hadn't said before. The conversation, which wasn't tape-recorded, was brief and for the most part unhelpful, although Stogsdill couldn't help wondering: Where was Mechele's husband?

She had had advance notice of the interview, and yet Colin Linehan wasn't there.

Stogsdill later observed, "If I'm her husband, I'm going to be hanging around there when police arrive. He's not going to come home for lunch and say, 'Hi, honey, how did the interrogation go?' It was a lot of weird things. She was far from being truthful."

After talking to Mechele, Jim Stogsdill wanted to give John Carlin III one more chance to talk. In October 2005, the detective flew to New Jersey and knocked on John's front door, and John answered.

They spoke briefly. The detective didn't tell him much, and certainly didn't tell him about his son talking to investigators, but Stogsdill wanted the elder Carlin to know that there was no reason to take the fall for Kent Leppink's murder—that Mechele was no friend of his anymore.

"She's a lying bitch," the detective said.

Stogsdill looked for a reaction, and he didn't get it.

Aside from John III's marriage to Julia, the eight years since Alaska had changed him little: he was still heavyset, living in his original house in New Jersey off that insurance payout, and fiercely protective of Mechele.

"I can give you one word that will solve the entire case," John said.

"What's that?" asked Stogsdill.

"Brick."

Stogsdill knew what he meant. Early on, the original investigators had followed a trail to Mechele's old boyfriend, Pat Giganti, who lived in Brick Township, New Jersey. Giganti's last name was similar to that of a local organized crime boss, but that was a coincidence. He was no more a made man than Jim Stogsdill.

The effort to reach out to John Carlin III was a bust. Stogsdill returned to Alaska with another plan of attack.

* * *

For the next year Mechele heard nothing directly from the authorities in Alaska. As each month passed, she and Colin tried to resume life as best they could.

In August 2005, Mechele and Colin took a vacation to Belize, only to hear on the news about a hurricane hitting Mechele's hometown. They returned at once to Olympia and tried phoning her family in New Orleans, but couldn't reach them. Not willing to wait for phone service to work, Mechele loaded her SUV with food, water, and supplies and, with Colin's mother as a passenger, headed for New Orleans, finally hearing from her own mother on the way when cell phone service was restored. Mechele's mother reported that nobody was hurt, but Hurricane Katrina had left her house under four feet of water and destroyed their three cars.

Mechele continued driving. Colin's mother, Judy Linehan, accompanied her as far as Omaha, where she was dropped off with family members. "The surprising gift for me in this experience, other than being touched by Mechele's intrepid spirit and energetic heart, was the gift of time," Judy later told the court. "For the first time in our relationship, I had concentrated one on one days with her. I saw her with new eyes. . . . I had not appreciated how much she had grown in emotional maturity and balance over the past year or so. The forced intimacy of our cross-country trek opened me even further to the dynamic of her being unfolding through time." If they talked about the murder investigation, Judy never did say publicly.

Arriving in New Orleans, Mechele helped remove the soggy Sheetrock from her mother's house. What tools she had brought but didn't need went to a nearby shelter. "When learning that the shelter was almost out of their diaper supply, she drove until she found them and brought them back to the shelter," her mother later said.

They returned to Olympia and to a seemingly normal suburban life. To the outside world, they betrayed no strain from Mechele being the apparent target of a murder investigation. When Kevin Shamel and his family moved into the

neighborhood, the first person to greet them was Mechele
Linehan. "First impressions mean a great deal to me. Mechele made a good one," he later told the court. "She adopted
us into her family from the get-go, making us feel welcome
in our new city. Mechele, her husband, and [their] daughter
invited us to go with them to the beach just days after we
met them."

For months, Mechele had refused to believe she was in as
much trouble as she really was. When her husband found that
she had spoken to the cold case detectives in May 2005, he
told her they needed to hire a lawyer. "Why?" asked Mechele, according to Colin. "I didn't have anything to do with it."

Colin remembered the cliché: If you're innocent, that's
when you really need a lawyer. A friend recommended a
local attorney named Wayne Fricke, who took on Mechele
as a client. Now, in the fall of 2006, Fricke had news that a
grand jury in Anchorage was taking testimony about Kent's
murder.

As with all grand juries, only prosecuting attorneys were
allowed in the sessions in the old courthouse in downtown
Anchorage: no members of the public, no family attorneys.
But from what Fricke could gather, the presentation to the
panel targeted Mechele. Fricke contacted the office of Pat
Gullufsen, a prosecutor based in the state capital of Juneau
and attached to the Cold Case Unit, to say that Mechele
would cooperate in any way, but the lawyer never got a return
call. Left in the dark, Mechele and Colin began imagining
worst-case scenarios. If the grand jury indicted Mechele, she
wanted to surrender in Alaska to spare her daughter the
trauma of seeing her mother arrested. Fricked passed this on
to Gullufsen, but again heard nothing. As the days passed,
the anxiety in the Linehan home increased.

"We did not know if bail would be an option or what the
amount would be and if it would even be possible to have
Mechele home in preparation for her defense," Colin later
told the court. "We pleaded for notice, via Wayne Fricke to
Pat Gullufsen, so we could prepare our daughter for the up-
coming ordeal. This was the main thing on our mind at the

time. How do you discuss this with a seven-year-old girl who adores her mother? We had to prepare her, yet we still had faith that the grand jury would see that there was nothing substantive in the allegations against Mechele."

Then came a phone call on the night of October 3, 2006. It was a reporter from the *Philadelphia Inquirer*, which was interested because John Carlin III lived in adjacent New Jersey. The reporter said a grand jury had just indicted Mechele and John for murder. Did Mechele have a comment?

Anger welled up in Colin. A soldier who believed in American ideals, Colin felt betrayed—and not for the last time.

Within hours, Bigelow Avenue would be rocked.

CHAPTER TWENTY

Although Mechele had heard nothing from the cold case investigators and the prosecutor's office, activity in the case had been quietly building momentum. Despite overtures by Mechele's lawyer, the detectives didn't need to talk to her anymore.

It took a while, but the forensic software probing Kent's laptop and the personal computer at John Carlin's house was at last getting hits off of investigator Linda Branchflower's suggested keywords. At first it found just a few words, then phrases, then entire pages. The letters were smashed together in long strings, with no regard for spacing or punctuation, but patterns began to emerge, and soon entire emails appeared. Detectives could now see what the emails said, who wrote them, and when they were sent, hundreds of pieces of correspondence materializing from the blackness. The investigators narrowed the search window to the months leading up to the murder. By the time the grand jury met, they had hundreds of pages of emails between Kent Leppink, John Carlin, and Mechele Hughes, a treasure trove of evidence that, combined with what John IV had said, provided authorities for the first time with enough ammunition to seek charges.

It would all be kept secret from the public and from Mechele and her attorney, but not from the grand jury. In the spring and summer of 2006, Stogsdill and Branchflower prepared for the presentation to the panel by hunting down witnesses, some of whom hadn't spoken about the case in a decade. They talked to Hilke again, and he agreed to cooperate. The search went on for others in the case, from the original investigators to people like Brian Brundin, the lawyer who drafted and amended Kent's will, and New York Life Insurance Company agent Steven Leirer, who shortly before Kent's murder changed his policy to remove Mechele as beneficiary. The investigators found Lora Aspiotis, who agreed to repeat her story about Mechele's identification with the heroine from the thriller *The Last Seduction*. And, most of all, they had John Carlin IV—and a stack of emails.

One by one they arrived in Anchorage. Pat Gullufsen laid out the evidence and questioned the witnesses.

When it was over, the people of the state of Alaska had their indictment.

After the *Philadelphia Inquirer* reporter called, Mechele still couldn't get any information about the grand jury, her lawyer's messages to the authorities in Alaska going unanswered. The next morning she went to work as usual but kept in touch with her husband, who stayed at home. They were on the phone when Colin heard a sharp knock on the door.

When Colin opened his front door on the morning of Wednesday, October 4, 2006, he saw what he later called a "squad of police" on his quiet street. Officers had stormed the house with guns drawn, according to news reports, a show of force that horrified and angered Colin, who had offered through attorney Wayne Fricke to have Mechele surrender quietly in Alaska if it came to that.

A cop stood in the doorway, told him they were there to arrest Mechele, and fed him a line from a B movie: "We could do this in a small way or a big way."

Colin phoned their lawyer, who picked up Mechele from work and drove her to the local police station within the hour. She was arrested and booked and held without bail on a charge of first-degree murder.

For Colin Linehan, the next few days were a blur of headlines, court dates, and indignities. In their statement to the media, the Alaska state troopers laid waste to Mechele's reputation as an all-American housewife and mother. She was branded the killer stripper from Alaska. Identified in press materials as "Mechele Hughes AKA Mechele Linehan," authorities alleged that the thirty-three-year-old Olympia, Washington, resident had been involved in the 1996 murder of Kent Leppink, who was shot three times with a .44 caliber handgun.

Although she had not stripped for money in years, Mechele was described as a "longtime exotic dancer" who had met Kent shortly after he moved to Alaska and got engaged to him within a month. The press statement said that Mechele also was engaged to a man named John Carlin, identified as a forty-nine-year-old department of transportation worker from Elmer, New Jersey.

Mechele, according to the press release, had purchased a $1 million life insurance policy on Kent, persuaded him to put his real estate and commercial fishing boat in both of their names (a partial error, since Kent had no real estate), and name her as beneficiary. Authorities contended that Kent became wise to Mechele and tore up his will, likely without her knowing.

Mechele and John then murdered Kent, the authorities alleged, unaware that Kent had provided a clue from the grave. The press release quoted from his letter to his parents urging them to "take Mechele DOWN. Make sure she is prosecuted." The letter, authorities let the world know, also named John and a third man who was also engaged to Mechele. This mystery man wasn't identified because he hadn't been charged, sparing Scott Hilke any immediate publicity. Within weeks of the killing, the authorities said, Mechele and John bought an RV and moved to Louisiana.

After a decade of languishing, the murder case was solved, authorities announced, thanks to advances in computer technology that helped them find deleted emails and because of new witness statements, including recent cooperation from John Carlin's son.

In addition to Mechele, John Carlin III was also arrested.

Colin was aghast: troopers allowed John to surrender quietly in Alaska.

While Kent Leppink's murder garnered only a brief mention in the local newspaper's police blotter, the arrest of the stripper turned homemaker and her New Jersey friend attracted wide attention and created sensational headlines. The first photo to be released was Mechele's mug shot, and even from that the public could see she was a beauty with big blue eyes, pert red lips, and hair—now brown—pulled back hastily and mussed. "Former Stripper Wanted for Murder Is Now Housewife, Mother," blared the *Anchorage Daily News*, quoting stunned friends. "She's a great gal," said Jan Henry, who had known Mechele for about a year. "She is one of the sweetest people I know. I don't think I've ever been so shocked in my whole life." The national media picked up the story: *People* magazine later headlined its article "Alaskan Temptress," while NBC's *Dateline* would do a prime-time show called "The Stripper and the Steelworker" and CBS's *48 Hours Mystery* called its piece "Love and Death in Alaska."

From the beginning, Colin Linehan seethed over the media coverage to the point of becoming hypercritical: he chastised one outlet for calling Mechele a "soccer mom" when Audrey had never played soccer. He repeatedly objected to the characterization of his wife as a "stripper," saying that was a job she had held for a short time a decade earlier. But what hurt him most in the early days was the coverage in the *Olympian*, the local paper he read growing up, which sent reporters to interview his neighbors and splashed a photo of his house on the front page.

"It's kind of frustrating because the only picture that's out and that is exposed is of my wife being someone she's not," Colin complained to reporters. "She's a loving mother; loving wife; valuable member of the community; friends and family support her. The allegations are inaccurate. An indictment does not mean she's guilty. She is completely innocent and that will come out." He said the family was "trying to stay as confident as we can," but it wasn't easy. "We're confident in the end really, but the process is uncomfortable," he explained. "Frustrating that we're not able to tell our side of the story, what will come out, and once that's done, we're not looking for any vindication. We're looking to get back to our life."

Family and friends rallied around Mechele and sought to protect her then-seven-year-old. Colin's mother later said: "The irony was that as Mechele's mother, Colin, and I along with aunts and uncles struggled to find the words to explain her mom's absence to my granddaughter, we simultaneously came to the same thought: 'If only Mechele were here, she'd have exactly the right words. She always does.'"

Halfway across the country, in Michigan, the Leppink family released a single statement: "After 10 and a half years, we are very happy to have this take place and are eager for the process to continue."

After Mechele's arrest, she was escorted by a King County, Washington, sheriff's deputy and an officer from the Alaska court services aboard an Alaska Airlines flight for Anchorage. She made her first court appearance at the Nesbett courthouse with Colin in the spectator galley, his head hung low. Wearing a yellow jail uniform and shackled to another prisoner, Mechele pleaded not guilty on Friday, October 13, to scheming to murder Kent Leppink, and was held on $500,000 bail. It was her first court appearance and the first time she'd face off with the prosecutor, Pat Gullufsen.

Gullufsen had a thatch of silver hair and a silver mustache and wore button-collared Oxford shirts with a buttoned-down demeanor to match: he spoke in measured tones, all business in the courtroom and no flash.

In a state where so many people come from somewhere else, Gullufsen was a native son. Born in Alaska to a father who worked in U.S. Customs and raised in coastal Juneau, in southern Alaska, he left for the University of Washington with the idea of never returning. "When I got out of high school, I hadn't been out of Juneau at all," he said. "I thought it was the armpit of the world, and I wanted to get out of here and live life and become famous and rich. After a time out of there, I found myself drawn back. I'd come back for the summers and work. I started to remember what I liked about it."

After attending law school, also at the University of Washington, Gullufsen clerked for superior court judges in Juneau and in a year went to the district attorney's office in Fairbanks, deep in the interior of Alaska, and "started out as a baby prosecutor." It was the late 1970s, and construction on the Alaskan pipeline had brought a surge in the population—and a boom in crime. "Fairbanks was like the focal point for all the workers coming in from the fields," he said. "It had gone crazy in terms of the number and kinds of criminal cases. I did everything from trials for failure to stop at a stop sign to first-degree murder."

Although he liked Fairbanks, Gullufsen yearned for the salty Juneau and got a transfer out of the landlocked city for the capital, where he worked as a prosecutor, then went into private practice for eight or nine years—much of his work spent on legal disputes over fishing grounds—before returning to public service as Juneau's DA.

About two years after the cold case investigation unit began, the state created the position of cold case prosecutor. The prosecutor originally assigned to the cold case unit went on to something else, and Gullufsen took the job.

The move meant new cases and broad jurisdiction—and only homicide cases. "Homicides are not typical cases" in Alaska, Gullufsen said, "maybe one or two a year. Over the years, I've handled as many as anybody. But if I were the county prosecutor in, say, Riverside County [California], I'd do more homicides in five years than I get here in fifteen."

Gullufsen showed no mercy for Mechele. At her bail hearing, he argued vigorously against letting her out of jail, opposing the lowering of her bail to $100,000, as the defense had requested. Judge Larry Card initially sided with the prosecution, and Mechele spent another weekend in jail. At her next bail hearing, the defense asked for a reduced bail with the provision Mechele wear an electronic monitoring bracelet and that her husband and another Army doctor serve as monitors responsible for watching her twenty-four hours a day. Kent's father monitored the hearing by telephone and spoke out against bail. "My son seems to have been forgotten and the accused has taken the limelight as if nothing ever happened," he told the judge. "I'm sorry, but I don't feel that Mechele Linehan should be allowed the freedom to go back to the state of Washington."

At one point Colin came to the stand to assure the judge that he personally would report Mechele if she jumped bail. Bringing his military bearing, the Army doctor sat ramrod straight and spoke of his long record of distinction in the armed forces, including service in Iraq. Gullufsen countered with an embarrassing episode he had dug up from Colin's past. When the Linehans lived in Maryland, shortly after Audrey's birth, Colin was arrested at a Nordstrom department store when he walked out without paying for women's clothing tucked in his daughter's stroller. Colin's face burned as he told the judge the incident had been a big misunderstanding that was quickly resolved, with the charges dropped. But the matter demonstrated how tough a fight lay ahead for Mechele.

Sitting at the defense table was a lawyer well acquainted with Gullufsen. Mechele had added Kevin Fitzgerald to her defense team. An Anchorage attorney with elite academic credentials—Harvard undergrad with a law degree from the Northwest's small and prestigious Willamette University in Oregon—Fitzgerald once worked as a prosecutor and knew the Alaskan courts from both the prosecution and defense perspectives. Gregarious and popular at the courthouse— staffers there call him "Fitzie"—he was the favorite uncle, bald and bespectacled, polite during even the most contentious moment, operating a one-stop law firm not far from the courthouse on Third Avenue that specialized in everything from environmental law to homicide.

"Ms. Linehan has made no effort to run, no efforts to discreet herself, and indeed why should she?" he told the judge. "Her family, her life, her existence, her community, is in the Olympia area." Mechele, he added, "has an interest in defending her good name."

Judge Card was convinced. He lowered Mechele's bail to $150,000 and approved one of her coworkers at her clinic to be third-party custodian, in addition to her husband. Both of her minders faced imprisonment if she fled and they didn't promptly notify police. The judge also ordered Mechele to wear a digital monitoring system, give up her passport, and check in with a bail bondsman weekly. Colin got a second mortgage on their house to make the bail payment and fund her defense.

Mechele flew back to Olympia to supportive neighbors, resuming life much as it had been before her arrest, moving forward with opening with her husband a Botox and laser hair-removal clinic. "She took the time and effort to continue get-togethers, making pizza for her friends and family," neighbor Kevin Shamel later said. "During that time, she still kept up her new business, still kept up her great mothering, still maintained friendships, still rescued animals, and worked, worked, worked." Neighbor Terri Plewa said Mechele "continued to go on with as normal of a life as possible," returning to her business, where she "worked incredibly long hours to make it thrive. She created a small family among the women who worked at her clinic. She has kept a positive attitude in this most difficult of situations and just worked to make it as good for everyone concerned as possible."

Meanwhile, John Carlin sat alone in jail. Soon after his arrest, he and his wife, Julia, separated, and she spoke with Alaska investigators about his visits to Mechele's doctor husband while they lived in New Jersey. He had spoken a couple of times to his son, but their relationship remained strained—and would only get worse. He even lost one of his original state-funded attorneys because of a conflict-of-interest issue involving one of the witnesses. Running out of money, John couldn't make bail and faced having to prepare for his defense from behind the jailhouse walls.

John clung to one thing. He said he was innocent, and he wanted to get the trial under way as soon as possible. His legal strategy from the beginning differed from that of Mechele, who had no interest in rushing to trial. John and his two new attorneys provided by the state of Alaska requested that his case begin within the 120-day speedy trial law. It sent the prosecution scrambling to find witnesses, many spread around the country and some aging and in poor health because the case was so old, and to organize thousands of pages of police reports, interview transcripts, and emails. The defense also kept the prosecution busy with pretrial motions to suppress evidence and limit the scope of witness testimony.

"I always look at a case as to whether they're triable or not," said Sidney Billingslea, one of John's defense attorneys. "I never make guesses other than that: a good triable ease, with a real defense, real things to say, a real shot. So I guess the mood going in was cautiously optimistic, which is all you can ask for."

Billingslea would be second chair in the trial, after lead defense attorney Marcelle McDannel. Both lawyers had vast criminal law experience. Until recently McDannel had made her living on the other side of the courtroom as a tough-talking assistant district attorney with a reputation for fierce cross-examinations and no sympathy for the convicted. Just two years before defending John Carlin III, she had appeared in this same courtroom and successfully prosecuted a man in the brutal murder of a woman. Judge Volland sentenced the man to ninety-nine years in prison, and afterward McDannel said, "I'm so thankful that he will now die in jail." She now worked for the Public Advocate, a government agency that provides legal assistance for elder abuse, child welfare, custody matters, and criminal defense. Billingslea was on an hourly contract with the state, a former Public Advocate lawyer now in private practice, with a caseload that included everything from domestic violence to murder.

John Carlin III played an active role in his defense, meeting with the lawyers regularly at the jail on East Fourth Avenue, about ten blocks from the courthouse, his emotions held in check. "John was always really calm in a lot of ways," Billingslea said later. "Mostly he would not appear to be too excited about anything, but he would say what he was feeling. Even though he appeared to be matter-of-fact, he was really angry at being charged, angry at being wrongfully accused, I'm sure he was really stressed—more stressed than a person should live with. He was mad at the way the system kind of screwed him up. He didn't want any delays. He just wanted to get to trial."

Along with maintaining his innocence, two other attitudes prevailed. "He had no animosity toward John IV," said Billingslea. "He was never disrespectful of Mechele." But as the case raced to trial, those two thoughts could prove detrimental to building a defense.

John's lawyers advised that he go on the attack against both.

CHAPTER TWENTY-ONE

Two twelve-and-a-half-foot-tall totem poles of carved red cedar stand in front of the Nesbett Courthouse, a raven and an eagle, serving as "resplendent reminders of the convictions and power of the people responsible for their own destinies," according to the artist, Lee Wallace. Everywhere in this building of stained glass, Native artwork, and clocks—everywhere clocks, from the whimsical to the abstract—can be found as reminders of Alaska past and present, of the infinite and the finite. The six-story, block-long edifice of pink stone and glass was designed, the architect McCool Carlson says, to reflect the "complex interaction" between the formal rule of law and humanity." In this noble setting come each day the thieves, drug dealers, prostitutes, pimps, wife beaters, child molesters, assault-and-batterers, and killers. The contrast speaks to the balance that totem artist Wallace and architect Carlson sought to express.

On the morning of Monday, March 12, 2007, prosecutor Pat Gullufsen stood before the jury and asserted, "There will be no reasonable doubt that John Carlin, as an accessory or as a principal, was responsible for the murder of Kent Leppink." Opening statements in the case of *The State of Alaska v. John Carlin III, Defendant* unfolded in the windowless courtroom in the center of the courthouse named after Alaska's first chief justice, Buell Nesbett, who took the bench in 1959, the year of statehood. John Carlin III sat at the defense table next to attorneys McDannel and Billingslea, taking notes and appearing unruffled.

The trial attracted a small crowd. Reporters from Anchorage's daily newspaper and television stations were there: still and video cameras were granted access to the courtroom. Nightly newscasts led with what was being called "the stripper murder trial," with the stations supplementing their telecasts with Internet reports. Before it was over, producers and camera crews from CBS's *48 Hours Mystery* and NBC's *Dateline* would be jockeying—and at times sparring—with the local TV media for interviews.

Kent Leppink's father, Kenneth, was allowed to attend even though he was on the witness list, taking his seat in the audience section. Kent's brothers would attend portions of the trial, as would his mother, all of whom were also expected to testify.

Mechele, however, was not there. She stayed home in Olympia with Colin. But her presence loomed, the John Carlin case being a dress rehearsal for her own trial, set for later in the year. Her attorney Kevin Fitzgerald would sit in on most days, taking detailed notes. By the time Mechele went on trial, her defense would know everything the prosecution had.

Presiding over the case was superior court judge Philip Volland. Calm and excessively polite, with the smooth voice of an easy-listening radio station DJ, Volland was one of those rarities among the nation's judges in that he hadn't come up through the ranks of prosecutors. Appointed to the bench in 2002 by a lame-duck governor, Volland began his law career in Alaska in the late 1970s working for the Legal Services Corporation, a private, nonprofit law firm providing free legal aid to the poor. He went into private practice in the 1980s, making a mark by successfully suing the state over overcrowding in prisons. When he was appointed to replace a judge who was retiring, Volland told the *Anchorage Daily News* he expected to be "energized" by the new job. "This will be a different way I can use my skills or knowledge or judgment to help the law get better," he said at the time. "I know it sounds kind of sappy, but I do think the quality of the judiciary is only measured by the people who are willing to do the job."

Despite a history that would suggest a defense bias, Volland dealt John's attorneys one setback after another before the trial. Later, when Mechele went on trial, her attorneys, too, would complain about the amount of prosecution evidence he allowed. Volland also could be distracted on the bench, typing at his computer on other trial-related business while testimony was under way. But his even-keel temperament set a tone. Despite the emotionally charged testimony, tempers never flared in court, and attorneys treated each other—and witnesses—with courtesy not often seen in such an adversarial setting.

And so it was in keeping with the courtroom protocol that Gullufsen would speak in a calm, businesslike tone about even the most heinous allegations. He could have been explaining to jurors their refinancing options rather than laying out what he called "a story that is going to involve passion, greed, manipulation, and deception." But rhetorical flourishes would have been superfluous. The case would provide all the passion required.

Gullufsen's opening statement presented what he believed the evidence would show: that John Carlin had owned a Desert Eagle .44 and lied about it; that Mechele had duped John into gunning down Kent with that weapon so she could walk away with $1 million and the freedom to frolic with Scott Hilke; that John had been a fool, a mark, a tool of a greedy seductress-stripper, but a murderer all the same.

"Jurors love cold cases," Gullufsen said later. "They really are fascinated with them, want to solve them. I think there is a general instinct to want to participate in the resolution of these cases."

The defense's case was outlined by Marcelle McDannel, whose folksy delivery to the jury belied her fierce pretrial legal battles—trying, but failing, to suppress large amounts of evidence, from Kent's letters to his parents to many of the emails extracted by cold case investigators. In her opening statement she highlighted what she called the many holes in the prosecution's case, not the least of which, she said, was the almost total absence of any hard evidence that John did anything other than fall in love with the wrong woman.

"What the state will never be able to disprove is that Mechele herself, the hub of everything, the center of the wheel, acted alone," said McDannel. She promised to portray Mechele as deceptive, manipulative, greedy, and prone to anger. Mechele didn't need John Carlin III, the lawyer said. This cunning stripper could have conned anybody into committing murder: Scott Hilke, Brett Reddell, or some dupe nobody knew about.

That is, McDannel said, if Mechele herself didn't drive to Hope one cold night and gun down Kent herself. "This is a case that frankly cannot be solved and certainly [cannot] be proved beyond a reasonable doubt with respect to Mr. Carlin," McDannel declared. "No way. Not even close. You will not get past a maybe."

In presenting the state's case, Gullufsen wasted little time getting to the first big witness. After testimony from electric company worker Michael Gephardt, coroner Norman Thompson, insurance agent Steven Leirer, and Detective Michael Sears established how Kent died and some of his activities before his death, the state called John Carlin IV on March 14, the third day of the trial. Dressed in a striped shirt and no tie, his hair parted down the middle and wearing glasses, John IV walked quickly into the courtroom, averting eye contact with his father at the defense table.

After John IV solemnly swore to tell the whole truth and nothing but the truth, Gullufsen asked him, "Are you nervous?"

"A bit," he said, and shot his first and only look at his father.

"Just relax," said the prosecutor.

Gently taking John IV through his history in Alaska, Gullufsen elicited how the Carlin family moved to the state around Christmas 1994 when John IV's mother was ill. The younger Carlin talked about a boyhood that started innocent and free; he kept a little wooden case in which he stored his treasures: firecrackers, photos, old shell casings he found—"nothing important," he said.

"Our intention when we first came to Alaska was to have a two-week vacation," he recalled. Then his mother's health worsened. "My mother decided she liked the doctor and wanted to stay, and we honored that request."

His father bought a new house, and John IV enrolled for his second semester of high school, struggling with a new-found freedom at a larger school with fewer rules than his school back home, and started dating follow student Adella Perez. John IV described the living room of the Carlsons' Anchorage home—with the sofa, wall unit, and entertainment center—then got to the heart of his testimony.

Gullufsen asked about something that had happened there in early 1995, something that the original investigators never knew and which John IV only revealed a decade later to the cold case detectives as he nervously smoked in the parking lot of his office in Seattle.

"You remember at some point, after moving into the house, that your father purchased a firearm?"

"Yes," he said.

"What do you remember about that?"

"It was purchased from a newspaper."

"A newspaper?"

"Yes."

"Were you there in the house when the transaction occurred?" asked Gullufsen.

"I was there, but I did not see it, though," said John IV.

"Do you recall someone coming there?"

"There was a man, yes."

"Afterwards, there was a firearm?" asked the prosecutor.

"Yes," John IV said.

"Do you remember there being a case with the firearm?"

"Yes."

"Do you remember that there was a holster with it?"

"Yes."

"And how about a belt?"

"Yes."

"Was there a firearm in that case when it was in the house?"

"At times, yes."

John IV could not remember exactly what the gun had looked like, nor could he positively identify it as a .44 caliber Desert Eagle model that killed Kent. He also couldn't say that the holster looked like the Desert Eagle holster found in Mechele's car after the killing. But his testimony marked not only the first time any witness could link his father with a gun—any gun—in Alaska, it also appeared to contradict his father's contention years earlier that the gun case and belt were left over from a stolen weapon in New Jersey.

John IV testified that about four months after his father purchased the gun, John IV's mother died. Within months two more people would enter his life: his father's stripper friend Mechele Hughes and her oddball fisherman pal, Kent Leppink, who called himself T.T.

"Titanium Testicles," John IV explained to the jury—not "Tennessee Taxidermist" anymore.

John IV remembered the time his father took Mechele to Europe for a couple of weeks, with John IV staying with his grandparents. Kent was strange, but the younger John recounted getting along well enough with him, playing video games together on the laptop. And he remembered the day around Christmas 1995 when his father told him that the relationship with Mechele was more than just a friendship.

"I remember being called aside and basically I was told that they were getting married," he testified. "I don't have a real strong recollection of the actual conversation."

"Was it both of them, though?" asked Gullufsen.

"Yes, they were both present."

The last time John Carlin IV saw Kent was in May 1996. He was uncertain as to the exact day but believed it was the

night before Kent's body was found, a night like any other
night in their Brook Hill Court home. "He was downstairs
with my father," he said, adding that they had probably been
watching TV.

Gullufsen then asked John IV about the days after the
murder, zeroing in on one day in particular and an event
the original detectives had not been told about.

"Was there a point in time when you came into the house
and your father and Mechele were near the bathroom?" the
prosecutor asked.

"Yes," John IV said.

"Do you remember seeing a pistol in the sink?" asked
Gullufsen.

"I remember coming around the corner and seeing Mechele and my father," said John IV. "And there was a firearm in
the sink. And the sink was about half full of a clear liquid."

By now, whatever nerves John IV had didn't show on the
stand. He spoke clearly and steadily.

"Could you smell anything that you associated with the
liquid?" asked Gullufsen.

"I did smell bleach," John IV said.

"Had you just come into the house?"

"Yes," said John IV, "I had just come home."

"What was the reaction of your father and Miss Hughes?"

"I don't think they expected me home at that point."

"And why do you think that?"

"I think that there was a look of surprise."

"Do you know the difference between a pistol and a revolver?" asked Gullufsen.

"Yes, I do," said John.

"What is the difference?"

"[A pistol] has a magazine, whereas a revolver has a re-
volving type magazine, I guess you could say."

"This would be . . . ?"

"A pistol."

"And it has a magazine that fits up into the handle, right?"

"As far as I know."

"Was it a pistol that you saw in the sink?"

"Yes, it was."

"Did you ever see that pistol again?"

"No, I didn't."

Sitting at the defense table, John Carlin III was as stoic as ever. He knew it was coming. His son had not only told the police about the gun in the sink but repeated the anecdote before the grand jury, transcripts of which went to his defense team before the trial. But even as his son testified against him, John III held no animosity. After years of estrangement, they had begun some semblance of a father-son relationship again. They had begun talking while John III was in jail. John III would never say anything bad about his son, never blame him for anything he did. It would be John IV who would feel the most pain and ambivalence.

Gullufsen wrapped up the direct examination asking John about his relationship with his father in the aftermath of Kent's murder.

"Could you be more specific?" asked John IV.

"I could try," said Gullufsen. "Did you get along well?"

"At times," he said. "At other times we argued."

"Would you describe your father as a private person?"

"Yes."

"What do you mean?"

"A private person means someone who does not like to divulge personal information."

After the murder, John IV said, he was abruptly shipped off to New Orleans with Mechele in the motor home. "I didn't have much choice in the matter," he said. He recalled the trip through Sacramento, where they stopped at Scott Hilke's house, and the stay in the campground before arriving in Louisiana. He spoke of leaving New Orleans and his accusation that Mechele had stolen his dog. And he talked of the surprise email from Mechele years later, asking him to stay with her in Olympia while her husband was stationed in Iraq.

John IV hadn't been the only visitor to the house. He

recalled seeing a male friend of Mechele's, a doctor who had worked with her husband.

"Was he there frequently?" asked Gullufsen.

"Yes," he said.

"And he was a friend of Mechele's?"

"Yes," he said.

In the direct examination, John IV didn't elaborate on the nature of Mechele's relationship. The prosecution left the inference to the jury.

Gullufsen's next question was "Did Mr. Hilke ever visit there that you recall?"

"I don't remember him ever being in the house," said John IV, "but I do remember him stopping by at one point, yes."

John Carlin IV ended his direct testimony, looking tired and spent. In one morning he had provided what DeHart and Belden had sought for months: evidence of a gun and a cover-up. He had tied up some loose strings.

It would be up to the defense team to try to unravel them again. One of John Carlin III's lawyers stood and looked John IV in the eye: "My name is Sidney Billingslea and I work for your father."

So began the cross-examination, drawing a line in the sand between father and son. Billingslea would straddle that line carefully, for before challenging John IV, she needed him. Seeking to show a lack of motive for murder, she asked about the relationship between his father and Kent Leppink.

"Did you ever see any fights or arguments?" she asked.

"No, I did not," said John IV.

"Did you ever hear your dad gripe or complain about him being around?"

"Not that I remember, no."

This lack of tension was evident despite Kent's obvious infatuation with Mechele, whom he had been told was his father's fiancée, John IV said.

"He had a crush on her, for lack of a better term," he testified. "I would say kind of by following her like a little puppy."

"What was her demeanor or reaction that he would follow her like a little puppy?" asked Billingslea.

"I think that she humored him to a certain extent," John IV said, "but I think it also at times—she was annoyed by it."

"How would she demonstrate her annoyance?"

"She would gripe, she would make fun of him."

"Was Mr. Leppink under the impression that he was going to get married to Mechele?"

"That's what I was led to believe, yes."

"Who led you to believe that?"

"He did."

"How did he give you the belief of that?"

"Pretty much by saying just that: that 'Mechele and I are getting married.'"

But John IV could see that it wasn't going to happen. "Mechele did not want to marry him," he said.

Through John IV, the defense sought to show that it was Mechele—not John Carlin III—who had not only the motive but the personality of a killer. Building on the prosecution's earlier line of questioning, Billingslea asked John IV about his months with Mechele in Olympia. He recalled her anger when she believed a contractor had stolen from her.

"How did she display her displeasure, temper, anger?" asked Billingslea.

"I remember she, you know, was pretty agitated by it," John IV said, "and was upset and cursing and hooting and hollering."

"She had volume?"

"Yes."

"Intensity?"

"Yes."

"Bad language."

"Yes."

It was the same darker side of Mechele he had seen, he said, when she stole his dog, Roscoe; the Mechele who clashed with him in Olympia over his living arrangements, ending with a second estrangement; the Mechele who confided that the doctor who visited the house while Colin served in Iraq was more than just a friend.

"You knew she was having an affair with that other doctor that would visit the house?" asked Billingslea.

"I never witnessed her having an affair, but—"

"She talked about it?"

"Yes."

"So she shared confidences with you?"

"Yes."

"And this is while her husband is away?"

"Yes."

And yet, despite her faults and despite their arguments—and despite his testimony now, which no doubt would be repeated against her at the second trial—John IV remained fond of Mechele. He considered himself closer to her than to his father. The relationship, he said, was "that of a sister."

During the cross-examination, Billingslea didn't revisit the two most damaging aspects of his direct testimony, the gun purchase and the gun washing, although she did lay the groundwork for explaining those matters, asking John IV if he ever felt he was a suspect in the murder. While John Carlin III felt no ill will toward his son, his attorneys knew they had to dirty him.

Billingslea asked John IV about a former friend who had claimed he had seen him, not his father, burying a gun after the murder.

"If you learned that he told the police that, would that have been a lie?" asked Billinslea.

"That would not have been truthful," said John testily.

The strongest part of the cross-examination came as Billingslea revisited that night John IV had told police about: the night before the murder, when John went to bed upstairs after seeing his father with Kent downstairs.

"The location of your bedroom in this house was over the garage, is that correct?" she asked.

"That's right," said John IV.

"And you slept with Roscoe, right?"

"Yes."

"And what would Roscoe do every time the garage door would go up if you guys were in the bed?"

"He would howl."

"Would that wake you up?"

"Yes."

"In your mind, is there any way the garage doors could have opened and closed—and opened and closed again—that night after you went to bed without Roscoe doing what he always did?"

"I don't believe so, no."

"When you got up in the morning, who was in the house with you?" asked Billingslea.

"My father was the only one there," said John IV. "He was still in bed."

"And outside was Mr. Leppink's car, but he wasn't there?"

"That's correct."

John IV wrapped up his testimony, then bolted from the courtroom, looking at no one, saying nothing, his nerves shattered.

He had provided the most damaging testimony of the trial against his father, but he had also provided, in the account of the non-howling dog, something of an alibi, albeit a rickety one. In a case with no witnesses to the murder, no murder weapon, no physical evidence at the scene or anywhere else, the defense hoped it would be enough to save John Carlin III.

But no sooner had the defense made that headway, a second blow came.

David Michael Stilchen was flown in from Phoenix, where he served in active duty in the Air Force. Prior to that, he had served for eight years in the 1990s at Elmendorf Air Force Base just outside Anchorage. Military to the bone, he sat straight and proper and answered in clipped "Yes, sir's" and "No, sir's" to Gullufsen's questions on direct examination.

"You remember," asked Gullufsen, "when you owned a particular firearm?"

"Yes, sir, I do," he said.

In 1991 or 1992, he said, he had purchased from a friend a Desert Eagle .44 caliber handgun, which he described as a large if temperamental weapon that had a habit of locking up after one shot. He said a gunsmith had replaced the springs and other parts, and while it resumed firing properly, it still was difficult to cock.

"Did you sell it eventually?" the prosecutor asked.

"I sold it in the early part of 1995," said Stilchen.

"How did you go about selling it?"

"I placed an ad in the local newspaper."

It was Detective Linda Branchflower who had found Stilchen. When John Carlin IV told the cold case detectives about his father buying a handgun from an ad in the *Anchorage Daily News* in early 1995, Branchflower followed through on what Detective Steven DeHart had considered doing: going through old classified ads. After a tedious search at the offices of the *Anchorage Daily News*, she finally found the item in the January 29, 1995, edition.

It read: ".44 Desert Eagle, holster, with belt, three clips and ammo, case and paperwork. $850 or best offer."

Branchflower called the phone number on the ad. It was a cell phone number that had been disconnected, but a search of phone records eventually linked the number to Stilchen, who had left Alaska in 1998 and now resided in Arizona.

Gullufsen showed Stilchen a copy of the ad. "Do you recognize that?"

"Yes, sir, I do."

"Is it the ad you put in the paper to sell your Desert Eagle?"

"Yes, sir, it is."

Stilchen said that within days he got a response to the ad.

"I received a phone call," said Stilchen. "A gentleman was interested in purchasing my gun. I talked briefly about the gun. We set up an opportunity for me to go over and show him the gun, to take everything to his house. He gave me directions. I believe I called him once or twice en route, I know it was night when I went over there, and it was a relatively new area to me."

After he arrived he was greeted by a man with his shirt off—in the dead of an Alaskan winter—"which seemed odd to me," said Stilchen. They went into the kitchen of a newly built home in South Anchorage.

"I showed him the gun, the case, everything associated with it, and we began just to have idle conversation, very briefly talked about the gun, what he wanted the gun for. [He said] just hunting—a big gun, which is the only reason I had it for. Back and forth a little bit. Didn't take long, and he gave me cash, and I sold the weapon to him."

"Do you remember how much cash?" asked Gullufsen.

"I know it wasn't what I asked because I got in trouble when I got home," Stilchen said. "But I think it was around $600 or $650, give or take."

"And it was cash you received?"

"Yes, sir, it was."

"Do you remember the denominations?"

"They were large bills, hundred-dollar bills."

The buyer had checked out the gun carefully. "I knew there was no ammo with it, and I didn't bring any ammo with me," Stilchen said. "He went through it, cocked it back, looked at it, dry fired it, and didn't seem to have any issues with handling the gun."

Gullufsen showed Stilchen the gun case and ammunition belt found in John Carlin III's house and the holster found in Mechele's car. "They look like the exact items I sold," he said.

Stilchen remembered the belt, made by Sidekick, because it had a large buckle useful when wearing gloves. The case, he said, had held two guns—he also had a .22 caliber pistol in there—and the holster was notable because it was the only one he could find big enough to hold the Desert Eagle.

During the gun transaction, Stilchen recalled, somebody was in the living room watching TV, though he couldn't remember if it was John Carlin IV or even if it was a man or a woman.

"He just wanted a gun for hunting, basically something that would drop a bear, and that's exactly what the Desert Eagle was," he said.

But while he could remember the interior of the house—the sofa, wall unit and entertainment center—he couldn't recall exactly what the man looked like. "He was a burly man, just kind of stout," he said. He also remembered the man saying he had recently moved to Alaska.

Gullufsen didn't ask him if the man sitting at the defense table was the gun buyer, and on cross-examination Stilchen said that when interviewed by Branchflower he was never shown a photo lineup.

"He wasn't fat, he wasn't muscular," he said. "He was just a stout person."

One more witness saw what the prosecution would suggest was the murder weapon.

"It was," Scott Hilke testified, "the biggest gun I have ever seen in my life."

Mechele's former lover came to court on March 19 primarily to lay the groundwork for the prosecution's centerpiece evidence—the extracted emails—by introducing jurors to Mechele's life as a $3,000-a-night stripper and a deft juggler and manipulator of men, particularly Kent Leppink.

"She was grooming him for economic purposes," said Scott. "He would always do whatever he could to get whatever she wanted."

And John Carlin III?

"Same situation," he said.

Confident and cocky on the stand, Hilke built on the testimony of John Carlin IV and David Stilchen, recalling his disgust at Mechele for thinking she could learn to use a huge handgun in a concealed-weapon course she took with other Bush Company dancers sometime in 1995.

"How did she appear to handle it?" asked Gullufsen.

"Not very well," said Scott. "She struggled to pull the slide back."

"What was your attitude in terms of her with that gun about to take the course?"

"I thought it was crazy," Scott said. "I thought the gun was far too large and unmanageable."

"Did you say something to John Carlin III about that?"

"I asked him: 'What makes you think she's going to be able to fire that?' " Scott recalled. "I expressed a concern in regards to the firearm."

"Did he deny having loaned it to her?"

"No."

Scott recounted that while Mechele moved in with John Carlin III in the fall of 1996, they continued to see each other, usually on out-of-town weekend trips, including one in the days before Kent's murder. At the condo in Lake Tahoe, he said, Mechele seemed tired but otherwise acted normally. He played golf; she made phone calls and sent emails—on a laptop computer.

He spoke of how their relationship collapsed, the low point coming with the ill-fated trip to Cancún in the spring of 1997, when he thought they'd never see each other again—until, to his surprise, she contacted him years later while she was living in Olympia in 2004.

"Tell us about this time when you met with Miss Hughes."

"I met her at a park a couple blocks down the street from her house, apparently, and met her child, and we just sat and talked for a while and then I went on my way."

"Did you make arrangements to meet again?"

"I'm not sure if I made them at that time," Scott said. "I did meet with her, though."

"What were the circumstances when you met with her again?"

"We had dinner in Tacoma."

"Did you have a sexual encounter on this occasion?"

"Not on that occasion."

"You did subsequently, is that right?"

"That's correct."

"How did that come about?" asked Gullufsen.

"I met her again in Seattle, and we spent the evening up there, and she spent the night in my hotel room," Scott said. "And not long after that, I flew her and her child to Minneapolis."

"To see you there?"

"Yes."

"And did you have a sexual encounter there?"

"I did."

"And where were you staying at that time?"

"The Crown Plaza."

"How long was she with you?"

"I think she came in Friday night and left Sunday afternoon," he said. "She and her child were in one room. I was in my room. And after her child was asleep, she would come into my room."

"Did you see her after that?"

"No."

"When was that?"

"I'm not certain."

"But it was in 2004?"

"May have been early 2005."

"Did your wife [Erin] discover that you had these encounters with Miss Hughes?" the prosecutor asked.

"She did," Scott said matter-of-factly.

"How did that happen?"

"By an email or finding information in regard to the communication on my computer."

"And what did she do?"

"She called Mechele."

"Were you present when that happened?"

"No."

"You and Erin are still together?"

"Very much so."

If nothing else, Scott Hilke had learned from his transgression. He had once thought he was Mechele's true love, a cut above John Carlin III and Kent Hilke.

"You called them both a moron?" asked Gullufsen.

with a sexy, beautiful young woman turned out, he said on
cross-examination, to be "a very, very bad, in all respects,
part of my life that I wished I hadn't dealt with."

Asked if he felt used by Mechele, he laughed bitterly and
said, "Oh, yes."

While the combined testimony of John Carlin IV, David
Stilchen, and Scott Hilke was used by the prosecution to
try to link John Carlin III to a Desert Eagle .44, one more
witness was called to connect him with a piece of evidence
that had only just surfaced. In early 2007, just weeks before John's trial began, an advertisement appeared on eBay
for a bronze sculpture of two deer, titled *The Greatest
Game*, by wildlife artist Rick Taylor. The seller was Julia
Carlin.

Julia, now separated from John since his arrest, testified
on March 22 by telephone from New Jersey, where she was
still residing in the three-bedroom home where she had
lived with John and her daughter by a previous relationship.
Speaking in a heavy Russian accent, she explained that she
had seen the statue when she first moved into the home after
leaving Russia in 2003.

"Where was it kept?" asked prosecutor Gullufsen.

"In the family room above the fireplace," Julia said.

When contacted by New Jersey State Police Sergeant
William Scull in February 2007, she turned over the statue.
Scull came to court to show the jury the twenty-pound art-
work.

"Is there a name engraved on the back of the base of that
statue?" Gullufsen asked Scull.

"Yes, there is," he said.

"And what is it?"

"Kent Leppink."

Along with the statue, Julia produced a certificate of au-
thenticity from the artist showing that the statue was sold to
Kent in November 1992.

She had also found a handwritten note titled, "People to notify if arrested." The first names were John's parents, now deceased. The second name: Mechele K. Hughes, with her Alaskan phone number.

Kent, of course, had complained that Mechele had stolen the statue and his laptop, and the prosecutor the next day produced a witness to testify about the computer. Appearing nervous and speaking in a soft voice, Mechele's sister, Melissa Hughes, testified on March 23, recalling how Mechele had sent her the laptop to erase the hard drive, then showed up at the campground where Melissa worked with her husband. Melissa described how the argument with Mechele climaxed with the latter's cruel pronouncement that the gunned-down Kent Leppink "got what he deserved."

When she finished her testimony, Melissa raced out of court and burst into tears.

As the prosecution's case neared its end, Stephen DeHart wrapped up his testimony, conducted over separate days because of scheduling issues with other witnesses. Now retired from the Division of Alaska State Troopers and working security at the federal courthouse, DeHart spoke of his theory of the case—that John Carlin III had been the gunman—but that Mechele had helped plan the killing for financial gain. Although the holster had been found in her car, DeHart never felt that Mechele had had enough time to get from the airport to the murder scene and kill Kent. He spoke of how Carlin had denied owning a Desert Eagle and how intent Mechele had been on keeping detectives from getting to her laptop.

And he spoke of his frustrations in never making a case against either one of them. It had not been a perfect investigation, DeHart acknowledged under cross-examination by Marcelle McDannel. Weeks and in some cases months had passed before some witness statements were taken or before search warrants were served on the houses and cars of those targeted in the case.

"There's lots to cover," he told her defensively. "It takes

time to get things done. And we worked it every day and every weekend and accomplished as much as we could."

"Isn't it your duty . . . to investigate all possibilities?" she pressed. "Or did you narrow your investigation so much that you did pursue your investigation in such a manner that you excluded Mechele as the primary suspect?"

"The investigation, first of all, was not narrow," DeHart said. "And secondly, my job is to attempt to find the truth to the best of my ability, and that is, in fact, what I did."

CHAPTER TWENTY-TWO

In the computer age, some things never die, no matter how hard you try to kill them. Old emails, Word documents, photos, Web pages and spreadsheets lurk in computer purgatory, the unallocated space on the hard drive. That was the message to the jury from Alaska state trooper Sergeant Christopher Thompson.

"Often when you delete something, it's still here and it's recoverable later," he said. "Sometimes it's recoverable partially, sometimes the whole thing's sitting there."

Thompson explained that, per a search warrant, he examined Kent's laptop and several zip disks in 2004, creating an image of everything in the memory using forensic software and transferring that image to a second computer.

Another high-tech investigator, Curt Harris, supervisor of the Division of Alaska State Troopers' Computer and Financial Crimes Unit, then did a search using twenty keywords selected by detective Linda Branchflower:

- "TangoPI" (Kent's email address)
- "AKmewell" (Mechele's email address)
- "JCarlin127" (John Carlin III's email address)
- "SHilke99" (Scott's email address)
- "Mechele"
- "Kent"
- "John"

- "Scott"
- "TT"
- "Little John"
- "Kill"
- "Alibi"
- "Gun"
- "Desert Eagle"
- "Hope"
- "Insurance"
- "Love"
- "Leppink"
- "Million"
- "Costa Rica"

Later, Harris also searched a memory image lifted from the personal computer used in John's house. The searches turned up thousands of pages of text, including much duplication; but when sorted out and limited to a time frame of between March and May 1996, the computers and disks yielded dozens of emails and several Word documents and Web pages. Taken together, the recovered text told a story.

It all began in March 1996, less than two months before Kent's killing. He had just found out that Mechele had been having a secret—from him, anyway—relationship with Scott Hilke and was acting suspiciously close with John Carlin, even though she had accepted Kent's wedding proposal. Kent confronted Mechele, who replied in a long email in which she sought forgiveness—and his love. In a letter addressed to "My Darling Kent," Mechele said that since they had decided to get married, it was "time for me to be honest with you about my past and my feelings. . . .

"Scott and I were involved both sexually and emotionally," she acknowledged. "When I met him, he was on the rebound"—he was in the midst of a divorce—"and I was confused. I thought I fell in love with him. We were engaged to be married for a while. We are not just good friends. It has been over and will stay over."

Repeatedly speaking of her emotional confusion, she

admitted that "there were times when I have treated you badly," but said she took note that "you still stayed with me" and that "this means more to mean than you will ever know. . . .

"The world seems to close in on me," she wrote. "I protect myself by running. If only for a week, I come back refreshed. You seem to always understand. I need that. You must be able to handle that. I will get over that. I need a simple life. I have never had a simple life and I want that life now. You can give me that life." She repeated that she knew she had hurt him, and for this she was sorry.

"As for John, you know we have never had sex, and you know that he can't," she wrote. "What you don't know is how sick he really is. You must NEVER tell anyone. I gave my word not to tell and I am breaking my promise for you. The lead did something to his kidneys, too. His blood is messed up somehow. He asked me to take care of John [IV] if something should happen to him. I have agreed."

John III, she insisted, "is more a brother or even a father to me" and "please don't worry about him. . . .

"I think if you still want to marry me, we should just go and do it," she concluded. "We don't need our families there. We just need each other and some trust between us. We don't need a big wedding or guests or the expense that goes with it. We should get married within the next month. We should just do it and start our life. We need nothing else."

Her reply satisfied Kent, who would call his mother in Mexico and announce he was planning to get married within weeks. He also continued with his application for the $1 million life insurance policy with Mechele as the beneficiary. But Kent also had to clear the air. He emailed Scott.

"For a long time I have wanted to write you this letter," he began. "Actually I wanted to talk with you, but I can normally say things better in a letter. I am glad that I have waited until now to get my feelings out, things are now settled, out in the open, and finished.

Telling Scott that he and Mechele "hurt me very much" by hiding their relationship, Kent now came to believe it was a waste of energy—"I know exactly how you feel," he wrote—and oddly took some of the blame himself. "By remaining silent, I am as guilty as you for not being open with me," Kent said. "I keep too much inside, and all the pressures build up until the only thing that is left is resentment. . . . I was a bundle of mixed-up emotions: desire for love, hatred, bitterness, confusion."

But now, Kent said, "Mechele and I have talked a lot in the past few days, and I am putting all of this behind me." He said he wouldn't ever bring it up again.

"I want to be your friend," Kent told Scott. "You still mean a lot to Mechele. So we can't have anything get in the way; no skeletons in the closet."

Kent then tried to create the same clean slate with John Carlin III. In a long email, Kent shared how much Mechele meant to him—and how difficult it was to love her.

"From the moment I met Mechele, I fell in love with her," Kent wrote on March 11, 1996. "It would seem pretty strange to say that, knowing where she used to work, but when she would do table dances for me, I was watching her eyes. Sure, it's hard not to see the naked body in front of you, but I felt more for her than just as a sex object. I knew that we would be married to each other almost from the beginning. I gave her a diamond one month after we met, and we talked about life together, sex—waiting for a while—having children, etc. I would have married her right then and there, but we talked and decided not to set any dates right away."

Then the first sign of trouble was when Scott came into Mechele's life. "I was told that Scott was just a friend and that he was gay: 'You have nothing to worry about[,] TT.' And I really didn't worry about it. I'm supposed to trust the one I love, and I believe everything she says," he wrote.

Then he found the faxes she had left lying around and "even a blind man could read what they said. . . .

"I felt as if somebody had hit me on the head with a sledge hammer," he wrote. "These faxes pretty much spelled out the fact that I was not the person I thought I was to Mechele, and that the gay friend that I didn't have to worry about was not only engaged to Mechele, but was also having a pretty steamy sex life with her to boot."

When Kent finished the fishing season in the fall of 1995, he thought that Mechele and Scott had broken up. "Then I saw the whole thing starting over again," he wrote. "Only this time it wasn't Scott. It was John." Finally, in around March of 1995, Kent and John had a frank conversation about Mechele and patched things up.

John wrote back that their talk did in fact clear the air about Mechele—and John confided he suffered "medical problems," apparently impotence, that made him no threat to Kent. "You are a true friend," John wrote to Kent. "I also appreciate your willingness in helping John [IV]. You will be assuming the role model for him. That is a serious commitment. I know that if you accept this, you will do well. . . . He is still getting over his mother and you know that he is not handling that well."

This was around the time when John Carlin IV was beginning to suffer severe problems at home and at school, the fallout from the death of his mother and his clashes with his father. Adella Perez, his girlfriend of six months, had just broken off their relationship because she couldn't deal with his mood swings and outbursts. Soon he'd check into the North Star mental health clinic.

John told Kent that they were kindred souls. "We both have not had the sex life we should have hoped for from a man's point of view," he wrote. "I don't know why you were worried about me. . . . I'm a fat bald man with no social graces. . . . It is also safe from emotional romance but not from loyalty to her from friendship."

In the second week of March, Mechele went on a trip, according to the emails. It's not clear to where, though in an email to John she told him she missed him. John was convinced she was in California—to see Scott Hilke—and it was driving him nuts. He told her that he and Kent would fight over the cordless phone when it rang in the hopes it would be her, and he wrote at length about taking care of her pets. "I want you home so bad," he wrote to her. He didn't want to call her, he said, because "it is Scott's phone and I know he would not like that."

Mechele didn't respond in kind, talking instead about her pets and travel logistics. She said Scott was making her reservations to fly back but "he won't send me first class" because he didn't have enough frequent-flier miles on Alaska Air. She planned to spend a few days in Anchorage before flying to New Orleans to see her family. The email made John resigned that he would never have her. "It is probably better for you to be in CA as you don't like Alaska that much and you do like Scott," he wrote on March 17. "Scott is a lucky man, a real lucky man. I only wish that I could be so lucky . . . Scott has something that I do not."

John then apparently got drunk and fired off a sexually explicit email: "I want you and am hard for you. I want to take you like I have never before. Fuck Scott and the horse he rode in on. I want you and will have you if you arrive."

John wasn't the only one aching for Mechele. In an email with the subject "Lost and All Alone," Kent seemed to think Mechele had gone to her hometown of New Orleans, based on his references to time zones. "I miss you, I miss you, I miss you. More than I love you," he wrote to her March 21. "It is making me crazy being away from you. Did you talk to your mom about the wedding? Is she going to be able to come?"

Mechele's full reply couldn't be found, only the closing: "Love always from your future wife." Kent was in heaven. The marriage was on track and Mechele was about to return from her vacation.

He emailed Mechele on March 26 to say that he had spoken to his parents and "I know what our surprise is" for the wedding.

"I'm not going to tell you what it is over the phone or in an email because it is best told over candlelight and a soft music. PS: I love it when you call yourself my wife."

While Kent was consumed with thoughts of love and marriage, Mechele privately harbored serious doubts about spending the rest of her life with him. These feelings were expressed in what would be a powerful piece of evidence for the prosecution.

In a long, sarcastic email to her mother on March 29, Mechele related what she said was a conversation with Kent's relatives when they had asked her about her own family.

"I told them my mother never loved me like she loved my sister," she wrote. "I explained to them that I wasn't your real daughter and that you were forced to take me on as your daughter because your third cousin had me when she was only 13 and that the whole family suffered because it was her brother that fathered the baby (me). So I think they understood.

"I also explained that a deal you made had gone sour because of my lack of talents and that is how I ended up in Alaska." Kent's parents, Mechele said, "naturally . . . begged me for more. . . .

"So with a little sobbing on the phone I told them the rest," she wrote, explaining to her mother that she had given Kent's parents a preposterous story of how Mechele had been sold into prostitution with Eskimos, only to fail and disappoint her parents, who refused to take her back. Until she was saved by meeting a fisherman from Michigan.

"And then my destiny became clear," she wrote. "All the clouds moved out of my small confused mind as the tears cleared my eyes, I began to see an angel appear: TT. He came and swept me off the street and accepted me and taught me how to love and be loved. He showed me the way of life. And, well, all of my dreams came true that day. I took one look at this man and knew I wanted to be pregnant with his children for the rest of my life. I was put on Earth for him."

Mechele said she then thanked Kent's parents for "producing such a god-given gift" who "showed me the way of life."

Then came the punch line. Mechele hit the caps-lock key and typed:

"HA HA HA HA HA HA HA HA HA HA HA HA HA HA HA HA HA HA HA HA HA HA HA HA HA HA HA HA HA HA HA HA HA HA HA HA HA HA HA HA HA HA. JUST JOSHING YA !!!!!!!! FUNNY, HUH? . . .

Mechele admitted that she had never spoken to his parents, "and they haven't asked to speak with me since I said I didn't know your home #. HA HA HA. I can't wait to come home."

The tone and those forty-four "HA's" flew in the face of her "Love always, from your future wife" email to Kent of just days before, providing the prosecution with loads of ammunition at John's trial—and Mechele's later—to show the depths of her nastiness and manipulation.

Mechele's mother replied saying she loved the "crazy email" so much that she had printed it out. "Hello, gypsy child," her mother wrote. "Think you should become a writer kind of like Stephen King."

On the same day Mechele sent what would become known as the "HA HA HA email," she received a note from John Carlin III.

John wrote of a seemingly far-fetched plan by Mechele—later discussed in other emails—to leave Alaska and build a bird sanctuary in Costa Rica. This, apparently, was why Mechele had just traveled to South America, scoping out property for the sanctuary. Mechele had discussed the idea with John but apparently not with Kent, and now Mechele was trying to get John on board as an investor. Whether she truly wanted to raise birds in South America, or had just cooked up the idea as a ploy to get more money from John, wasn't known, but John was seriously considering it.

"It would require the liquidation of all or most of the assets that you and I have in Alaska as well as liquidation of my assets in Jersey," he wrote to Mechele. "This commitment is easy for me. I find no happiness in life with the exception of you."

Despite his love for Mechele, John worried that he'd be stuck in South America, just himself and Mechele's birds, while she would periodically take off with Scott Hilke. He also worried about the heat and humidity, though said he wouldn't mind the seclusion. In the end, a maudlin John concluded it was better to have some of her in his life than nothing.

Mechele appeared to be going full steam ahead with the idea.

"I just spent three weeks in Costa Rica. Nice. I found a great piece of land there," she wrote March 31. "Anyway, I am off tomorrow for New Orleans. I am bringing my new laptop."

By now Mechele was back in Alaska—and itching to hit the road again. Her mother emailed to say that gumbo, Caesar salad, and French bread awaited her in New Orleans "when y'all get home." And in late March 1996, Mechele told Kent and John that she was traveling again. This time she was headed for Louisiana.

John's spirits sank once more. He complained about never being able to love Mechele the way he would want to, only this time he didn't only blame Scott Hilke.

"This atmosphere here is very unhealthy, and I will never have a fair shot at winning your heart. It frustrates me so much," John wrote to her on the evening of March 31, after she had left. "TT is here. He is very weird. He intercedes in any time I have with you. I cannot openly talk to you as he might hear.

"I blame it on TT," he continued," Sometimes I think you don't understand how this affects me with TT here. How really, really frustrated I'm going to be with him finally gone and you're not being here. This will kill me."

Just how weird he considered Kent was spelled out in other emails, including one written to Mechele after John went on a drinking binge with Kent. "I'm so high," John began, then announced, "TT wants me to fuck him. I don't know what I said. He threw up and I am confused." At another point John said, "TT wants me to stick it up his ass." John drunkenly and graphically assured Mechele that he had no interest in Kent. "I want you. I love you. I am going to throw you on the bed and fuck you like no other," he wrote. "You might not want to come home."

But there were signs that John was sexually confused himself. A couple of weeks after sending this email, he forwarded to Kent information about a gay Web site called MALE Club. "I received this today and thought I would share it with you," wrote John. Kent professed to be puzzled. He emailed Mechele, "What's he think I am?" And in another email, John grumbled to Mechele that "you really enjoy telling people that I was with a whore that was a man, don't you? Hmmmmm. Oh, well, humiliation, I guess."

Whatever actually happened between John and Kent while they went on tequila benders would be left to the lawyers to debate at trial. Based on the email evidence, Mechele commiserated with John about having to be around Kent. "It's a shame TT is going to be gone the same time I am gone," she wrote, a reference to Kent deciding to join his parents and brother's family in Florida for Easter vacation. "I love you. I don't know what to say to you. I feel that I need to make a decision now and I am a little pressured by that. . . . I think we need to investigate more into the Costa Rica thing before either one of us makes any fast decisions. . . . I love you dearly and I don't want you to think that the space between us is changing the feeling I have. It is not."

Shifting gears—and men—Mechele then sent an email to Kent, telling him that the "time we are spending apart is healthy" and that "although it may hurt a bit, it will make everything stronger."

"I am not trying to procrastinate our wedding. I am just concerned that everything will be rushed, and it worries me because I will only have one, and you know I want it to be perfect and well, like you," she wrote.

"I knew you cared, but I didn't know it had no boundaries.

And I hope I can make you a happy husband. I will try my hardest to keep our family strong, loving and sturdy."

Then, she sent a third email—to Scott Hilke.

"Hi, how is my baby?" she wrote. "Well, I've got the $ for Costa Rica. Just don't pee your pants. OK, I almost did. Let's do it. Why not? We don't have to move there now. Maybe later."

Scott addressed his reply to "LOML"—Love Of My Life. "Sounds good to me," he wrote. "Sybil [Mechele's bird] wants to make sure she can still be a baby and not have to hang out with the wild birds in the jungle. I told her she would always be our baby."

He signed it "AML"—All My Love.

This email was sent the day before Mechele went to the offices of the New York Life Insurance Company and delivered a check for Kent's $1 million life insurance policy and her smaller policy. She then flew to her mother's house in New Orleans.

Late on the night of April 3 or early on the morning of April 4, when Kent was with his family in Florida—his mother had been shocked by how thin he was, and how infatuated he was with Mechele—Kent was at the computer, emailing Mechele. She was in Louisiana, and he was trying to make arrangements for her to fly to Florida to join him. "Thanks a lot for doing everything that you were doing," he wrote.

Mechele replied angrily. In a message in all capital letters, with no punctuation and full of misspelled words, she accused him of looking through her personal belongings, including her phone book, which had numbers of men she knew from the Bush Company days. "I have a lot of things to do before we settle down, so please stop snooping and asking all these questions," she wrote. "If you continue to rummage through my privacy and snoop through my belongings I will not marry you. While we are not married, nothing is ours. Do you get it? When we get married you will know where everything is in the house, but when you go through my purse and my bags and my computer, you are invading my privacy and I will not tolerate it. So remember, I think you owe me an apology."

Kent replied with a long, contrite message. "I was wrong," he wrote. "I should not have looked through your stuff. I should not have taken any of your things. I am 100 percent to blame. I had no right to do what I did, and won't do it again. Will you please accept my apologies for doing this?"

But, he suggested that in his snooping he had found something on her. He doesn't say what it was, although when his body was found he had been carrying the Scott Hilke documents, including the reservation form for the Natchez resort from August 1995.

"Another thing I want to talk you about is our wedding," Kent continued. "We really need to decide on a date and stick to it . . . If you need time for one thing or another just tell me. I have waited a long time to marry you. While I have only known you for one-and-a-half years, I have waited for you for 36-and-a-half years. A few weeks will not make any difference to me."

Kent reminded Mechele of how their relationship had started. "A long time ago, you asked me not to tell my parents about where I met you and I haven't. It seems like everybody else knows where you work though, and it is very hard for me sometimes. If you could remember, I wasn't there to see all the naked women, I was there to see you, to be with you. . . .

"Yes, I have seen you naked before, and you have seen me naked before, but that is not why I went to the Bush," he went on. "As a matter of fact, I don't like to go there, but while you were there, I went just to see you. God works in mysterious ways."

In a postcript, he added, "When you get down here I'll tell you another secret. It's about why I moved to Alaska and my family problems. It might really surprise you"—an apparent reference to his embezzling money from his parents' grocery store.

A cheery Mechele wrote back: "I'm so lucky. Send me the number you are at . . . I cut my hair. I'm very happy with it. I love you."

But there would be no meeting in Florida between Mechele and Kent's parents, as his father balked at paying for Mechele's airfare to come down for Saturday only. Kent couldn't reach Mechele again, and frantically emailed her from the mobile home. He tried to find John in a chat room without luck. By Friday, April 5, Kent was back on the computer, pouring out his heart. "Mechele, my love. I love you," he wrote.

Finally Mechele replied, in no mood for sweet talk. She demanded money for the wedding. "You said you would wire it but you have not," she wrote. "I need $2,000 for the dress and $500 for the headdress. That is the cost of the headpiece. You need to wire or Western Union it. . . . I would not expect you to follow through. You have not."

She told Kent that by not sending the money, he had embarrassed her in front of her relatives and violated her trust. "Stop putting me off and give me a definite time and place where the money will be," she wrote. "Tell me by 8 o'clock."

Her email enraged Kent. "I WILL NOT ARGUE ABOUT MONEY," he replied. Although Mechele often wrote with the all-caps key down, this was unusual for Kent. He explained that he was pestering her with wedding plans "because my parents are paying for a lot of things . . . and they don't like being left out in the dark."

"As far as procrastination," he continued, "Where's the money that you told me you would get to me for the tile work at the house or for the vet bills or for the things I do to Brett's truck, etc.? I ask you about the money, and you tell me not to worry about it, that you'll get it to me. I wait and ask and wait and ask and no money.

You show me a picture of a birdcage and ask me if it's ok to get it. That makes me responsible to pay for it? Is

my wallet supposed to have a one-way path on it? Am I
supposed to just pay bills and not know where the
money is going to or help make plans for its use? I don't
think so.

As far as people covering other people's asses, I guess
I have done my share and then some. Enough of this
bullshit.

Mechele appeared stunned that he had stood up to her,
firing back that he had promised that she wouldn't have to
work. "Why didn't I have a job? [Because] you'll support
our family. If the cage were not ordered, I would not have
had to pay for it. It was out of your commitment that I ordered it, remember? And as far as all the other shit, I told
you: You could be part of everything. Sorry, not my dress.
That is mine," she wrote early on the morning of April 7,
Easter Sunday. "And you told me your parents wanted to pay
for everything. If this is changing, you need to tell me."

It was after this email argument that Kent had the long
talk with his mother, who urged him to put off the wedding
and told him that the family would contribute only $2,500 to
the ceremony. A defeated Kent emailed Mechele. "You are
right," he wrote. "You do not have a job and I will support
our family . . . All week long I got questions about you and
when you would be coming. Needless to say, I think it's best
to hold off on the wedding."

Kent left Florida late that Sunday night arriving in Anchorage early Monday morning. He went back to John
Carlin's house, and sat down at the household personal computer, scrolling through old emails—doing more of the
snooping that had so angered Mechele.

Again he was caught, this time by John.

"I just noticed that TT went through all my letters on the
computer when I was gone," John said in an email to Mechele, who was still with her mother in New Orleans. "He
does a bad job of covering his tracks now that I know to look
for."

But what was most on John's mind was not email security but love, desire, and a tender memory. "The last night you were here was so special to me," he wrote, one of several gushing emails. "I know that you did not want to do what was done, but yet you did it for me. I will remember that night until I die. I will never forget. I was truly happy that night. I have longed for that for so long. Happiness. It felt very good, and I now know the feeling of spending the night with someone you love."

He loved her so much, he wrote in another email, that it had strengthened his resolve to make their lives better—and take action.

"I am not going to wait," he wrote. "I'm going to end this soon. I am the one who will take the risk. I cannot wait. It will end. You know what I'm saying here."

Their secret remained between themselves, for no other emails elaborated on John's cryptic but ominous message.

For Kent, returning to Anchorage meant facing his financial problems. He wrote to Mechele that his father "hit the roof" when he found out she wanted $2,500 for a wedding dress. "He said that if you added up the cost of the dresses of all my brothers' wives that they would have been less than that. Then he asked me a lot of questions about you and me."

Kent said he was in the process of taking out a loan for the fishing season. "My advice right now is that we had better start looking at a budget," he wrote. "Let's do it right, but let's do it within the limits of our pocketbooks. I want you to know that I am going to find a way to pay for your dress."

His note triggered another argument. "Sorry, the dress is already ordered and paid for," she snapped in an April 9 email. "You should have told me that two weeks ago when I asked about it. I don't want to discuss it now while I'm this upset."

"I'm sorry," Kent wrote back. "I'm sorry for a lot of things. What I'm really sorry for, I'm sorry that I misled you. From the very beginning I have misled you by letting money be a bigger part of our relationship than love. It is my love for you that has kept me around. By spending every dime that I had and then asking my dad for more money only put up a false front to you. It made you feel like you had an unlimited budget by which you could just go out and do anything you wanted to."

Mechele emailed back: "My grandfather has given me the $, so stop now while we're fighting." Then she added: "Did you get our policies for life insurance?"

She told him that a copy of the policy was supposed to go to her grandfather, but he hadn't received it yet. "I am losing his trust and I don't like it," she wrote. Mechele had apparently told Kent that her grandfather had paid for the policies when in fact she had, explaining why Kent had told his family that the policy was a wedding present.

"I went in and signed for my insurance policy yesterday," Kent replied. "I have copies here. I want very much to talk to you. I've talked to John about the money, but I am waiting for you to get home. Do you want me to call in the morning about sending paperwork to your grandfather?"

Her reply couldn't be found, but the answer was apparently yes, because it was the the next day that Kent called the New York Life office and had the receipts for the policies faxed to him at John Carlin's house.

Three days later, on April 12, 1996, Mechele was back in Alaska, where she underwent tonsil surgery. Investigators uncovered a rare email from Scott in which he wished her well before the procedure. Addressed to "LOML," it said, "I have become accustomed to holding you at night and waking up and stroking your hair and kissing your cheek. I miss you very much."

The surgery left Mechele with pain and trouble eating, but that was only part of her troubles. Something was brewing between her and John. In a note with the subject line "Missing You and Your Mail," Mechele wrote on April 12: "I wondered where you were tonight, so far away. You did not want to spend any time together. You chose to be alone.

I don't know why. Maybe I need to be with you after being
away. I am being insecure and I should act stronger, but I do
miss you so bad. I just want us to be like we used to . . . Why
are you pulling so far away? Did I do something to cause
this?"

They had apparently argued when Mechele returned from
Louisiana. "The other day I upset you a great deal," John
wrote in a letter to her. "I cannot believe you said you were
worried about me telling you that you would have to leave
me as I have found another. I want to reiterate that I will
never leave you, cheat on you, desire anyone but you, and I
will worship the ground you walk on, the air you breathe, the
words you speak and the glow of your being."

Mechele responded, "You say that I am too good for you,
but the truth of that is not what you say. It is that you give me
just a reason to be, a reason to live."

It was not known if, while snooping through John and
Mechele's emails, Kent Leppink saw this exchange, but at
about this time his mood darkened. His financial situation
was dire—he had just borrowed another $10,000—and his
doubts about Mechele's love for him were growing.

"Awhile ago you wrote me a letter," he wrote to her on
April 16. "To refresh your memory I'll reprint it for you." He
attached her email from weeks earlier in which she told "my
darling Kent" how lucky she was to have a man who has
"stuck with me during all my confusion" and suggested they
forgo a big wedding and get married within the month.

His email arrived the same day John and Mechele were
professing their love for each other. She replied brusquely:
"Dear Kent, why did you send me a letter that I wrote. I do
not need it. Remember, I wrote it. I felt I needed to explain
those feelings and let my emotions and sorrows be known,
not to be thrown back at me in the future."

She told him that if he wanted to talk—and not "beat
around the bush and whine"—then he needed to answer
"direct questions with direct answers, and I will be respectful of our intelligence and do the same." The words fore-

shadowed Mechele's comments to Alaska state troopers after Kent's death that he "sounded stupid" and wasn't answering directly.

"Until you stop snooping, which you are doing as of last Friday, you and I will not get married and will not have a life," she wrote to Kent. "This is not a request anymore. This is a threat. The first time was a warning. . . . Three strikes and you are out and stay out. I won't have it in my life."

It was after she sent this "Dear Kent" email that Kent's feelings toward Mechele flew in all directions. It was in those days in late April 1996 that they argued in front of lawyer Brian Brundin, with Mechele suggesting that Kent was gay; that Kent returned to Brundin's office to hear the attorney liken Mechele to a scorpion; that Kent removed Mechele from his life insurance policy; that Kent put her back on his insurance policy; and that he quarreled with her at the hardware store over the cabinets, then paid for them anyway, drawing down on that $10,000 loan.

By now a change had also come over John, who was grappling with ending whatever semblance of a relationship he had with Mechele. "Please be happy and don't let me cause you to be unhappy," he wrote in a letter saved on his computer April 24.

"I will be the one who will take the loss," he continued. "You have asked me several times to tell you what to do, and that you will do it. OK, I will do this."

John did not specify what he was planning to do for Mechele, a woman for whom he would give his life. The phrase gave the prosecution grounds to suggest that John was referring to murder, even if his anger wasn't directed toward Kent.

John ended the letter with another provocative statement. "You will be just fine, Michele, just give it a few weeks, your life is about to get a lot better," he wrote. "You will see. Now the ball's in your court. You are now making the decisions, not me. You will decide what will happen."

Events now were unfolding quickly. It was the next day,

Thursday, April 25, that a $3,100 check to Mechele drawn on M&K Enterprises cleared, but the signature of Kent Leppink appeared to a bank employee to have been forged. This was also the day that Kent found his laptop and statue missing and possibly discovered the "Go to Hope" note.

And it was the day that Mechele left on a 3:16 p.m. flight, bound for Sacramento for an assignation in a condo with Scott Hilke, while Kent thought she was in Hope with a lover in a cabin owned by John Carlin III.

"Where is the laptop computer?" Kent wrote to Mechele late that night. "I've been home all day and you didn't say anything about taking it to do anything. I think it would be considerate of you to wake me up if you wanted to take it to do something. The way you unhooked it may have damaged it. If you would like I would show you how to work it so that nothing happens to it."

Mechele replied with the email that would be found in Kent's pocket, telling him the laptop was "finally working" and that the rugs were being cleaned, claiming she would "see you tonight or in the morning," and complaining that she was a "a little pissed off" because she couldn't find him and suspected he was smoking pot, taking pills and drinking.

The next morning, on Friday, April 26, Kent alerted Mechele that his father had arrived in Anchorage to help sort out his taxes. "He would like to see you," Kent wrote. "We have a lot of things to talk about, and I would appreciate it if you would make it here soon."

By now Kent had had it with Mechele. That was the day he went to Eagle Hardware to cancel the cabinet order, telling the salesman that Mechele had found cabinets she liked better elsewhere. It was also the day that he met Brian Brundin, who would later tell investigators that Kent had related that "the night before had been an upsetting one for him." This was the office visit in which Kent had Mechele removed from his will and left everything to his parents, filling out the change-of-beneficiary form that would be found in his pocket at the murder scene. It was also this day or the next that Kent drove to Hope, showing the photo of Mechele to the cook at the Discovery Café and alarming his mother with his story about Mechele's grandfather buying them a life insurance policy as a wedding gift.

Mechele and John had begun to sense that Kent was taking action—and they were worried. Kent had not been at John's house recently, and the pair didn't know where he was or what he was doing.

"He will pop up soon," Mechele wrote to John on Saturday, April 27, in an email from Lake Tahoe, typing on the computer that Kent had accused her of stealing. "Good luck. Things are to be easier, I thought."

In a second email that Saturday, she added, "I can't imagine where TT is . . . He is such a shit. He sent me a letter asking where the computer is—said I may have damaged it the way I unplugged it. It should be easier than this. Things will go smooth. I hope he shows up before his dad." In other emails to John, she called Kent "stupid" for complaining she took his computer and asked, "Why are things getting so messed up? . . . Has his pop called to confirm the time? I bet he has called him. Bye bye, love you Mechele."

It was important, Mechele wrote again to John, that Kent not know that she was out of town with Scott. If Kent saw her car at the airport, perhaps he wouldn't believe she was in Hope—and start to suspect she was in California with Scott. "You should tell TT I flew to Barrow," she wrote.

She then forwarded to John her previous email to Kent about the computer and surmised what Kent had done with it. "Did you get this one?" she asked John. "He must have printed it then." She was correct: this was the email found in Kent's pocket by police.

John tried to reassure Mechele. "You know you can call here if you need to, OK," he wrote back. "I will be in tonight. I am going to relax, get a rental movie. Love you, John, Bye."

Phone records also showed a flurry of calls from the condo in Tahoe to John's house. From the emails it appeared that in one of the calls, Mechele and John continued to discuss how to handle the elder Leppink. Kid gloves seemed the best option. She suggested that John, Kent, and his father might all want to "eat a nice dinner somewhere," but if the topic of money—and all the gifts lavished on Mechele by Kent—came up, John should be wary.

"You know where we have money spread out," Mechele wrote. "He [Kent's father] won't like the insurance and my coats and jewelry, you know that sort of stuff, so he will probably try to stop some of those purchases, although some he can't. We cannot return some."

The next morning, Sunday, April 28, Mechele followed up. By now John had spoken with Kent, and Mechele worried again that Kent had somehow intercepted their emails. She asked John how Kent reacted when John told him that Mechele was "2½ hour [sic] away," an apparent reference to their efforts to keep Kent from knowing she was really in Lake Tahoe by telling him she was either in Barrow—a two-hour flight from Anchorage—or in Hope.

She spoke of the future, the next lines of the email providing the prosecution with some of its strongest evidence against Mechele.

"I can't wait to go on our getaway," she wrote to John. "Did you know that you can buy a citizenship in the Sacheles [sic] for around ten mill? And no matter what crimes you have committed they will not extri [sic]. They are the only country that won't send you back to the U.S. I found that out yesterday. . . . Have you given any thought to where you want to go," she added. "Learn to dive, maybe? Cancun? Cabo? Anywhere."

Mechele had misspelled "the Seychelles," an Indian Ocean archipelago nation off the coast of Africa northeast of Madagascar, and abbreviated the word for "extradite," but prosecutors would argue the inference of a post-murder getaway.

Later that Sunday morning, Kent emailed Mechele to say he had spoken with his father at his motel and he would be "going there right now to talk more, have breakfast, go to church. It would be nice to be able to go to lunch with you. We are in room 229. Give us a call."

Mechele promptly forwarded this email to John. "Such a shit," she wrote.

The next day, Monday, April 29, was the one Kent spent holed up with his father at the Best Western, sorting out his finances, his bank account down to just $656.32 with the fishing season about to begin. It was the next day, Tuesday, that Kent brought his father to the airport, then spoke to his brother Lane about having the "bull's-eye" on his back before mailing the package to his parents. That was the same Tuesday that Mechele called the New York Life office from the Tahoe condo, saying that her wedding had been postponed and asking if she and Kent could get refunds on their policies. No emails surfaced from these two days, although a number of phone calls were made between John's house and the Tahoe condo.

The email trail resumed on Wednesday, May 1, 1996—the last day that Kent Leppink would ever see. It began with a message from John to Mechele:

> Maybe we can invite TT and discuss our conversation you had with him last night. I don't think John is crazy about his sexual comments anyway...Please be well, safe and happy. You know that's all I want for you, no matter how much it hurts me.

The email referenced what John IV would tell authorities: that he had complained to his father about Kent's sexually inappropriate behavior, which included the strange pelvic thrusts.

The prosecution presented one more document that it said held evidentiary value: John's will.

"It is my desire and I hereby direct that Mechele K. Hughes shall be the guardian of my minor or incompetent child," said the document, written not as an email but on a word processor. "I hereby bequeath 50 percent of my residual estate to Michele K. Hughes and 50 percent to John Carlin IV."

The will was originally dated April 4, 1996, when Mechele was in Louisiana and Kent was in Florida. But according to the forensic software, the document was modified on Thursday May 2, 1996—the day Kent's body was found.

CHAPTER TWENTY-THREE

Linda Branchflower presented the emails to the jury on Wednesday, March 28, reading some in their entirety, giving excerpts of or paraphrasing others. The prosecution also assembled the messages into a packet for jurors to read during deliberations. Only a couple of emails sent after the murders were presented. "There is a huge emptiness in my life right now," John wrote to Mechele in one. "I will find a way to deal with it, I guess. Well, until we meet again." In another, Scott Hilke wrote to her: "I miss you like I have never missed you before and fear things are as they have never been before. Please tell me I am mistaken." None of the emails spoke directly of the murder or of any cover-up. Nobody mourned the loss of Kent Leppink.

Pat Gullufsen then called his last witness, Jim Stogsdill, who provided more details about the cold case investigation. After eleven days of testimony, the state rested its case against John Carlin III.

Going into the defense case, John's lawyers believed the prosecution had presented an interesting, even lurid case but legally failed to meet its burden of proof to convict John of first-degree murder. As compelling as the emails were, defendants have walked on a lot more than what Gullufsen had brought into court. The cross-examinations of the state's witnesses, particularly John's son, had in the defense's view raised more than enough reasonable doubt for an acquittal.

During summations, when the defense could present its interpretations of the emails and other evidence, John's lawyers hoped to put to rest any lingering thoughts in jurors' minds that there were sufficient grounds to convict John Carlin III of murder.

Such was the strategic thinking in considering whether to have John take the stand and testify in his own defense. "I thought we had gotten enough momentum coming out of the prosecution case that we didn't need him to," John's lawyer Sidney Billingslea said later.

It wasn't that John was reluctant to testify. He wanted to. And it was, legally, his decision in the end. But his attorneys advised against it. Along with their perceptions of weaknesses in the prosecution's case, his lawyers worried that John's mind was not as sharp as it would need to be to survive a Pat Gullufsen cross-examination. John had begun suffering memory losses, Billingslea felt, and there were too many dangerous areas for him to speak about—too much to explain—that it seemed not worth the risk.

The defense called just two witnesses, an evidence technician and a trooper investigator, then rested on Thursday, March 29, confident it had scored all the necessary points during the prosecution's case and could wrap it all up in summations.

Closing arguments were held on Friday, March 30. As in all trials, Pat Gullufsen, as the prosecutor, would have two opportunities to speak, with time for rebuttal remarks after the defense's summation. The practice afforded Gullufsen an advantage—he would literally have the last word—but he faced another challenge unique to this case. His summation was really two summations: one for this trial, and one for the trial that was to come. Gullufsen wanted to show the jury that John had murdered Kent Leppink, but he also needed to show that John hadn't acted alone—that Mechele had played enough of a role that, when she went on trial in a few months, she, too, could be convicted. It was a balancing act: blame Mechele too much, and John Carlin could get off the hook; put too much of the murder on John, and Mechele could walk.

And so, as Gullufsen stood and addressed the jury, he began by acknowledging the point on which both the prosecution and the defense agreed. "Mechele Hughes wants money," Gullufsen said. "She was obsessed by it. She had a drive to get it, and she had no moral qualms about how to get it. Throughout the evidence in the case, that's apparent. I don't think there's going to be a dispute between the parties on that issue."

Then he showed where he believed the two sides differed. "John Carlin had an obsession that almost matched Mechele's," he said. "It was different, though. It was an obsession for her. He would do anything to make her happy, including giving up his life. You find that in his words and his actions."

The prosecutor then recounted the emails between Mechele and John, highlighting the correspondence in the final days of Kent's life, when his money was nearly gone and his suspicions were mounting. The fishing season loomed, and soon Kent would be on the water in Cordova or Whittier or Valdez. His life insurance was in effect, and as far as Mechele knew, she was still the beneficiary of $1 million. It was, Gullufsen argued, now or never for John and Mechele.

"Kent is not going away quietly, let's put it that way," the prosecutor said. "He's got his family involved in this marriage. He's got his whole ego and being involved in this marriage. He's obsessed with it. He's not going to walk away, and they know that."

Gullufsen said John and Mechele together left Kent the Hope note—a note, he argued, that forced Kent to ask John where the fictional cabin was because the letter offered neither an address nor any directions. Protecting herself, Mechele took the alibi trip to Lake Tahoe, leaving the dirty work for John Carlin III, the former Marine, of gunning down Kent with military precision. With Kent out of the way, John Carlin felt that he was on the road to having Mechele to himself.

Convict John now, he urged the jury, and leave the unfinished legal business for later.

"Mechele Hughes is going to have her day of reckoning," the prosecutor told the jury. "It's going to be before a different jury. She's also charged with first-degree murder for her participation, her responsibility, her role in Kent Leppink's death. But that will be before a different jury. Obviously you have to assess her behavior, her actions and her role in all of this. But it's his guilt or innocence that we're here to decide. This is his time of reckoning."

The defense had one last opportunity to speak to the jury. Marcelle McDannel had to make it count. Through his attorney, John would follow Kent Leppink's directive: "Bring Mechele DOWN."

"She's the only one in this trial," McDannel said, "who has the type of nature capable of executing this cold-blooded, nasty act of rage."

Not so John Carlin III, she said. Describing him as a huggable teddy bear of a man, the lawyer said John had neither the disposition nor motive to kill Kent. John was "selfless" and "friendly," letting Kent crash at his house, loaning him money, picking his dad up at the airport. "These guys are two peas in the pod," suggested McDannel. "They are both being used by Mechele. . . .

"There's no motive of jealousy between the two of them," she added. "Mr. Carlin knows what's going on. He knows about Hilke. He knows about Brett Reddell. He knows about Mechele's scams. He knows about T.T."

No amount of money would convince John to kill Kent, because no amount of money was coming to him from the murder, said McDannel. For most of their time together, John, with his lawsuit payout, was the only member of this psychodrama who had any money, and he used it at every turn to keep Mechele with him. An insurance payout would be the worst thing that could happen. "Making Mechele wealthy just removes Mechele's dependence on Mr. Carlin," said McDannel. "She's not going to share any of that money. That's Mechele's $1 million."

And besides, John has an alibi: the non-barking dog. Had he snuck out to kill Kent in the middle of the night, Roscoe would have yelped, and that didn't happen: the state's own star witnesss, John Carlin IV, testified under oath that he never heard a thing, the lawyer told jurors. "Mr. Carlin III is the only one with an alibi actually verified by another witness," she said.

As for the evidence presented by the prosecution, McDannel said what little there was all pointed to Mechele, starting with the email about the Seychelles. Mechele wrote it, not John. He never even responded to it, McDannel said. As for the gun case and belt, the fact that police actually found it spoke to his innocence. Why, asked the lawyer, would he leave it around just hours after committing a murder with the gun associated with those items?

She turned then to the most damaging testimony.

"What Mr. Carlin does for Mechele, he cleans up her messes," said McDannel, explaining to the jury that under the law, behavior described by John IV should be not considered aiding and abetting in a murder, since it happened *after* the crime. "Even washing a gun," said the lawyer. "In Alaska, that's a separate crime. It's called evidence tampering. It does not make him an accomplice to murder. The state chose not to charge Mr. Carlin with evidence tampering. They wanted to for murder. But helping Mechele for whatever reason she gave him, whatever line she fed him, whatever lie—who knows?—to get him to do that for her does not make him an accomplice because it happened after the fact. The state has presented no evidence that he ever acted to help Mechele kill Kent Leppink before."

It was a risky move, essentially conceding that John Carlin IV had told the truth, then hoping the jury would be sophisticated enough to differentiate subtle differences in the law between aiding and abetting before the fact and evidence tampering after.

McDannel then listed what she called the many deficiencies in the police investigations, shortcuts that McDannel claimed were taken in a rush to focus only on John and Mechele, suggesting that other people besides John had more motive to kill Kent, with just as much—or as little—evidence to prove it.

Take Scott Hilke, she said—a man who openly called Kent a "moron," who had no alibi, who spent time with Mechele right after the murder, and who reconnected with her as late as 2004, right after the cold case unit began its work. "If Mechele finds out she's being investigated again, who's the first person she's going to want to sink her claws into?" asked McDannel. "The guy she collaborated with, the guy she needs to keep close, the guy she needs something on—perhaps like cheating on his wife. Hilke is who she goes to."

Or even John Carlin IV could also have killed Kent. "He certainly had a motive," she said—and that the fact that he was a seventeen-year-old boy living with a stripper in her early twenties. Maybe he wanted to be more than just a little brother to her. Plus, "he was very vulnerable to manipulation by Mechele Hughes," McDannel said.

But the most likely scenario, she claimed, was that Mechele committed the murder herself, meeting an agitated Kent at the airport late at night after her trip to Lake Tahoe, driving with him to Hope, where they argued about money, before she gunned him down at close range—close because she's a lousy shot and because this was personal. She left his body on the ground with none of her own footprints, because she didn't weigh that much.

The defense said she even had proof that Mechele was with Kent that night. It was her longtime knowledge that Kent had mailed his parents the letter implicating her in his death. Police had never disclosed that fact publicly, and yet Mechele had later told her sister that she knew all about the letter.

"Who knows about that letter?" asked McDannel. "The killer. Because when the gun was to his back, when he knew Mechele meant business and he was going to die, he whips out his final life insurance policy [and says], 'I sent a letter to my parents and it names you.' "

And he was killed anyway. The insurance policy was worthless.

"John Carlin in this case, ladies and gentleman, is just the man who cleans up Mechele's messes," McDannel said. "And he's done it throughout his entire, unfortunate association with her. . . . Don't you bet that Mechele is sitting down there in Olympia right now hoping John Carlin cleans up one final mess for her?"

In her final words to the jury, McDannel acknowledged the jury's impulse to want to hold somebody accountable for the murder. Reminding the jury of what Kent Leppink's lawyer had called Mechele more than a decade earlier, McDannel said, "The day of reckoning is coming for the scorpion, and it's coming in September. Mechele Hughes will be forced to be held accountable for everything she's done to all of these people, but most importantly to Mr. Leppink. The day of reckoning for the scorpion is coming. In the meantime, ladies and gentlemen, don't kill the turtle. Find him not guilty."

Gullufsen used his rebuttal to reject the theory that Mechele had acted alone. First, he told jurors, John Carlin III himself had told police that he, not Kent, had picked her up at the airport when she returned from Lake Tahoe.

And if she had murdered him overnight, the crime scene would have looked different. Noting that the ground was frozen overnight, he asked: "How do you get Kent Leppink's footprints in the . . . mud between 2:30 a.m. and 8 a.m.?" The murder, he said, had to have been committed during the daylight or evening when the ground was thawed, rendering the non-barking-dog testimony moot.

If Mechele had killed Kent, and John only found out later, "why is John Carlin III sending John Carlin IV alone with a murderess in the new RV that he has just purchased for her?" Besides, the prosecutor insisted, this wasn't Mechele's style. "Does anyone in this courtroom believe that Mechele Hughes is going to dirty her hands by doing the deed herself?" he asked.

It was now Gullufsen's turn to ask the jurors to look closely at Alaska law, which the judge would later read to the jury, urging them not to confuse a circumstantial case with a weak case. As the defense had said many times, prosecutors do have to prove the elements of a crime beyond a reasonable doubt, but they don't, Gullufsen told jurors, have to prove "each fact that will lead you to guilt." The prosecution didn't even have to prove that John was the shooter, only that he had aided and abetted in the killing. Gullufsen said that by law if some jurors felt John had fired the gun and others thought Mechele had, the panel could still convict John of murder.

"We urge you to go down all the roads [the defense has] suggested," said Gullufsen, concluding his rebuttal. "We want you to look at everything, to look at the so-called other suspects, to take the evidence, turn it inside out, and really take a hard look at it, because we believe you'll come back here to John Carlin after that, and your conclusion will be even stronger. . . . You'll put it all together. And when you do, there will be no doubt, no reasonable doubt, that he committed this crime of first-degree murder in the killing of Kent Leppink."

CHAPTER TWENTY-FOUR

The jury retired to deliberate that Friday afternoon and went into the weekend without reaching a verdict. On Monday the foreman sent a note to the judge asking for two things. First, the panel wanted to inspect a Desert Eagle .44 that had been used during the trial as a model, the real murder weapon having never been found. The judge agreed and sent the weapon into the jury room. The second concerned the testimony of John Carlin IV: the jury wanted to hear it again. The panel was brought back into the courtroom, and an audiotape of the younger Carlin's two hours of testimony was played.

The next morning the jury had a verdict.

The day and a half of deliberations was unusually short, and the verdict on Tuesday caught everybody by surprise. This was a busy day in local government. Voters had gone to the polls to cast ballots in state and local elections. Judge Volland, who had guessed the jury would come back on Wednesday at the earliest, couldn't make it to court. Nor could prosecutor Pat Gullufsen, who was out of town. Nor could defense attorney Sidney Billingslea, who was hiking in the mountains. The reading of the verdict would proceed anyway, with half the trial's participants out of the courtroom.

A van brought John Carlin III from the jail to the courthouse, where he was unshackled and escorted to the defense table next to lawyer Marcelle McDannel. Another assistant DA sat at the prosecution table and a different jurist, superior court judge Michael Wolverton, took the bench.

After jurors walked into the jury box, the fill-in judge told them, "You may be seated. . . .

"The record should reflect that the jury panel is in the courtroom and seated," he began. "Good afternoon, members of the jury, my name is Mike Wolverton. And I'm here because Judge Volland had to be called away. Judge Volland is, however, on the line telephonically, as is Mr. Gullufsen, who tried the case."

The judge turned to the jury box. "Mr. Fullerton, it's my understanding that the jury panel reached a verdict, is that correct?"

"Yes, we have, Your Honor," said the jury foreman, Patrick Fullerton.

"What I'm going to do is I'm going to have you hand the jury form to the bailiff," said the judge. "I'll review [it], I'll return it to you, and as soon as he's done that, if you'll just stand and read the jury verdict and the remainder of the page, please."

Fullerton did as instructed, and after the bailiff handed the jury form to Judge Wolverton, he read the page without expression. The verdict form went back to the bailiff and then to the foreman, now standing.

"The State of Alaska versus John Carlin III, Defendant," he read. "We the jury find the defendant, John Carlin III, guilty of murder in the first degree as charged in the indictment. Dated in Anchorage, this Third day in April, 2007."

John's demeanor didn't change, his face blank, one eye barely twitching. He accepted the verdict as he had accepted every other development in the trial: impassively, without emotion.

The judge instructed the foreman to hand the verdict form back to the bailiff, then said, "Do you wish to have the jury polled, Ms. McDannel?"

In a wavering voice, she answered, "Yes, Judge."

"Members of the jury, Mr. Fullerton as your foreperson

has advised us now what the jury verdict is," said the judge. "What I'm going to do now is ask individually: Is the verdict that has just been read your true and correct verdict?"

One by one, he read off the juror's names, and each of the eight men and four women answered "Yes" or "Yes, it is." Two of the women dabbed away tears and spoke with halting voices.

That completed, the judge asked, "Is there anything, Ms. McDannel or Mr. Gullufsen, you want to take up before I give concluding remarks to the jury?"

"I have nothing, Your Honor," came Gullufsen's voice over a speaker.

"Nothing," said McDannel.

"Judge Volland," asked his stand-in, "is there anything you want to add at this point?"

"There is not," said Volland over the speaker.

"Members of the jury," said Judge Wolverton, "I want to thank you for your service here. I always tell people after jury trials—and I've said the same thing for many years because I truly feel it—you know it seems to me that this is really the most direct form of participatory democracy that we have because that vote, as it were, that you exercise in the jury room has an even more of a direct impact on fellow citizens than that important vote we should all be exercising today on Election Day. We know it's not an easy thing we ask of one another as citizens in this community. But it is vitally important what your service has been and very, very much appreciated."

Noting that throughout the trial prior to deliberations they had been ordered not to discuss the case with anyone, Wolverton told the jurors, "Now that I'm going to discharge you from further service in this case, I'm going to advise you that you are permitted if you want to talk to individuals about this case."

The jury was excused, a sentencing date for November was set, and John Carlin III was led back to jail.

Later, jurors revealed that they had always leaned toward guilt. Their initial vote after the first day of deliberations was 9 to 3 in favor of conviction. Panelists said they had been influenced by Carlin's lying about owning the pistol, which persuaded the remaining three to come around to guilty, but the process took a toll: "Traumatic" was how foreman Fullerton summed it up.

As the verdict was read, juror Donald Sanford locked in on John. Sanford caught the eye twitch but nothing else. "He expected it," Sanford later told *Dateline*.

Outside the courtroom, Betsy Leppink said, "God is good, all the time. And we are very much at peace, thank you."

John's attorneys seemed to take the verdict harder than his client did. "I don't think I've been that surprised by a verdict before," said Sidney Billingslea, who found out in a cell phone call. "I thought that after the closing arguments we had really made our points. I thought that in Pat Gullufsen's closing arguments, he was inconsistent—he was trying to accommodate all different government theories."

Lead defense lawyer Marcelle McDannel was devastated. She not only thought she had the case won, but now she feared that justice would never be done. "What this means is the real bad player in all of this, the real evil participant in all of this, has a chance of getting off," McDannel told reporters after the verdict. "My prediction is that this will substantially diminish her chances of being convicted, which is tragic. I mean, if anyone was involved in this case—anyone—it was her."

CHAPTER TWENTY-FIVE

"Her."

In the end Marcelle McDannel couldn't even say Mechele Hughes Linehan's name. Mechele wasn't in the courtroom when the verdict was announced—she had stayed home with her family in Olympia—and her reaction was relayed by her attorney. "She holds no ill will toward anyone," Wayne Fricke told the *Anchorage Daily News*. Her feeling was "not one of jubilation. She is just worried about her case."

As Mechele's trial date in September 2007 approached, the defense's tactic of delaying her trial had ramifications. After John's trial, Marie Homer, the secretary to Kent and Mechele's insurance agent, had died. Another witness, Brian Brundin, was in poor health. Two other witnesses appeared to be getting cold feet. The first was Mechele's sister, Melissa Hughes. She told prosecutors that she wouldn't testify a second time because of the stress it was having on her family, then she disappeared.

"While we certainly continue to look for her and try to obtain her, she will know that all she has to do is lay low for about a month until the trial's over," Gullufsen told the judge at a pretrial hearing on Wednesday, September 5, just days before jury selection was to begin the following Monday.

Even more troubling to the prosecution was the reluctance now of John Carlin's son, John IV, to testify a second time. Filled with regret after his father's conviction, the younger

Carlin told the *Anchorage Daily News*, "I'm pretty upset at the moment because I believe they have an innocent man in prison." He added: "There's always going to be that part of me that realizes that a big part of why he was found guilty was because of my testimony. And I know there was emails and other things like that. But in my heart I know that's what did it. And I think that's the toughest part to live with." After much uncertainty, John IV surfaced that day, but Gullufsen worried that the younger Carlin could avert a prosecution subpoena by invoking the Fifth Amendment or, like Melissa Hughes, by just disappearing.

With Melissa Hughes missing and John Carlin IV on the fence, Gullufsen asked Judge Philip Volland to delay the trial. Proceeding without Melissa Hughes or John IV could be "very, very risky" for the state's case, the prosecutor said.

Mechele's lawyers, who had originally been in no hurry to begin, now objected to any delay. They blamed the failure to subpoena Melissa Hughes on police incompetence, for which the defense should not be punished. As for John Carlin IV, his lawyer, Darryl Thompson, insisted that while John IV was upset, in the end he would reluctantly show up to take the stand. "I think emotionally, he's kind of drained of this whole situation," Thompson told the *Anchorage Daily News*. "So, is it his desire, does he want to do this? No. But he knows he has an obligation and he doesn't want to see the state go through a bunch of rigmarole and hassles and warrants. . . . He doesn't want to do that. He will come and if asked questions, he will answer."

The judge granted a slight delay, saying the trial would begin later in the next week instead of the following Monday, and by September 11, 2007, more than 120 prospective jurors—twice the usual number called for a trial—were summoned to the courthouse. The screening of jurors would be more extensive than before because of the large amount of publicity, much of it negative for Mechele.

As the prospective panelists poured into Judge Volland's chambers for the first round of questioning, or voir dire, which was done in private, the judge asked all potential jurors to stop watching the news. "We can pick out and deal with, individually, those who are going to answer media issues. Answer the questions on media exposure and indicate they had one, because I want to do those individually. I don't want them talking in front of the whole panel," said Volland. The initial questions focused on everything from whether prospective jurors ever sent emails they later regretted to whether they had ever dated more than one person at a time.

To blunt a large portion of the pretrial publicity, the defense requested that the judge not allow anybody in court to call Mechele a "stripper." Her attorneys said that the term, while technically accurate, carried too prejudicial a punch. "They get she made money, they get everything else, what they don't get to do is essentially rely on cultural archetypes about women, that women are either Madonnas or whores, they're either gold diggers or doormats," defense attorney Carmen Clark said at one pretrial hearing. Mechele's lawyers wanted the lawyer to say only that she had "worked in a bar." The prosecution objected. "It is relevant and weaves throughout her relationship with these men who are pertinent in her life at the time, who become accustomed to and know her, as one who they are going to give money to, and lots of cash to. That's the whole relationship," Gullufsen said. In the end, the judge reached a compromise: instead of a "stripper" or "bar worker," Mechele could be called an "exotic dancer."

By the third week of September a fifteen-member panel of jurors and alternates had been chosen: twelve women and three men—a gender imbalance that would prompt great debate over whether it was helpful or harmful to Mechele.

On September 20, 2007, the day of opening arguments, Mechele took her seat at the defense table next to attorneys Kevin Fitzgerald and Wayne Fricke across from the prosecution table, where Gullufsen took his position. For the duration of the case, she would wear conservative business suits, her hair styled, her makeup spare and discreet, putting as much distance between her life in Bigelow Avenue and the Great Alaskan Bush Company stage. Her husband, Colin, sat in the audience section. Kent's mother, Betsy, also attended the trial. His father, Kenneth, stayed home for health reasons but listened to the proceedings over the phone.

From an evidentiary standpoint, the trial would be a rerun of the John Carlin III case, with the only unknown being whether Mechele's sister and John Carlin IV would ultimately show up. The trial did promise a face-to-face between Mechele and the now-bitter men from her past, Scott Hilke and Brett Reddell, as well as a courtroom showdown with her former friend, ex–Bush Company dancer Lora Aspiotis.

In fact, as Pat Gullufsen rose to address the jury for the first time in Mechele's trial, the prosecutor announced that both sides had actually agreed on much of what would be presented to the jury, beginning with what had happened in early May of 1996 in Hope, Alaska. "John Carlin shot and killed Kent Leppink," Gullufsen said. "I don't think there will be any dispute about that."

A new trial brought a flip-flopped defense. John had blamed Mechele, now Mechele would blame John. The prosecution case remained the same.

"If it wasn't for Mechele Linehan, Kent Leppink would still be alive today, because she set the stage, and she at least wrote the ending," said Gullufsen in his opening remarks. "All she needed was somebody to help her fill in the blanks, somebody to do the dirty work, somebody to pull the trigger. And she found an able and a willing partner in John Carlin III."

The defense opening, by Wayne Fricke, also signaled the agreement between the adversaries. "A lot of what you're going to hear in the next few weeks is not going to be disputed as far as it relates to who killed Ken Leppink," he said. "We're not here to dispute who shot, who killed T.T. We agree with Mr. Gullufsen that it's John Carlin Sr. Where we part ways is the suggestion that Mechele Linehan—then Mechele Hughes—is in any way responsible for his death."

And so the prosecution's case against Mechele unfolded much as it had against John. And as in John's trial, the lawyers for Mechele tried to build their case primarily through cross-examination. During the testimony of Brian Brundin, for instance, the defense sought to bolster the contention that John Carlin III alone killed Kent by claiming the elder Carlin was motivated by a homosexual relationship gone sour. Attorney Kevin Fitzgerald read back Brundin's original comments to police that he believed an angry Mechele had "caught [Kent] in some homosexual relationship."

And when ballistics expert Robert Shem testified, the defense tried to erase any lingering doubt that Big John, not petite Mechele, was the shooter.

Describing the bulky Desert Eagle pistol, Fitzgerald asked Shem, "It's not a fun gun to shoot, is it?"

"Not at all," said Shem.

"It would perhaps be comfortable for a big wrestly type, not for somebody who might be smaller or more slight?"

"I would agree with you. I would go even further to say it would be an unpleasant gun for anyone to shoot at a target. It might be a reasonable gun in a hunting situation. It would be a very unpleasant gun to shoot at paper targets."

But Shem then left open the possibility that in the adrenaline-fueled rush of the moment, anyone could handle the Desert Eagle.

"When you get into the excitement of the event, hunting or what have you, you tend to be so focused on what you're doing, the gun becomes an afterthought," he testified. "The typical person in the heat of the moment could fire the gun without noticing the recoil or report."

Fitzgerald quickly added, more as a statement than a question: "The parties are not disputing that Mr. Carlin fired."

It was an early setback for Mechele's lawyers, and not the last. The defense stumbled again with the testimony of Michael Hull of Eagle Hardware, who testified how Mechele hadn't seemed upset when she talked about the violence to a man once so close to her.

"It was pretty much no emotion, no anything, that he was deceased and she wanted her cabinets," said Hull at trial under direct examination.

Fitzgerald tried to score defense points by suggesting during cross-examination that Hull didn't know enough about Mechele's personality and character to make such a conclusion, having met her only once in his life.

Hull agreed, but still found her demeanor odd.

"His death did come up in the conversation, and she just—it was—there was no emotion," he said. "That, to me, being that soon, in figuring they were buying cabinets together, there was some relationship, even if it was just friends, that being that close to the time of death, you would still assume there would be some kind of sorrow or something. It didn't show. There was just no emotion."

Fitzgerald tried another tack, but only got into more trouble.

"One of the things that she had related to you was that the family had indicated to her that Mr. Leppink had essentially bilked the family out of a large amount of money?" asked Fitzgerald.

"Yes, sir."

"Because it didn't appear to be the image in her own mind of who Kent Leppink was?"

Fitzgerald didn't get a helpful answer.

"She had said he was kind of a shy, quiet type of guy—at least portrayed himself as not real intellectual," said Hull. "And I kind of thought it was strange Ms. Hughes was even saying it. And I found it even stranger that the family would be saying something at the time of death. They supposedly were up here to arrange for the funeral and relayed this story to Mrs. Hughes about [how] he had written some program to—evidently, they owned some stores or something in the Lower Forty-eight—and he had written a program when you rang up the sale, all the sales didn't show in the register. And he had bilked the family out of some money. I kind of thought it was strange that something like that would even come up in a family discussion in a time of preparing to bury a son."

After Hull left the stand, the prosecution shifted the focus from Kent's alleged theft to that of Mechele's, calling the

Russian woman John Carlin married after leaving Alaska. She was now going by her maiden name, Julia Chernikova, having filed for divorce. Tall and beautiful, she walked into the courtroom, and all eyes were on her, including Mechele's. Several observers described Mechele's stare as "like daggers."

Julia repeated her testimony about turning over to police the statue with Kent's name engraved on it, but she had new information that had not come out at her ex-husband's trial.

"Ma'am," asked Gullufsen, "you have never met Mechele?"

"No," she said.

"Have you heard her name?"

"Yes," she said.

The first time was 2000, not long after their July marriage, when she saw her husband exchanging emails with Mechele. She saw another email in 2003 when they lived in New Jersey.

"For a period of time, was he traveling to Maryland to see Mr. and Mrs. Linehan or their baby?" asked Gullufsen.

"Yes," Julia said.

"Was it more than once?"

"Yes, he used to call me from this house and send emails."

"What was he doing there?"

"He told me he was babysitting."

"Babysitting who?"

"Their child," said Julia.

John claimed that he was exchanging babysitting for medical treatment by Colin.

"That was his explanation when I asked: Why you doing this?" she said.

On cross-examination, she acknowledged that she had had her doubts that this was really why he was visiting Mechele.

As for the statue, which Chernikova said she had never liked because it clashed with the decor of their house, that they had never talked about where John had gotten it, and that she had seen Kent's name on the bottom only after she was contacted by the New Jersey State Police.

Julia left the stand, but the day got no easier for Mechele. Next up was Scott Hilke.

When he took the stand for his second round of trial testimony in the murder of Kent Leppink, Scott repeated much of what he had said before, telling jurors how he had met Mechele at the Great Alaskan Bush Company, become her boyfriend and later fiancé, then abandoned their wedding plans even as they continued to see each other at John's house or in hotel rooms around the country, including their trip to the Tahoe condo before the murder and the disastrous getaway to Mexico afterward in the spring of 1997.

Then, as Colin Linehan watched from the audience, Scott recounted his hookups with Mechele in 2004 while Colin was in Iraq: their talk in the park, dinner in Tacoma, and overnights in Seattle and Minneapolis. He made no excuses and offered no justification: Mechele had called him, and he had gone—until his wife found out after the Minnesota overnight when Mechele brought daughter Audrey.

Under cross-examination, Scott could offer no information about Kent's murder and no hint from Mechele that she was involved, even the day before it probably happened, when she was in Tahoe.

"You didn't see any indication that Mechele was nervous during that trip?" Fricke asked.

"No, I didn't."

"There was no indication that she was worried about anything?"

"That's correct."

"As far as something—murder—going to occur?"

"Right."

And while Mechele had held a low opinion of Kent, Hilke acknowledged she hadn't been alone. Hilke said that when police told him of Kent's death, it made little impact on him.

"You had no love for him?" asked Fricke.

"That's correct," said Scott.

"And you certainly didn't feel sorry for him or anything like that?"

"No."

Scott Hilke left the witness stand, but Mechele's past continued to reassert itself, this time in the form of former stripper Lora Aspiotis. Now forty-three and a mom living in South Carolina, Lora emphasized that she, like Mechele, had long since distanced herself from the Bush Company stage. Before getting to her substantive testimony, she said her several days in Alaska for the trial was a burden her family.

"You're anxious to get back?" asked Gullufsen. "You have a child with a disability, is that correct?"

"Yes, he's autistic," she explained.

With that established, the prosecution got down to the real reason Lora was in court: to show that Mechele Linehan had not always been the happy homemaker described by her attorney in opening statements. Although barred from using the word "stripper," Lora left no doubt about where Mechele worked while in Alaska—or how adept she had been at making men happy.

"I would say that she was one of the top—one of the girls that earned a great deal of money," Lora told the jury. "I was making in the hundreds, and I think she topped that easily."

Mechele's regular customers included John Carlin, Scott Hilke, Brett Reddell, and Kent Leppink, whom Lora also called T.T.—and who seemed to her to be deluded about his relationship with Mechele.

"T.T. was under the impression that they were going to get married," she said.

"How did she treat him?" asked Gullufsen.

"Not very well," said Lora.

"Could you be specific about that?"

"It seemed to me, by my observation, that T.T. was just— well, he's a puppet on a string for her. He did everything that she asked him to."

She recounted the dinner gathering in early 1996 that Kent wasn't invited to, but when he showed up Mechele made him pay the bill. Another time, Lora said, Kent drove Brett Reddell's red truck to California to buy "a large amount of tile" for Mechele's house in Wasilla. She believed Kent paid for the tile. In all, Kent told her that he spent $40,000 to $50,000 on improvements on the Wasilla house.

While they were friendly, Lora said that she and Mechele spent evenings at Mechele's house watching videos while Lora's husband worked at a restaurant.

"Was there one movie in particular you recall watching with her?" asked Gullufsen.

"Yes, I do," Lora answered.

"Why is it that you recall a particular movie that you watched with her?" the prosecutor asked.

"Because [of] what she said when we were watching the movie," said Lora.

Repeating what Scott Hilke had testified to the day before, Lora said the film was *The Last Seduction* and gave her recollection of the plot: that a woman talked her doctor husband into selling pharmaceutical cocaine for $700,000, only to double-cross him by stealing the money while he showered and running off to hook up with a young man in a bar. "She could tell right away he was very naïve," Lora said. "Eventually she talked him into trying to murder her husband for the insurance."

Gullufsen asked: "How did it end?"

"He ended up in prison and she went free with all the money."

"What did she say about it?" asked Gullufsen. "What was her reaction to that movie?"

"She told me that was her heroine," said Lora, "and that she wanted to be just like her."

The parallels between the movie and the court case were obvious, making the cross-examination of Lora Aspiotis one of the most important defense tasks of the trial and raising the question of how aggressive Mechele's attorney's would be. Mechele's animosity toward her former stripper friend could be felt throughout the courtroom as she focused a glare on Lora.

By nature, Mechele's counsel, Wayne Fricke and Kevin Fitzgerald, were gentleman lawyers, never raising their voices, never taking the cheap shot, deferential to the judge, respectful to Gullufsen, even during private sidebar conversations when they didn't have to impress the jury.

When Fitzgerald began his cross-examination of the person who the most damaging witness so far, and possibly of the trial—with Melissa Hughes and John Carlin IV still question marks—the defense lawyer began by maintaining his calm, professional demeanor.

Fitzgerald established that Lora had danced for six years in Alaska and Las Vegas, going by the names Zoey, Allison, and Mystique, and made the not-so-subtle inference that she was comfortable with untruths. He also suggested that Lora felt something other than admiration for Mechele's skills at the Bush Company.

"You were a little bit jealous of that, were you not?" asked Fitzgerald.

"No," insisted Lora.

"Didn't you think it was somewhat unfair to the customer if Miss Hughes was just socializing with them instead of dancing?"

"No," she said again.

In fact, suggested Fitzgerald, Mechele's interaction with her regular John Carlin III was little more than being sociable—friendliness rather than a serious attachment.

"Wasn't it a running joke between them that they were going to get married?" he asked.

"I don't think it was a joke," said Lora.

"Wasn't there a bet between them, that if Miss Hughes lost the bet that she would have to marry Mr. Carlin?"

"I don't know."

As for another regular, Scott Hilke: "You didn't like him, did you? You thought [he was], to quote you, an 'A-hole'?" he asked. (It was a testament to Fitzgerald's restraint that he couldn't even bring himself to use profanity in open court.)

"Right," said Lora.

She acknowledged that she hated Scott so much that she once felt he could have had something to do with Kent's murder.

"I said he's capable of it," she corrected. "I think Mechele *and* Scott had something to do with it."

At this point it was now 1:30 p.m. The judge interrupted her testimony and raised the issue of Lora's schedule, telling the jury, "Ladies and gentlemen, I would like to be able to let Ms. Aspiotis go home today rather than keep her here until Monday, but it will take another twenty minutes. Will you all stay?" Jurors nodded that they would, and the cross-examination resumed.

The defense now focused on the *Last Seduction* testimony, suggesting that Lora had made it up. Through the pretrial process of discovery, in which the prosecution must hand over evidence, the defense had been provided a copy of Lora's diary from the time she was friends with Mechele.

Fitzgerald had Lora confirm that the diary listed a number of movies she had watched in January and February 1996: *Showgirls*, *First Knight*, *Grumpy Old Men*, *Leaving Las Vegas*, half of *Mr. Holland's Opus*, and *Nine Months*.

"There is no reference to any view of *The Last Seduction*, is there?" asked the lawyer.

"No," Lora said.

"When is it you claimed to have watched the movie that isn't reflected?"

"I don't know when it happened."

Fitzgerald suggested that even if she and Mechele had watched the movie, Mechele's intentions had not been devious.

"Isn't it true, ma'am, that she told you that with regard to the movie, *[The] Last Seduction*, that she liked the actress, Linda Fiorentino?"

"No," countered Lora.

"Now, I like movies. I like Al Pacino in *Scarface*, but that doesn't make me a drug kingpin, trying to kill rivals?" asked Fitzgerald.

Gullufsen stood. "Your Honor, I object to the question. It calls for speculation."

"I'll allow the question," the judge said.

Fitzgerald continued. "Just because I've watched that and

enjoy Al Pacino doesn't make me a drug kingpin killing rivals, right?" he asked.

"Not necessarily," said Lora.

"Do you like Julia Roberts? Ever see her in *Pretty Woman*?"

It was the nastiest the defense would ever get. Roberts plays a prostitute in the film.

"Uh, no, I haven't," said Lora.

"The fact of the matter is, ma'am, you have no personal knowledge that Miss Hughes solicited any murder, do you?" asked Fitzgerald.

"For sure? No," she said.

"You have no personal knowledge that she planned any homicide, do you?"

"No."

"You have no personal knowledge that she solicited any murder, do you, ma'am?"

"No personal knowledge."

You have no personal knowledge that she assisted in any way in any homicide, do you?"

"No."

Lora wrapped up her testimony and left the courtroom, but that didn't end her involvement in the case. The questioning about *The Last Seduction* was about to trigger a major legal fight, one the judge knew was coming. In dismissing the jury, he told the panel, "You've heard reference and testimony . . . to a movie by a specific title. Don't go check it out."

After the jurors filed out of the courtroom, the battle began. Gullufsen implored the judge to let the jurors watch *The Last Seduction* in its entirety in the courtroom as part of the prosecution's case against Mechele. The movie, he said, had not only inspired Mechele to kill but presented a road map for how to do it, a model to follow. "There is someone she admires, wants to be like, and the wheels start turning. She can apply that plan to her circumstances," Gullufsen said to the judge. "It's a real-life way of getting the idea for this crime."

Fitzgerald, showing a rare flash of anger, snapped, "I have to admit, Judge, I have been a little too preoccupied to sit down with a bowl of popcorn and view that movie," and objected to the jury seeing it. "I believe it is unfairly prejudicial. I think it is not only potentially but probably going to lead to a confusion of the issues and mislead the jury with regard to what the evidence is in this case," Fitzgerald said.

Judge Volland said he had not seen the film, either. "Strikes me in order to reach that issue, I think I need to watch this movie or at least a significant part of it to know whether having the tape actually here as an exhibit for the jury is going to be unduly distracting or misleading," he said.

And so the judge retired for a weekend of watching an R-rated thriller.

CHAPTER TWENTY-SIX

Sitting in the audience section of the courtroom, holding his tongue, Colin Linehan seethed. He had already listened to his wife's old boyfriend, Scott Hilke, speak of intimacies with Mechele, then bash her as a manipulative slut. This was not the Mechele whom Colin had fallen in love with and knew, he felt, better than anybody in Judge Volland's courtroom.

But no witness infuriated Colin more than Lora Aspiotis and her testimony about *The Last Seduction*. Colin, too, had spent many hours on the sofa watching movies with Mechele. He knew in his heart that she admired Linda Fiorentino as an actress and not as a femme fatale. That the movie provided a script for murder struck Colin as absurd. This anger and disgust toward Lora festered. He questioned the legitimacy of a legal system that would allow her to give that testimony.

However, Lora Aspiotis's role in trial had an even bigger impact than angering Colin Linehan. A mistrial was at stake.

The judge had arguably erred when he allowed Lora to testify about the film before ruling on its admissibility. During a hearing outside the jury's presence, he acknowledged as much, saying he now had second thoughts. He then watched the movie, giving it a nice review but worrying about the effect it would have on the jury.

He asked Gullufsen: "Isn't the risk—this two-hour movie,

Hollywood style, good actors and actresses—is a very emotional movie in a lot of respects—isn't that adding a gloss to Ms. Asiotis's observations and comments and Scott Hilke's that aren't there when you look at their comments?"

Gullufsen repeated how important it was to introduce the movie into evidence, and said that if anybody was to blame for bringing in the movie, it was Mechele. "She has looked at this character and she has said: I want to be like that person who is pretty bad, and I want to do something like that person has done, which is pretty bad," said the prosecutor. "And then she has carried it out in this case. . . . She is the one who looked at it, she's the one who adopted it, the deal. She said: that's what I want to be like and that's what I want to do."

Once again, Kevin Fitzgerald strongly argued against its introduction. "I hear Mr. Gullufsen's legal analysis and it seems to be devoid of any legal analysis," he said.

Fitzgerald said there simply wasn't enough of a link between simply watching the movie—and liking it and the character—and the murder of Kent. "It still doesn't bridge the enormous gap," he said. "The state wants this movie because it fills an enormous gap in its case with regard to plan and motive."

In addition to this, he said, there was no reliable evidence that Mechele had ever even seen the movie. "I'm going to provide the court with an additional piece of evidence which I believe demonstrates unequivocally that Ms. Aspiotis perjured herself," said Fitzgerald, citing an entry from her diary dated September 1995 that she had watched *The Last Seduction* with her husband, not Mechele.

In making his decision on whether to screen the movie for jurors, Judge Volland relied on previous cases, primarily involving the movie *Natural Born Killers*, the 1994 Oliver Stone–directed movie about two serial killers played by Woody Harrelson and Juliette Lewis. The movie garnered controversy when it was alleged to have inspired copycat killings. In one murder case, the jury was allowed to see the movie because the defendant himself had watched it nineteen or twenty times, referred to himself by the name of the character in the movie, and shaved his head like that character. In another case in which a jury saw *Natural Born Killers* the number of stab wounds in the film were virtually identical to the crime charged, and newspaper articles about the movie were found with the defendant.

As for Mechele's trial, the judge said he had no issue with the quality of filmmaking behind *The Last Seduction.* "It's a well-done movie, and it has all the Hollywood gloss that you would expect," he said. "The characters are handsome, the pace is intense. It has all the attributes of a movie that's well done. I'm not going to say it's easily viewed. It is not an easily viewed movie. It left me with a feeling of discomfort, so I won't say it's easily viewed, but it's certainly a very well-done movie."

But, he said, "there are too many differences" between the movie and the murder of Kent Leppink. The judge noted that Mechele would have seen the movie about fifteen months before the murder, a fact he hadn't realized when he originally allowed Lora's testimony. "I made the ruling on the assumption that there would be closer proximity to the acts in the case and the viewing," he said.

Also, he said, "Bridget in the movie certainly commits more crimes and more directly than Miss Linehan is accused of," the lead character being so evil that it might wrongly sway jurors. "There's just Hollywood gloss to it," he said. "We're used to seeing evidence here in its real natural state, with all of the normal human attributes to it, not in a way where it has a lot of Hollywood gloss. . . . I think that can cause jurors to reach a verdict based on that tendency, based on their reaction to the Hollywood in the movie rather than what the movie is offered really to prove. I don't think a limiting instruction can do that, not with a movie with this intensity and length. . . .

"For those of us in this room who at least work the dark side," he added, "we may not be surprised about that intent or particularly upset or affected by it at all. But, you know, I sat here thinking about how Juror No. 12"—a recent high school graduate—"might feeling watching the content in that movie with Juror No. 7, who is probably old enough to be her grandmother."

The judge found that Hollywood murder might strike jurors as more heinous than a real murder and that "showing the movie will be more prejudicial to Ms. Linehan than it is probative of the evidentiary value."

The Last Seduction would not be screened for jurors—but the fight over the movie wasn't over.

CHAPTER TWENTY-SEVEN

John Carlin IV still didn't want to testify. Not only did he wrestle with guilt over his father's conviction, he continued to worry that he, too, could be implicated in the murder of Kent Leppink. His father's lawyer had alleged as much at the first trial. But after consulting with his attorney and speaking to both Gullufsen and Mechele's lawyers, John IV reluctantly announced that he'd testify, this time against a woman he once loved like a sister.

Taking the stand on Monday, October 1, John IV covered familiar ground: his family's move to Alaska, his mother's death, his relationship with Mechele, his father buying the gun, and—of great value to the prosecution—his father and Mechele in the bathroom after washing the gun with what smelled like bleach.

But it didn't end there: John IV had a surprise. He had not told authorities everything—not in his initial police interviews, not before the grand jury, and not at his father's trial. Now, for the first time, he said he had seen the gun not only when it was being washed in the bathroom but another time after the murder.

"And what were the circumstances?" asked Gullufsen.

"One morning I was coming out to walk my dog and I went to the front hall where we kept leashes for the dogs," John IV said, "and at that point we had retractable leashes with the big handles on them, and I went to pull one down, and the leash snug—got snagged on what I would describe to be a plastic grocery bag, and [I] pulled it down, in which there was a handgun."

"A pistol?"

"A pistol, yeah, fell to the floor in the bag. What happened from there I do not have a clear memory."

The defense jumped on him. Suggesting that his story only seemed to get better with each telling, attorney Wayne Fricke elicited under cross-examination that this was in fact the first time John IV had ever testified under oath about seeing the gun a second time.

When he suddenly remembered it, John IV said, he worried that if he told authorities it would be used as evidence against him, of covering up a murder. This explained his reluctance to testify again.

He had talked to his lawyer about whether he should take the Fifth before deciding to go ahead with his testimony. John IV also said he had felt that if he mentioned this additional information he would again hurt somebody he loved. Mechele had helped keep him straight in Alaska and supported him when he needed counseling. And now he was placing a gun in the house in which she had lived—a gun she had denied to police that she had seen after the murder, just as John's father had.

"I had forgotten about it for years," John IV said, but when he came across a court document, it "spurred my memory."

After John IV left the stand, his heart filled with more regret, prosecutors brought back Brett Reddell to talk about how Mechele had used him and his truck, but his testimony didn't go as smoothly as it had at John Carlin III's trial. Under direct examination by Gullufsen, Brett's memory of what he'd told investigators in 1996 failed repeatedly, and the prosecutor had to get permission from the judge to ask leading questions to get the information into the record.

Then, on cross-examination, Brett began a slow meltdown. Although he had told police in 1996 that he had been Mechele's boyfriend and had loaned her large amounts of money, defense lawyer Kevin Fitzgerald played a scratchy August 2006 recorded interview with cold case investigator Jim Stogsdill in which Brett said that Mechele had never actually asked him for money and that he had only spent a couple of hundred dollars on her.

"Isn't it true, sir, that Miss Hughes was only an acquaintance to you?" asked Fitzgerald.

"Not from the way I understood it with her," he said. "It's hard because I was—it was a long-distance relationship was what it was. And that's the way I looked, you know. It was going to be a tough relationship with her being down here and me living up here."

On redirect, Gullufsen tried to rehabilitate Brett.

"Do you think your memory was better about these events in September and October 1996 than in August 2006?"

"Yes, it was," said Brett.

But the oil worker from Barrow was rattled. There would be no post-testimony statements to the press as he had given during John Carlin's trial. Brett ran out of the courtroom past reporters. The next day's headline in the *Anchorage Daily News* read, "Linehan Trial Witness Caught in Contradicting Statements."

It was a rare high point for the defense. For on Monday, October 8, the trial took an emotional turn with the appearance of Kent's mother. Betsy Leppink testified about meeting Mechele over dinner in Alaska in the summer of 1995, telling jurors about her son's excitement over his engagement before he sank into despair over his inability to find Mechele. Betsy recalled her shock when Kent said Mechele's grandfather had bought them a $1 million life insurance policy, and her fear when he drove to Hope looking for Mechele, frustrated at not knowing where she was. "He said John Carlin knows where she goes and he won't tell me."

Her voice wavering throughout her testimony, she broke

down when she spoke of how her worst fears were soon realized.

"Do you recall what day of the week you were informed Kent had been found dead?" asked Gullufsen.

"I believe it was Saturday morning, very early," Betsy said.

"And how were you informed?"

"It was about five o'clock in the morning," she said through tears, "and my son Ransom and his wife were banging at my door screaming. And the sheriff had come to their house and told them Kent's body had been found."

The judge called a break so Kent's mother could compose herself and so attorneys could discuss one last time a piece of evidence that Mechele's attorneys strongly objected to presenting to the jury: Kent's letters to his parents. The defense contended that the letters violated Mechele's constitutional right to confront her accuser: since Kent was dead, there was no way to cross-examine him about his allegations against her to test the truthfulness of his claims. But as he had in the first trial, Judge Volland overruled the defense and allowed the letters to be read—but with a limitation, which he read to the jury after the break.

"Let me read to you this cautionary instruction," the judge told the panel. "You are about to hear and likely see the letter Kent sent to his parents on April 30, 1996. The statements and the opinions contained in the letter are not being offered for the truth of the statements or opinions or conclusions expressed therein, and you cannot consider them for that purpose. Instead, the statements are being offered and can be considered by you only for the limited and sole purpose of understanding Mr. Leppink's state of mind at the time that he wrote the letter."

Even with the instruction, the evidence was a blow to Mechele's defense. Gullufsen read the letters while Betsy remained on the witness stand, the power of the evidence intensified by her pained expression and moist eyes.

The gentle cross-examination by Wayne Fricke brought a change of demeanor in Betsy. No longer tearful, she spoke in a firm voice, complaining about answering the same question more than once and taking issue with the way Fricke worded his questions, especially when he broached the subject of Kent's letter.

"So you got this letter, which you indicated, and it expressed your son's thoughts, correct?" asked the lawyer.

"Which letter?"

"The sealed letter."

"Yes."

"He had never expressed any fear about Mechele prior to this time, is that right?"

"*He* had not," Betsy answered.

"And he certainly didn't seek to move out of that house, apparently, from what you understand, is that correct?"

"He wanted to make that relationship work," she said sternly.

"He didn't seek to move out of that house?"

"I don't have a clue."

Gullufsen returned for one more round of follow-up questions.

"With respect to contact with Miss Hughes after your son's death, did she ever send you a card or condolences or anything like that?"

Fricke stood and said, "I would object as to relevance."

"Overruled," said the judge.

Betsy Leppink said bitterly, "We had no contact from her ever."

Following Kent's mother to the stand was his older brother Craig, who recounted Kent's infatuation with Mechele going back to the Christmas of 1995, when he drove to Michigan in her Volvo, talking about her nonstop "like a lovesick puppy."

"It was the last Christmas our family ever had with him," said Craig.

Detective Linda Branchflower of the Division of Alaska State Troopers' computer and financial crimes unit took the stand to show how smitten Kent was by reading into the record dozens of emails between him, Mechele, and John

Carlin, documenting Kent's roller-coaster emotions leading up to the days before his murder—and Mechele's private communications with John and Scott Hilke. The defense had little to offer to counter the emails during cross-examination, taking Branchflower instead through the efforts to locate and interview John Carlin IV.

"Was he in fact a suspect?" asked Wayne Fricke.

"He was not a suspect in the murder," said Branchflower, "but we were concerned. The information from the 1996 investigation indicated it was possible he might have had something to do with the evidence after the fact."

Her cold case partner Jim Stogsdill took the stand next to read for the jury transcripts of Mechele's police interviews, quoting Mechele as telling troopers that in her last phone call with Kent he had sounded "stupid" and how Kent had died in woods just like the animals he had stuffed and "Yeah, he deserved it."

The defense sought to show that Stogsdill had been no more open-minded in his investigation than Steven DeHart or Ron Belden before him, suggesting he had focused from beginning to end on Mechele without looking at other alternatives. In cross-examination, Kevin Fitzgerald suggested that Stogsdill had revealed his anti-Mechele bias when he went to New Jersey to talk to John Carlin III.

"With regard to the schooling you've received, how many schools have you attended on interviewing?" asked Fitzgerald.

"Several, I couldn't tell you. It was a long time ago," he said.

"Could you tell us what school would ever condone investigators conducting an interview with a witness and calling another person a 'lying bitch'?"

Long pause.

"Well, I don't know, I mean—" started Stogsdill.

"You would agree that that would be inappropriate?" asked Fitzgerald.

"In some cases, yeah."

"Can you think of a situation when you would be interviewing witness X and be calling Y a 'lying bitch'?"

"You know what, I think I used those very words in an interview with Mr. Carlin, I believe," he said.

CHAPTER TWENTY-EIGHT

Jim Stogsdill was the last prosecution witness, and on October 11, 2007, the state rested its case against Mechele.

The presentation had been a virtual replay of the case against John Carlin III, and as with the first trial, the defense believed it had made its points during cross-examination. Mechele's defense, although brief, began on a surprising note, addressing a provocative question lingering for months. At John's trial, the defense had bolstered its Mechele-shot-Kent-herself theory by saying that she knew about Kent's letter to his parents long before police disclosed it to the public. John's attorney suggested that Kent had revealed the presence of the letter—his "insurance policy"—to her to stop her from pulling the trigger. The only people who knew about it were Kent's family, and his mother said that Mechele had never talked to them after the murder.

It turned out, however, that Mechele did have a pipeline to both the Leppink family and the police investigation.

The defense called Lane Leppink.

The youngest of the four Leppink boys took the oath and settled in to testify for the woman accused of killing his brother, although Lane didn't have to face his family in court. Explaining that he was estranged from his family at the time of Kent's murder, Lane said he had struggled to find out what had happened to his brother. Police in Alaska were communicating mainly with Lane's parents.

"It was pretty bleak to get any information," he said.

Lane had a contact phone number for Kent, and when he dialed it on the Saturday that the family was informed of Kent's death, Mechele picked up the phone.

"She ultimately was the one I wanted to pass condolences on to," he said. "She was to be my future sister-in-law. And I told her that it was a very awkward phone conversation, probably the most awkward I had ever made."

Mechele seemed "pretty mortified" at Kent's death, but like Lane had been left in the dark by investigators and Kent's family. Lane thought he knew why.

"I indicated to her she should be careful because [my] parents would blame her," he said.

The next day, Lane learned about the letter from Kent to his parents—then told Mechele about it.

In time, the family found out he was talking to Mechele and cut him off completely, depriving him of what little information they had been giving him. Lane and Mechele spoke occasionally about the case: Mechele gave him the names and phone numbers of Kent's friends and life insurance agent, and Lane told Mechele about Kent embezzling money from the family store.

Three more witnesses remained for the defense. The first was a private investigator who had made the drive from Anchorage to Hope and clocked it at one hour and forty minutes—testimony to support a fact that both sides agreed upon: that Mechele didn't have enough time to get to Hope and kill Kent.

Next to testify was Colin Linehan. Aside from remarks to the media in the days after Mechele's arrest, Colin had said little publicly and avoided reporters, whom he came to loathe as much as Lora Aspiotis.

In his first chance to finally give his side, Colin brought jurors through his relationship with Mechele: their meeting in the park, their marriage and baby and move to Olympia— contrasting the unsavory portrait of Mechele painted by Brett Reddell, Scott Hilke, and others.

Linehan also confirmed that he had treated John Carlin

III in Maryland but insisted it was merely a doctor-patient relationship. Kevin Fitzgerald asked him about the testimony from John's ex-wife, Julia, who claimed that John also babysat Colin's daughter, Audrey.

"Did that ever happen?"

"No, sir," said Colin, the Army doctor answering in military style as Air Force man David Stilchen had earlier.

"And did you ever exchange medications for babysitting?"

"No, sir."

"Would that have been inappropriate to have occurred?"

"That would have been more than inappropriate."

"At some point did your wife, Mechele, become aware that you were seeing Carlin?"

"Yes, sir."

"Was she in favor of you seeing [him] or discouraged it?"

"She didn't like it," said Colin. "She discouraged it."

But he did acknowledge that John's son had lived at their Olympia house while Colin was stationed in Iraq, although he wasn't asked about John IV's claim that Mechele had affairs with two men during that time. Instead, he heaped praise on Mechele, talking about how she used her business skills to help him open a Botox and laser clinic for hair removal and other cosmetic procedures a year earlier—at almost exactly the time they found out she was charged with murder "by a state trooper knocking at my door."

"The final matter I want to address with you, Mr. Linehan, is a difficult one," said Fitzgerald, "but do you feel compassion or sympathy towards the Leppink family?" asked Mechele's attorney Kevin Fitzgerald.

"Objection," said Gullufsen.

"Judge, I think this is appropriate," said the defense lawyer.

"I'll allow it," the judge said.

Colin turned to look at Kent's mother and brothers in the courtroom.

"I'm thirty-six years old, and Kent was thirty-six years old," he said. "He was a brother, friend, I mean, of course I do. There's nothing more precious than a human life. . . . We forget that. It kills me that in their hearts that they think Mechele had anything to do with that, because I know from the bottom of my heart and soul that she did not."

"I've got no further questions," said Fitzgerald.

"Move to strike," said Gullufsen.

"Granted," said the judge. "Ladies and gentlemen, please disregard that last comment."

For cross-examination, Gullufsen was polite—and opportunistic. Going back to Colin's testimony about his early years with Mechele, Gullufsen directed his attention to Maryland in late 1999 or early 2000 when Colin treated John Carlin III.

"How is it that you came to see him as a patient?" asked the prosecutor.

"He came to see me, sir," said Colin.

"Could anybody then come and see you?"

"If they had insurance and they knew where I worked and they wanted to make an appointment."

"So he apparently tracked you down?"

"Apparently."

Colin also revealed that Mechele had not told him everything about Alaska.

"You knew that your wife had known Mr. Carlin Sr. in Anchorage, Alaska?"

"Not until I saw him as a patient."

"Did you learn that from him?"

"No, he told me he was a friend of Mechele's."

On October 15, Mechele's lawyers called two of the original investigators. Steve DeHart got a friendlier welcome than during the previous trial, when the defense suggested he had railroaded John. The retired detective recounted his work on the murder investigation and stated his belief that it was John who pulled the trigger.

The defense next recalled a prosecution witness, investigator Dallas Massie, who had broken the news of Kent's death to Mechele. It was through Massie that the defense introduced the most dramatic evidence at its disposal, an eleven-year-old tape recording of Massie's interview with Mechele. On that day, May 5, 1996, at Mechele's house in Wasilla, Massie was heard telling Mechele that Kent had been killed.

Mechele's wails echoed through the courtroom.

CHAPTER TWENTY-NINE

The tape recording was the closest jurors would get to hearing Mechele speak for herself. Like John Carlin III before her, Mechele decided not to testify in her own defense. In a hearing outside the jury's presence, Judge Volland ran her through a series of routine questions to confirm that she was waiving that right.

"Thinking clearly today?" he asked.

"I believe so, yes," Mechele said in her soft voice.

"Did you make this decision today?"

"I've had the last year to think about it," she said, putting her hair behind her left ear.

"Do you feel you've given it enough thought?"

"Yes, sir."

All that remained now were summations and a verdict.

On Wednesday, October 17, the fifty-seat gallery was packed with members of Kent's and Mechele's families, along with reporters, attorneys taking a break from other cases, and spectators. So many people turned out for the closing arguments that the judge opened the back doors of the courtroom so another dozen people could listen from the hall.

After two trials with much of the same evidence, Gullufsen knew the case intimately. Few facts were in dispute. Both sides agreed that John Carlin had pulled the trigger. Where they differed was the role played by Mechele, and Gullufsen

outlined a scenario in which Mechele didn't need a gun to
commit murder: she had other weapons in her arsenal. Under
Alaska law, a person who aids and abets in a crime is just as
guilty as the actual perpetrator.

"This person manipulated the circumstances with her
guile, with deception, and she created a situation where Kent
Leppink's life was worth nothing to her," said the prosecutor. "His death was worth a lot to her. And in these circumstances she had Mr. Carlin to accomplish the result that she
wanted, which was Kent's death."

Like all those men she used to dance for at the Great
Alaskan Bush Company, according to the prosecutor, John
Carlin III was a dupe: dumb enough, insecure enough, in love
with her enough, to do anything for her, up to and including
murder. And the target was no exception. Kent Leppink, the
prosecutor said, "was obsessed with her. And to some extent it's his own inability to see what was happening to him.
But to a great extent it was her ability to deceive him about
the relationship. All he can see right now is that she has
agreed to marry him, dates have been talked about." In his
final days, Kent was consumed with fears that Mechele is
"off at a cabin with somebody"—all because of the note that
Mechele and John had left for Kent to find. The "Go to
Hope" note sent Kent to his death.

"He had blinders on about as thick as you could possibly
get," Gullufsen told the jury. "He wasn't perfect. And if this
didn't result in his murder, and now our business, maybe we
just would have said, 'Hey, bud, you know what, you ought
to keep your eyes wider open, tough luck. Next time around,
be a little smarter.' But he was murdered as a result of this,
and it is our business now."

Mechele had Kent's number from early on, the prosecutor said. She first used him for pocket cash at the Bush Company, then increasingly. "He's getting stolen blind the last
two weeks of his life," said Gullufsen, pointing to the suspiciously signed check on the business account, the cabinet
purchase, the stolen rugs, the bronze statue, the laptop computer. "By the time he dies, his M&K account is down to

$655. They're going to kill him, but they have to take everything he has before they do. That's the kind of people we're dealing with."

It was always about money, the prosecutor said. "Look at the astounding 'Ha, Ha, Ha' email at the end of March," Gullufsen told the jury. "You can see that she is ridiculing the idea of marrying Kent. She is disdainful of the whole idea." But to get that money, she had to string Kent along, and at each stage Mechele kept watch over the insurance, even hand delivering the check for the premium before she left for her mother's house in April 1996. "Throughout this case, ladies and gentlemen, you're going to be hard put to find anything she pays for," said Gullufsen. "But she pays for this life insurance. . . . She wants to get that insurance paid for and up and running." Then, just days before Kent's murder, Mechele called the New York Life agent's office on April 30 to make sure the insurance was still in effect, because "there's going to be a dead body if the insurance is still in play," Gullufsen said.

She was, Gullufsen pointed out, a cruel multi-tasker. "At the same time . . . that she is telling Kent how much she loves and wants to marry him, she is writing emails to John Carlin that she cannot live without him," said Gullufsen. "What we have going on here basically [is] these fellows are being set up for her ultimate goal to get to collect on the insurance policy, to use one of them to kill the other."

Even if the plan goes awry, Mechele still can get money because Carlin has left her half his money in his will. "It's almost as if she can't lose," he said. After baiting Kent with the "Go to Hope" note, the prosecutor said, Mechele was smart enough to blow town. "She's down in Lake Tahoe with her real boyfriend, Scott Hilke, having a nice rendezvous by a beautiful lake," Gullufsen told jurors. "This is a getaway to Lake Tahoe, a place to be with Scott Hilke, and she's intensely in contact with Carlin here in Anchorage—the guy who kills Kent Leppink just before she gets back." But the flurry of phone calls and emails showed the plan being set in motion, with a few kinks, then things got better, with likely word that Kent had already been to Hope once, looking for her and the cabin. "She now knows the Hope note is kicking in. She now knows that Kent believes he has to come to Hope and get her," he said.

The clincher, the prosecutor argued, was the Seychelles email: "Clear as a bell. She's thinking about the crime they're about to commit." By the time Mechele got the last email from John, "Most likely, right now, Kent is laying on the trail with three bullet wounds."

After the murder, Mechele showed consciousness of guilt by not telling troopers about John washing the gun in the sink, by trying to wipe the memory off the laptop, and by abruptly leaving Alaska with the potentially weakest link: John Carlin IV. "They want to get him out of the state because he has some things to say," said Gullufsen. When troopers interviewed her, she tried to play them the way she played other men. "This woman is not without brains. This is an intelligent woman who knows exactly when she should admit and when she should not admit." She only "slipped up" once when she told a detective that Kent deserved to die. "'He kills animals so he should die a torturous death.' What sense does that make?" asked Gullufsen. "She's wearing the furs of these animals around."

The prosecutor closed by reminding jurors of *The Last Seduction*. "She wanted to be like that person, remember?" he said. "John Carlin pulled the trigger and he's going to pay for it. And we all agree that he's guilty. . . . He had a partner. He had someone who really set this up neatly. He had someone who promoted it, facilitated it and aided and abetted him in doing it. And that's Mechele Hughes—Mechele Linehan. If she's going to write the script, if she's the one who's going to write the ending to this, it's going to be just like the movie, isn't it? Problem is: You're going to write the ending. She isn't. And it's not going to be a false and contrived ending, one that she would have. It's going to be a true and it's going to be a just ending because the proof is beyond a reasonable doubt that she aided, abetted and solicited the murder of Kent Leppink, and it's time to hold her accountable for that."

* * *

Kevin Fitzgerald gave the defense summation, his single opportunity to address the jury. The onetime prosecutor acknowledged that "at first blush" the state's case against his client had a "certain attractiveness." He likened it to what looked from afar like a pretty package but upon closer inspection "you find that the paper is old, and it's fastened together with bobby pins, thrice-used tape and ten-year-old tape" and contains "old newspaper clippings" and "some movie popcorn."

"Conjecture, speculation, innuendo and even gossip—that's the package that the state has presented to you in an effort to try to convince you that Mrs. Linehan is guilty of murder in the first degree by being an accomplice," he told jurors. "That's the package, and the package has no value. It certainly doesn't have value to prove that Mrs. Linehan was an accomplice, either by soliciting or being an aider and abetter."

Fitzgerald sought first to explain key aspects of the prosecution's case, addressing the question of the many emails and phone calls from Mechele to John Carlin III from Lake Tahoe. "That's an easy answer," he said. "The reason why there was communications with regard to what Mrs. Linehan was doing in that period of time is the same reason why the Hope note was created. . . . She didn't want Mr. Leppink all of a sudden showing up in Incline Village." As for why Mechele had been so seemingly eager to secure Kent's $1 million life insurance policy in April 1996, he said, "It shows the business purpose. It shows the very thing the state doesn't want to acknowledge. . . . It's a fishing business. There isn't fishing in September, October, November, December and January. There's no need for life insurance [then]. He needs it when he goes out and faces the risk." The $1 million payout, he said, "was not that unusual" for a policy involving a business. The reason she called New York Life on April 30, he said, wasn't because she was planning to kill Kent but because they were "short of cash." That was the same reason, Fitzgerald argued, that Mechele had called on April 26, asking for the money back. Mechele, he said, was "not ferreting out whether [she was] the beneficiary. That is just a figment of the state's imagination."

As for why Mechele left Alaska with John Carlin IV after the murder, the defense attorney said her behavior reflected her concern for the troubled teen, not a consciousness of guilt. "Here's a boy who has serious problems," he said. "He wants to stay in Alaska and Alaska has not been good to him. Mrs. Linehan was seriously concerned about [John Carlin] Jr. What was she going to do? She was going to put him in a Catholic school in Louisiana."

And the emails? "What the email evidence really shows," he said, "is it shows a very odd and bizarre relationship. I mean, this isn't the Brady Bunch. There are very odd relationships, and they are very difficult to understand. They were complex and ebbed and flowed. And you know, the fact of the matter is: There is a lack of candor among all the players."

The liars included John, Kent, "and Mrs. Linehan," the defense attorney conceded.

"Not honest," Fitzgerald said matter-of-factly. "Let's own [up to] it. Not honest at all. Not honest in relationships at all. But that doesn't make her a killer."

It was the heart of the defense's case. Whatever character flaws Mechele may have possessed more than a decade earlier as a stripper in her early twenties didn't provide proof beyond a reasonable doubt that she had aided and abetted in murder.

"What's really significant about the emails is that there's no information," Fitzgerald said. "You look through those with a fine-toothed comb, bring out the microscope. What you want see is: You won't see any request, any counseling, any inciting. You won't see any solicitation or aiding and abetting. You won't see it in the emails."

Mechele never told John Carlin to kill Kent, Fitzgerald said. The emails instead showed three flawed people in dysfunctional relationships, writing and saying things they would later regret, as when Mechele told her sister that Kent had "deserved to die."

"It is a lousy thing to say, really lousy," Fitzgerald acknowledged, "but doesn't make her a killer. . . . If anybody who was really involved in a homicide, would they really say, 'He deserved to die'?"

And as badly as the Mechele Hughes of the 1990s had acted, her behavior reflected something much less sinister than murderous intent. "It shows immaturity in relationships," Fitzgerald said. "It shows confusion in relationships. It shows lack of honesty in relationships. It demonstrates she said some lousy things. But you know what, she is not charged with any of those things."

Mechele, he insisted, was no worse than many people at that age. "To some extent, as we make our way through life, yeah, we make mistakes," said. "There are things that I said and didn't [say] back at twenty-three that I'm sure, if you put them under the glare, I wouldn't be happy about either. And I'm sure every one of you can say the same thing. And you know what? It is legally irrelevant."

Fitzgerald then went back on the attack. Take away the character evidence, he argued, and the prosecution had nothing. That contention about Mechele modeling herself after the femme fatale in *The Last Seduction* reeked of prosecutorial "desperation," he said. Lora Aspiotis, the defense attorney maintained, was a liar who had been jealous of Mechele's skills at the Bush Company.

And Kent's letter to his parents implicating Mechele from the grave was "non-evidence," said the defense attorney. He noted that Kent had also named Scott Hilke, but the salesman wasn't on trial. All the letter showed was Kent's state of mind in the spring of 1996. "Who knows what his state of mind was?" said Fitzgerald. "It's perplexing."

Fitzgerald returned to another important document in the case, the "Go to Hope" note, again saying that it looked worse than it really was. "Miss Hughes admitted it right off the bat. She admitted it was . . . to prevent Mr. Leppink from tracking her down," he said. Fitzgerald told jurors that Kent had followed Mechele and showed up unannounced at least once when she was with Scott Hilke. She didn't want it to happen again.

It was John Carlin III who had taken things too far, Fitzgerald said: "He carried it out." Mechele had no idea that John was going to kill Kent—and knew nothing about his actions afterwards," he explained. "When John's son testified that Mechele was with John Carlin III in the bathroom while a gun was being washed, the young man was simply lying, for reasons only he knew.

"Could it be to help himself?" wondered Fitzgerald aloud. "To provide a diversion, because by this time he's a suspect?" He noted that young John's story changed every time he told it, becoming more incriminating against his father and Mechele along the way, leading up to his claim at Mechele's trial that he had suddenly remembered seeing a gun falling out of a closet after the murder.

"Forget?" asked Fitzgerald incredulously. "That's just unbelievable."

The defense attorney now neared the end of his summation, addressing two final aspects of the prosecution case. The first was the email from Mechele to John Carlin III about possibly going to Seychelles, where there was no extradition. He suggested that Mechele had heard about the Seychelles from Scott Hilke, not in the context of a murder plan, but as general information. Scott, he said, was a "news nut" who kept article clippings in his house and "in all likelihood told her about the Seychelles." The email also mentions scuba diving and Cancún. "This whole idea that the Seychelles is some significant piece of evidence just falls on its face," he said. "All you have to do is look at the email itself."

And finally, Fitzgerald sought to show why Mechele had sent the laptop computer to her sister. The defense attorney had saved the weakest part of his summation for last. "There's no evidence that anything was deleted on it," he said, although it appeared that hundreds of pages of emails and documents had in fact been erased. "This doesn't show consciousness of guilt. It doesn't show hiding."

In the end, Fitzgerald said, the evidence in the murder of Kent Leppink did point to somebody, and it was the person both sides agreed was the killer. According to Fitzgerald, John Carlin III "had unilateral intent and he had unilateral action." His motive? According to the emails, some probably written while John was drunk, "talks about having sex with T.T."

"Carlin Sr., who is probably homophobic, had in a moment of weakness engaged in this conduct, and the self-loathing, and the teasing he's getting isn't going to be directed so much at him out at T.T.," said Fitzgerald. "He's going to blame T.T. for that, for this moment of weakness."

So John "has decided on his own plan," said Fitzgerald. "He went down there and killed Kent Leppink on his own."

By now Fitzgerald was tired and the jury was growing restless.

"To be sure, ladies and gentlemen, Kent Leppink didn't deserve to die," said Fitzgerald, who after a smoothly crafted presentation began to ramble. "But Mechele Linehan doesn't deserve to be convicted. Now you've heard good and bad about her. You've heard a lot of bad. And I could relate a lot of good. . . . But you know what?—The good and the bad really isn't that important because what you need to focus on—you need to focus on whether the state has proved beyond a reasonable doubt that she did some act and that she had the coupling intent [*sic*] with the act."

Fitzgerald paused, looked at the jury, and then looked at the courtroom clock. "I'm running out of time and you're running out of patience," he said. He took a breath and made his final plea.

"You literally hold Mrs. Linehan's life in your hands," he said. "Ladies and gentlemen, what we ask is—we ask that you return Mrs. Linehan to Olympia. We ask that you return her to her family and her friends, and to her husband

and her daughter. And we ask that you return the only true and just verdict in this case, which is to find that Mrs. Linehan is not guilty."

In his rebuttal, Gullufsen insisted John Carlin III did not—and emotionally could not—have acted alone. "He would never cross her," Gullufsen said. "He would never take something like this and do it on his own without her approval, without knowing about it. His relationship with her just was not of that nature." Urging jurors to go through the evidence carefully, Gullufsen asked them to do what he knew cold case jurors often loved to do: solve the case.

"You're going to come to the conclusion that there's no reasonable doubt that this whole thing was orchestrated by her, using Carlin willingly," the prosecutor said. "He was ready to help her in whatever she wanted to do. She encouraged it, facilitated it, aided and abetted it to happen."

CHAPTER THIRTY

The alternate jurors were excused, leaving a panel of nine women and three men to decide Mechele's fate. The jurors deliberated Thursday and Friday without reaching a verdict. The judge told the panel to resume on Monday, beginning a trying weekend for Mechele and her husband Colin. "As I sat and listened to Mr. Gullufsen's closing argument . . . my insides clenched," Colin later said. "I felt: How is it possible that a man, representing the people of Alaska, could be so disingenuous? He does that in the People's name?"

But it wasn't only the media and the prosecutor lining up against Mechele. For weeks, John Carlin III had been conducting jailhouse interviews with the *Anchorage Daily News*, and on Friday—day two of deliberations—the paper printed its article. Mechele's former housemate didn't go as far as his attorneys had in the first trial by pinning Kent's murder on Mechele, but he came close.

Reminiscing about her days as a stripper, John said, "Mechele has a captivating voice for the males, for whatever reason, and a look too." Among those she ensnared were not only him, Kent, and Scott Hilke, but "a local lawyer, a pilot and a film producer," all unnamed.

John agreed with the prosecution's contention that Mechele was engaged to Kent at the same time she was seeing Scott Hilke, taking advantage of Kent's weaknesses, including a "masochistic personality" and confusion and unhappiness over being a homosexual. While Kent sincerely believed Mechele would marry him, John said, "I think Mechele was just conning him for the $2,300 or whatever it was for the wedding dress."

John strongly rejected Mechele's lawyers' claims that he killed Kent because Kent made a pass at John IV. "Never, never, never, never," John told the newspaper. "T.T. was never a threat to any child, that I can see. . . . If I felt that way, I would have kicked him out of my house, not killed him." While the article made no mention of John's response, if any, to the defense contention he killed Kent because of a homosexual encounter, he denied that he committed murder to get a share of the insurance money.

"Let's say she was going to get a million dollars because I killed T.T.," he said. "Where would she be? With Scott, with the million dollars. That doesn't get me her."

The following Monday after the article appeared, the jury—which was instructed to avoid media accounts of the trial—resumed deliberations. After a morning session, the panel sent a note to the judge: twenty hours of talks had produced a verdict.

CHAPTER THIRTY-ONE

The attorneys and Judge Volland were ready this time, all arriving in court at noon on October 22, 2007.

Mechele, dressed in black, took her place at the defense table. Behind her sat her husband, Colin, and friends and family, as well as Kent's mother, Betsy Leppink.

"Counsel," began Judge Volland, "as you can see we have a note from our jurors dated 11:16 a.m. that they've reached a verdict. Are we ready to take our verdict, counsel?"

"We are, Judge," said Fitzgerald.

"Yes, Your Honor," said Gullufsen.

"Right," said the judge, "let's get our jurors into the courtroom."

It took three long minutes for the panel of nine women and three men to get to the courtroom and take their seats.

"Mr. Hagler," said the judge to a man on the panel, "I see from your note that not only are you the foreperson but you've indicated that the jury has reached a verdict, is that true?"

"That is correct," he said.

"You just hand the verdict form to the bailiff and he'll bring it to me."

For a few excruciating seconds Judge Volland looked over the paperwork, his face betraying nothing.

"I have examined the jury form," said the judge. "It is properly dated and signed by our foreperson. Miss Linehan, would you please stand while I read the verdict. And your husband may stand with you if you wish." Colin rose in the audience section as the judge said, "You can stand next to her, Dr. Linehan."

Colin made his way to the counsel table and stood next to Mechele, his arm around her, his eyes closed, as the judge—not the foreman this time—read from the form: "We the jury find the defendant, Mechele K. Linehan, guilty of murder in the first degree as charged in the indictment."

A look of disbelief flashed across Colin's face. Mechele's mother gasped and then shed tears, which she wiped with a tissue. Other family and friends quietly cried.

Mechele didn't flinch, her face in repose. As the courtroom still cameras whirred, she stared straight ahead, expressionless, with the same frozen look as John Carlin III had had before her.

"Please be seated," said Judge Volland. "Counsel, do either of you wish to examine the verdict form?"

"The state does not, Your Honor," said Gullufsen calmly.

"Do you wish to examine the jury form, Mr. Fitzgerald?"

Barely able to speak, defense attorney Kevin Fitzgerald choked out, "I do, Judge, and if I could have the jury panel polled as well."

Judge Volland explained the polling procedure and had the clerk ask each one if his or her verdict were the true and correct verdict. As a dozen yesses followed, Colin slumped, his military bearing at last deserting him. Mechele looked straight ahead, no reaction.

"Counsel, do either of you see any reason why our jurors cannot be discharged at this time?" asked the judge.

"The state does not, Your Honor," said Gullufsen.

Somberly, Fitzgerald replied, "No, Judge."

"Ladies and gentlemen," the judge said to the jury, "please accept my respect and appreciation—and I believe I speak on behalf of the court system and the parties as well—for your service and dedication. This has been a long trial, and I know how difficult it is for you to serve as jurors in this type of case. One of the things you learn very quickly from where I sit is how dedicated jurors are, how they take their responsibility seriously and how weighty it is on you all to reach such a decision. Please recognize that we respect you, we thank you for it. Our system cannot work unless people like yourselves are willing to give this sacrifice and the commitment that you have. So, please, thank you."

After telling them that the case's lawyers and reporters might want to talk to them later, Judge Volland said, "With those remarks, I will formally discharge you from your service."

The panelists left the courtroom and Volland addressed the issue of sentencing, asking Fitzgerald if he needed more than a day for the hearing. "I don't know," he said quietly.

"I know on the basis of the jury's verdict, this is a non-bailable offense," the judge said. "I'll need to remand Ms. Linehan presently. Ms. Linehan, you can have one final embrace with your husband, but then I'll need to have [the] officer separate you and take you downstairs. I'll wait until that is complete."

The Linehans clung to each other, Colin burying his head in her shoulder, both arms clasped around her, his hands joined at her waist. Mechele lightly stroked his shoulder as the pair swayed unsteadily. In audience section, women cried.

"All right, Officer," the judge said to the court security officer, who then led Mechele out of the courtroom to jail after a year free on bond.

"Anything further, Counsel?" asked Judge Volland.

"No, Your Honor, nothing," said Gullufsen.

Fitzgerald didn't answer.

When interviewed later by reporters, jurors said the case was never a slam dunk for the prosecution. The initial vote was tied, six for acquittal, six for conviction. The jurors then trudged through the evidence, primarily the hundreds of pages of emails, and opinions changed. "It was emotionally challenging," juror Lisa Pagano told *Dateline*. "For three days, I could not think about anything else." They considered whether John Carlin III had acted alone—as the defense had argued—but the emails convinced them that Mechele was pulling the strings in a quest for money. While the prosecution's case was "well presented," juror Sherry Slade told the *Anchorage Daily News*, "We looked for the balance of that on the other side, and it just wasn't there." Robin Ruttle told local television station KTUU, "We went through [the defense case] with a fine-toothed comb, and there was nothing. "In the end, jurors felt secure in their decision, but were still emotionally spent. "I'm not ashamed to say I had a hard time going to bed last night," juror Christine Eagleson said the morning after the verdict. "I said to my husband: 'You know, I helped send someone to prison.'"

Legal analysts would suggest the gender balance on the jury had doomed Mechele—that the nine-woman female majority was swayed by her job as a stripper. Ruttle said, "It didn't faze me at all one bit." But another female juror, Eagleson, found Mechele's past relevant. "When you're table dancing or you're stripping or you're lap dancing, what you are doing is soliciting yourself to get money from men by pleasing them," she told *Dateline*. "The whole point is you're manipulating feelings to get something in return. If you're doing well at that as an occupation, you must be pretty good at it. It doesn't imply that if you're good at it, you're going to be a killer. But it just so happened to work out that that's what she did. She was good at it."

Prosecutor Pat Gullufsen called the verdict the "right decision" and expressed relief that "we have both of them convicted now." Kent's family released a statement thanking the Division of the Alaska State Troopers and the prosecutors, among others. "We firmly believe that 'Our God Reigns' and has blessed our family with the services of the finest of Alaskan people," the statement said. Whatever relief they had was tempered by the fact that nothing would bring back Kent Leppink.

"God is good, one more time," said Kent's mother, Betsy, as she walked away from the courthouse. "I guess we are just going to go on, make it a new beginning." Rather than anger, Betsy expressed pity for Mechele. "I'm just sorry for her

choices," she said. "In Kent's letter, he asked us to pray for
her. I have over the years. I don't take that lightly at all."

Kent's brother Craig told reporters that it was difficult on
the family to return to Alaska "and know Kent's not here."
That the two trials had finally ended brought a measure of
relief, but nothing more. "I guess you'd say justice is done,"
he said. "And we're done." His thoughts also went out to
Mechele's family. "We'll never forget, but heal a little more,"
he said. "I guess for the Linehan family, they just start today.
They've got a long way to go."

Indeed, Colin left the courthouse shaken. When asked
how he felt, he said: "It's one of the stupidest questions I've
ever heard." Their daughter, Audrey, was hysterical, asking
her father, "Why did they vote Mommy guilty?" She would
later go into counseling with a therapist trained in dealing
with children who experienced trauma.

CHAPTER THIRTY-TWO

After Mechele was convicted, John Carlin III spoke to the *Anchorage Daily News* from his jail cell, saying her attorneys "shot themselves in the foot by not presenting the truth" behind the murder of Kent. "The truth gets muddled when both sides are making things up." At the time, he didn't say what the truth was as he saw it. On January 17, 2008, the day before he was to be sentenced, Carlin elaborated.

Although he continued to claim his innocence, calling the prosecution's case against him a "fictitious scenario" dreamed up by original investigators Steven DeHart and Ron Belden, John acknowledged some of the actions of which he was accused. He admitted, for instance, that he had in fact washed a Desert Eagle .44 handgun in the bathroom sink after Kent's murder, but not for the reasons suggested by prosecutors. John told the newspaper he had purchased that model of gun but it had disappeared months earlier, only to be found by his son John IV in a hall closet after Kent's killing. He had no idea if it was the murder weapon—only that he hadn't used it—but he didn't think DeHart and Belden would believe him. "I wanted to make it go away," he told the local paper. "I didn't trust the Troopers. . . . No matter what I told them, they would use it against me." After scrubbing the gun clean with ammonia, as he had learned to do in the Marines, John Carlin III tossed it in the trash can at a nearby Carrs grocery store to cover the crime.

The day after the article appeared, John appeared before Judge Philip Volland to plead for mercy. Speaking for the first time in court, John, wearing a yellow jail uniform, his hands cuffed in front of him, denied shooting Kent or knowing who did.

"I can't tell you how he died," he said. "If I could I would."

As for the email from Mechele about the Seychelles, telling him they could buy a citizenship "for around ten mill" and not worry about extradition, John told the judge, "Essentially [you're] saying you're trying to rip off an insurance company for $1 million and to get away you want to buy two $10 million citizenships on some island somewhere. And that just doesn't make sense."

Rather, John speculated that Kent—broke, depressed, in love with a woman who would never love him back—found somebody to kill him to end his pain and get revenge on Mechele.

"I have come to believe that T.T. orchestrated his own death to be in close proximity to a cabin that he actually believed was in Hope."

The judge wasn't convinced. After hearing from Kent's family, including mother Betsy, who called Kent's death "the most hell-like experience of my life," Volland came down hard on John. He characterized the murder as a "deliberate, cold-blooded homicide for money" and declared, "I believe the maximum sentence is warranted. I sentence Mr. Carlin to serve ninety-nine years in prison."

John accepted the sentence with no emotion. With prison credits for good behavior, Carlin still stood a chance of getting out of prison on parole, if he lived into his eighties.

Afterward, Betsy said, it was the first time she had ever heard John's voice. "So far, God has watched over us through this whole thing," she said. "It's been a long time. He's taken care of it, He will, He just will."

Mechele's sentencing was eventually set for three months later, in March 2008. She faced the same maximum ninety-nine-year term, with parole after thirty-three years. In the months leading up to the hearing, she, too, went to the media, cooperating with CBS's *48 Hours Mystery* for a program airing just weeks before she would go before the judge. It was one of the rare times Colin would speak to the media at any length—he would also give an interview to NBC's *Dateline*—and the only time that Mechele would grant an interview (although her family and friends spoke to *48 Hours Mystery*.)

Mechele didn't speak directly to the facts of the case. "I just feel like there is nothing I can do to make people believe me or make people like me," she said on the show, which aired on March 3. "A witch I may be, but a psychopath I am definitely not."

When her two-day sentencing hearing began on March 28, Kent's family predictably had a different view. "Mechele Linehan is an evil lady who continues to do deeds of deception and manipulation," Betsy Leppink told Judge Volland. "I fear for her next victim if she's ever permitted to enter society again." She went on to say that Mechele had never loved Kent, never showed the slightest affection for him, instead only causing him pain, torturing him the way she had once accused Kent of torturing animals. "We've had twelve Christmas days without Kent's chair at our table," Betsy. "Twelve seasons of listening to Christmas songs like 'I'll Be Home for Christmas,' knowing very well that Kent will never share another holiday with us."

In her plea for leniency from the judge, Mechele's defense hired a forensic psychiatrist who concluded that while Mechele was naïve and in denial about the severity of her circumstances, she was "unlikely to be someone who schemed or planned the murder of anybody."

Then came remarks by Colin Linehan. Bitter and angry, he contended that Mechele fell victim to a media obsessed with her stripper past and a prosecution bent on winning at any costs.

"This media narrative shows she's a manipulative spider queen evil person that I have heard over and over again.

That is not who she is," he said, "and nobody knows her better than I do. I say that on my honor and at my word, that is not who she is."

Colin would return repeatedly to that word—"narrative"—convinced that Mechele was convicted not on the basis of evidence but on the power of a tawdry story constructed with old and misleading details.

"Mechele told me about the tragedy that happened in Alaska in 1996," he wrote in a letter to the judge for the sentencing hearing. "Her story has never changed and the details fit perfectly into all circumstantial evidence that the prosecution, representing the State of Alaska, used to convict Mechele of first degree murder."

He didn't say what she had told him—early in their relationship or over the years—or why, if Mechele's story was consistent, she had initially left out any mention of John Carlin III, a man unknown to Colin until he walked into the Maryland clinic. Rather, Colin asserted that "our legal strategy never involved getting into the details of her relationships and experience" in Alaska "because it legally didn't matter."

"Mechele's character was already trashed by the tabloid media mindset, and our counsel and Mechele both felt that, by her explaining the details of the relationships with Ken, John and Scott, it would only be used to reinforce the narrative concocted by the prosecution," he wrote. "More importantly, we didn't need to defend Mechele from inaccurate and slanderous untruths leaked to the media from the prosecution. The issue was not Mechele's lifestyle or her complicated relationships. The issue was whether Mechele was guilty beyond a reasonable doubt of First Degree Murder within the confines of the trial. . . .

"We strongly feel," he wrote to the judge, "this was not accomplished."

Colin used his letter to the judge to set the record straight on what he saw as inaccuracies reported about Mechele. "Mechele was an exotic dancer at the Bush Company for less than two years," he wrote. "She worked hard, never did drugs, was not promiscuous and saved and invested most of the money she earned. Her goal, the entire time, was to save enough money to finance her education. But her entity was reduced to 'ex-stripper' in the media, with all the negative connotations to go with that." As Colin saw it, being an exotic dancer "was not dishonorable and was completely legal." Mechele, he said, "would sit and talk with customers and try to get to know the person that was hiring her for her time." Mechele "learned so much about the world and life" by listening to her customers.

"I hardly see this as manipulative," he said. "The men who would pay for her time knew what they were paying for. It's not like the customer would be shocked that Mechele wouldn't come home with them or be their girlfriend." She wasn't even employed there at the time of the murder, he noted, but attaching the "stripper" label "had an impact on the collective consciousness that, I believe, leaked into the courtroom." While the prosecution mounted its media campaign, Colin said, Mechele took the high road, granting only the interview to *48 Hours Mystery*. Colin said he had "gracefully rebuffed" *The Oprah Winfrey Show*, *Dr. Phil*, and *Good Morning America*, mindful of the harm that could be caused by contributing to the hysteria, even though he knew that the real Mechele wouldn't be known.

"Mechele never asked me for any extravagant gifts. She always prefers gifts that are made, and as she says, 'from the heart,'" wrote Colin. "She has never asked for jewels or baubles. She has also instilled this in Audrey and has taught her the things most important in life are respect, love, and family. I have never seen Mechele exhibit any emotion or behavior associated with greed."

He wrote to the judge that the media attention and the incarceration of Mechele had traumatized his daughter. "Audrey is an innocent child with a heart full of love and compassion," he wrote. "I don't want her heart and soul damaged. She is so precious, and her love and need for her mother is searing."

He said he sympathized with Kent's family. "I am sure that the subsequent media crush has been dreadful for them," he wrote, although he added: "It is nothing compared to the loss of a family member and the subsequent agony. Mechele told me at one point that the hardest part of the trial was to have Betsy Leppink think that Mechele had anything to do with the murder of her son."

In his remarks to the judge, Colin repeated most of what was written in more detail in the letter. In court, he made a last person-to-person plea to Kent's family. Colin turned his back to the judge to face Kent's parents in the audience.

"I don't know the hole in your heart—what it's like to lose a child. I can't imagine," he said. But he said he wife was innocent. "I just want to say my prayers are with you." He paused. "OK?"

Kenneth and Betsy Leppink didn't answer.

But later, outside the courtroom, Kent's father told reporters, "We don't have a vicious bone in our bodies, but this has to come to a halt. She is guilty as sin and we know that, and we've known that for a long time."

After a break for the weekend, the sentencing hearing resumed on Monday, with one person left to speak.

There was no jury left to impress. Mechele arrived to court wearing a red jail uniform over a white T-shirt, her hair pulled back in a ponytail.

"I have a letter I wrote that I would like to read," she said in soft voice.

The judge asked Mechele's attorney Kevin Fitzgerald to move the microphone closer so she could be heard.

"Your Honor, I would like to introduce myself to you. I have sat here in the courtroom and I never had a chance to tell you about myself.

"I am not the monster that has been painted by the prosecution," she said, her voice cracking, "I have not lived a life of greed, manipulation, or that of this fictional character of a Hollywood movie that has been portrayed by the prosecution. I am thirty-five. I'm a wife to a wonderful man who I love dearly. I'm a mother to a bright-eyed little girl who always will be the brightest star in my life. I'm a business owner. I work overtime every week.

"My husband and I, my daughter, we live a simple life. We live in a home, which was built in 1904. We drive old vehicles. We spend our weekends and evening at home preparing and repairing our home, gardening and cooking. We enjoy skiing and running, cycling and camping, and watch *Star Wars* movies together. Our home is always bellowing with life."

She paused, shook her head slightly, inhaled. "On the weekends and holidays, our home is always filled with people," she said. "The kids make their own pizzas, carve pumpkins and ice Christmas cookies. The adults flow through the rooms and have conversations by the fireplace. Our life is never being decadent or extravagant or lavish."

Looking at the judge, she said, "I'm telling you this so you can have a visualization of how we live our life from me. Our home is simple, our life is not empty, it is not lacking anything. We do not fit the narrative, nor have I ever fit the narrative of the prosecution."

Mechele urged the judge to read the letters from "those who know me, those who lived with me, those who worked next to me." Pleas to the judge had come from a host of supporters, including her mother, Colin's mother and sister, their neighbors in Olympia, and former Bush Company stripper Honi Martin. These people, Mechele said, could speak best to her character, morals, and nature and draw a "stark contrast" to how she'd been portrayed in court.

"More than a decade ago I made the choice to work at the Bush Company," she continued. "While working there I made poor choices. I never asked for anyone to be hurt. I worked there for under two years. I saved money to finance my education. I did not continue to work there. I went to school."

Spelling out what she said she had done wrong, Mechele said, "I accepted gifts and money from men. I accepted gifts and money from Kent Leppink. . . .

"But," she stressed, "the prosecution would only have you focus on this three-month period of my relationship with Kent. And the fact is I considered him a friend. My reaction upon hearing of his death was horrible. My reaction was genuine." She acknowledged that "later in anger I said things about him that were not kind. By that time I had learned things that I didn't know, and I shouldn't have said those things."

Saying that the previous ten years "should speak volumes about my character," Mechele told the judge: "I was defined as an ex-stripper. In fact, I've worked many different jobs prior to that, during that and after that." She paused to pull a tissue from a box and wipe her nose. "None of these jobs were mentioned. That job is actually a small part of my work history and an even smaller part of my being. None of these other jobs were put forth as a definition of me and my character by the prosecution. And this portrayal of me is not who I am. It only serves to fit them. Because if they were to be honest about me it would not fit their theory."

Through sniffles, she asked the judge again to listen to her family, friends, and neighbors and said, "I beg you from the bottom of my heart to allow me the chance to go back to my family as soon as I possibly can."

She told the judge that she understood that he was bound by the verdict to give her a stiff sentence, but appealed to his sense of mercy. "You sat here during the whole trial, you've seen everything, and I know that you're a separate entity from both of these tables," she said, "and I ask you to use that power and do what you can from your heart."

After weighing nearly two days of statements and dozens of written statements from friends and family of Mechele and Kent, Judge Volland provided his analysis of the murder—and Mechele's role in it.

"It was a calculated homicide accomplished through deceit, deception and manipulation," the judge said. "It was done for the most venal of reasons and it was dismissed by the two participants in the most casual of ways. It was a man killed by his friend and his fiancée."

In hearing the competing descriptions of Mechele's character, the judge concluded: "There are in my judgment two Mechele Linehans wrapped into one." But at issue in the case, he said, was not the Mechele of Bigelow Avenue—the loving wife, mother, neighbor, volunteer, businesswoman— but the Mechele of the time of the murder. He noted the evidence of her obtaining a life insurance policy on Kent as she was deceiving him about her intentions to marry, and her deception to lure him to the murder scene. "Just those facts are ones that support complicity in the event," he said.

"In my mind, I can find no principled distinction between the puppet who pulls the trigger and the puppeteer who pulls the strings," he said. "And in my judgment, Ms. Linehan was the puppeteer who pulled the strings."

And so he made no distinction in punishment: "I sentence Mrs. Linehan to ninety-nine years."

Mechele again showed no emotion. Listening to the judge, Colin shook his head and appeared to be quietly laughing.

After her sentencing, Mechele hired prominent appellate attorneys Jeff Feldman and Susan Orlansky to seek to overturn the verdict on the basis of mistakes by the judge. In a seventy-three-page brief and later in oral arguments before the appeals court, Mechele's new lawyers argued that Judge Volland improperly allowed into evidence information about Mechele's work as a stripper, Kent's letter to his parents, and testimony that she wanted to like the heroine of the movie *The Last Seduction*.

The appeal put into legal language what Mechele and Colin had been contending: that the prosecution had so sullied her that it was impossible to have a fair trial. The stripper evidence, according to the appeal, "served only to cast Linehan in the stereotypical role of an immoral and seasoned manipulator of guileless men" while having no bearing on her guilt or innocence of the murder charge. The testimony about *The Last Seduction* was merely "character evidence" that proved nothing; and Kent's letter, while intended only to show his state of mind, in fact influenced the jury about Mechele's thinking and motives.

During her appeal, Mechele remained at Hiland Mountain Correctional Center, an all-women's prison just off the highway halfway between Anchorage and Mechele's former home in Wasilla. She was accepting books and well wishes through a Web site called Free Mechele set up by friends. Colin occasionally submitted messages to the site, mostly to rant against the media and prosecutors for perpetuating the "narrative" that had doomed Mechele in court.

"Not to beat a dead horse, but, Mechele's character is well known and defined by the people who know and love her," he wrote in a December 2009 post. "A three-month thread of emails and circumstance doesn't define anyone. Unless you are a TV or movie character. Or a cartoon villain with super powers to control men—but I digress. Bottom line: we are still fighting, and we still have hope."

John Carlin, meanwhile, was transferred from the Anchorage jail to the Spring Creek Correctional Center in Seward on the southern shore of the Kenai Peninsula, where he spent his time reading histories and biographies (one of his first books checked out from the prison library was Winston Churchill's *History of the English-Speaking Peoples*) and giving more media interviews.

In a segment of *48 Hours Mystery* that aired in September 2008, John continued to claim his innocence but expanded on what he had done with that Desert Eagle .44 that had suddenly appeared when John IV found it in a closet after Kent's murder.

"I heard Mechele yelling, 'Don't touch it . . . don't touch it!'" John said. When he went around a corner, he faced Mechele glaring at him, and they worried that with John IV's fingerprints left on it, it could spell trouble for his son, so they washed the weapon and the elder Carlin threw it in the trash.

While John asserted something that Mechele never has—that she knew about the gun after the murder and said nothing about it—he still insisted, "She didn't pull the trigger."

Asked who did, he said cryptically, "Good question, but it wasn't me, but it's one that should have been looked at."

After the episode aired, John was beat up in prison. "Some people here apparently didn't like the way I looked, so I got a prison makeover of sorts," he said in a letter to the *Anchorage Daily News*. He was temporarily moved to protective custody—"the hole," as he called it, "like living in the primate section of the zoo."

A couple weeks later, John was moved into the general population, to a part of the prison housing new inmates. On Monday, October 27, 2008, John spent the day speaking with his appellate lawyer. That night he was found dead.

At first a prison spokesman said only that John had died "under suspicious circumstances." Then authorities announced that John had been beaten to death. Although prison officials had suspects in mind, the investigation was stymied by a lack of cooperation by other inmates. At press time, no arrests had been made.

"The first thing I thought about was John's son," Kent's father, Kenneth Leppink, told Anchorage TV station KTUU. "He's been banged around quite a lot. This is not going to be very helpful in his life, I don't think, right now."

"I don't care who it is, that's not right," added Kent's brother Craig. "I wouldn't wish that on John or anyone else."

On the Free Mechele blog there was this message: "It was with sadness that we learned today of the passing of John Carlin III. Our deep condolences to his friends and family."

In Hope, Alaska, not far from the shores of the Turnagain Arm, the Discovery Café burned down three years after Kent's murder. There was no insurance, but the locals banded together and rebuilt it. Just off mile marker 13 of the Hope Road, the communications tower still stands at the end of the steep access road, although over the years many of the trees were cleared away to make it easier to reach the power lines. One stump was left standing. On it is nailed a brass cross with a small plate. It reads: *Kent Leppink. May 2, 1996.*

New York Life eventually paid the $1 million death benefit. After attorneys' fees and estate costs were covered, the remainder went to Kent's parents and his brothers Ransom and Craig. His brother Lane refused to accept any money.

AFTERWORD

In February 2010, the appeals court made its ruling: Judge Volland erred in allowing testimony about *The Last Seduction* and by allowing into evidence Kent's letter to his parents. It found harmless the testimony about Mechele's work as a stripper. As a result, Mechele's guilty verdict was overturned. Colin wrote on the Free Mechele Blog: "I am grateful that the American justice system checked and balanced."

The state of Alaska announced it would try Mechele a second time.